THANKYOU! SNEAKERFREAKER would not be possible without the help, advice and hard work of many, many people. Thanks most of all to my sweetpea Virginia, Sonny Ray and Cheech for putting up with the late nights. Also to Matt Fenton from monkii.com for being a best friend and for everything, especially all the incredible effort you put into the SF site. Thanks also to Carl and Brett for getting me started, Sean and Larissa @ Penguin, Hans DC, Jason Le, Rift-Trooper, Heppler and Iori (my bestest writers), Alex Jarvis, Reuben, Andy 79, Seggie, Simon Prestridge, Chicken Strips Jenkinson, Bridget, Austin, Chicken, Flick, Alex Burkart, Jazz the Forum-mod, Tull & Rodney & Josh FEIT, Sarah at Colette, Phil and Karin Footage, Thomas G & Marc ADN, Steve Jump, The McAulisses, Ivo Fokke & Remko Nouws, Hikmet Solebox, Glorias, Tim Easley, Joerg BH, Matt Clear, Trent Dakota, Dmote, Natlee Wood, Jeff and Nico Reed Space, Priscilla & John Rbk, Colin B, Sam, Michelle & Dennis GenPant's, Joe T, Chloe, Daniel & Misha adidas, Anne Tiger Beer, Jock Pony, Shawn Supply, Mr Cupcakes, Kara Messina AA, Marti CREC, Lars Zoo York, Lochie Vans, Olivia Kswiss, Kerry DC, the NB team, Melles & Chris Provider, Sherrin & Sophie X 2 Puma, Philipe +41, SVD & Chris O, JDS007, INSA, Craig Leckie, Lori Lobenstine, Gary Warnett, Simon Ramsay, Briony at Vice, Dave Ortiz, Eric Q, Dom Smith, Ivan Tang, Hughy, Kano & Kab, Linlee, Yu Ming, Deluded Monkey, Quincy, JC, Gary Warnett, Mark Ong, Terrence & Ed, Rinze, Logan, Matt, Olle, Adrienne & Andrea, RRR breakfasters, Alasdair, Ossberto, Dominique, Andrew Printlinx, Weapon X, DJ Peril, everyone at Revolver, Agent Paul S, Ben & Anita, Olger, Monster Children, Cyril, Dave Rare-Air, Felicity, Billie, Rinzen, Dave & Chris White, Nikon D70, Jester, Gonzo, Luca, Ben Frost, Anthony Kolber, Zoe, Brendan, Alfons, Andy G, Nails, Trauma 12, JB, Dave Stone, Kicks 101, Peter Fahey, Nikki Hudson, Ben Monroe (OG SF), Mark Johnston, Andrew at DIK, John Barbour, Nate T, Sandy B, Jesse, Fraser, Alife, Mark Smith, Air Elijah, Regular Product, Lupy, Charlie M, PMH, Corey, Eriq Q, Brett G, Steele/Ken, Justin, Omar, Jeff Carvalho, Brendan, Regular Product, Amy C, Veskovich, Hiro, Chris Gurney, Opium, Steve Varga, Proper Shop, Andy Bear, Bret Dougherty, The Yok, Phunk Studio, Luke Prowse, everyone who entered K99 and everyone who lent shoes to photograph and everyone who stocks the magazine! Sorry if I left anyone out, thanks a million!
Keep your laces loose and your tongues tied....

THE BERKLEY PUBLISHING GROUP
Published by the Penguin Group
Penguin Group (USA) Inc.
375 Hudson Street, New York, New York 10014, USA
Penguin Group (Canada), 90 Eglinton Avenue East, Suite 700, Toronto, Ontario M4P 2Y3, Canada (a division of Pearson Penguin Canada Inc.)
Penguin Books Ltd., 80 Strand, London WC2R 0RL, England
Penguin Group Ireland, 25 St. Stephen's Green, Dublin 2, Ireland (a division of Penguin Books Ltd.)
Penguin Group (Australia), 250 Camberwell Road, Camberwell, Victoria 3124, Australia (a division of Pearson Australia Group Pty. Ltd.)
Penguin Books India Pvt. Ltd., 11 Community Centre, Panchsheel Park, New Delhi—110 017, India
Penguin Group (NZ), cnr Airborne and Rosedale Roads, Albany, Auckland 1310, New Zealand (a division of Pearson New Zealand Ltd.)
Penguin Books (South Africa) (Pty.) Ltd., 24 Sturdee Avenue, Rosebank, Johannesburg 2196, South Africa

Penguin Books Ltd., Registered Offices:
80 Strand, London WC2R 0RL, England

The question I get asked all the time is 'why sneakers?' I dunno how to answer that. Why do people race lawnmowers or study the art of mime? Because they dig it and they get off on it! I don't understand the urge for performance poetry either and if you have to stop and ask why, you obviously don't get it and never will. Sometimes you can't rationalise an obsession, but in this case, I now have a whole book of evidence to answer the original question.

I got to this point because my sneaker habit had made me bit of a joke amongst my friends. A few years ago, well before it was 'way cool', my collection was smaller but it was still enough to fill a whole closet. Some were mint in boxes, some trashed, some loved, some hated and some were potentially valuable. But most were simply worn round the block a few times and loved to death. People were always amazed and called me Imelda Marcos like it was an original joke, but I knew it was nothing to brag about. There is always some cat waiting at the next bus stop with more knowledge, deeper pockets and extra time to dig deep down into the dirty. I met a dude with 300 pairs and I thought that was a benchmark til I ran into DJ Clark Kent who has thousands of Air Force sitting on ice. Crikey!

The first issue came out in November 2002. To be honest, it was all done in a month and was pretty simple. 40 pages, some good pieces, interviews with local guys, a bit of stuff felched off the internet and out it came. I gave away a few thousand copies and kept about ten for myself. Funnily enough, those original issues are now going for around $70US on eBay. And worth every penny I might add!

Since the first issue came out I've watched as 'sneakers' evolved into a highly contagious pop-culture virus. The symptoms are swift and devastating. You want those shoes so bad you spend hours sweating on eBay for obscure pairs, hanging in shops to get ahead of the game, raiding factory outlets, clocking the sales, logging on to forums, getting hookups in Asia... Man, unless you are flat-out loaded, it's bloody hard yakka being a sneakerfreaker! Limited editions, samples, Japan only colours, quickstrike, hyperstrke, Hong Kong knock-offs, deadstock, customs, vintage, small-runs, one-offs, artist collabs, retailer tie-ins, player-protos, retro reissues... all this fans the flames, keeps us fiends fiending and not eating for weeks so we can afford our sneaks.

The primary goal from my point of view was to get free stuff. Loads and loads of free shoes, all for me. The best, the rarest, the most illest sneakers, all in size US11 and hand delivered to my door by a man in a van - that's not too much to ask is it? That original dream did come true and I still love the thrill of a new arrival, I won't lie to you. But I had absolutely no idea that those same sneakers would take over my life and send me around the world many times, making friends everywhere like some international sneaker gigolo.

With every issue of the magazine totally sold out and it deemed imprudent to reprint, I was delighted when an offer came through to put the best bits from over the years into a book. Some of the content has dated but small changes have been made and a bunch of new images added to keep it fresh, without taking away the charm of the original. So when you read this almanac, please bear that in mind.

In the very first editorial that I wrote, I promised that the magazine would be "funny and serious, meaningful and pointless, all at the same time." That article is reproduced on the next page and although it's well and truly old news now, it still reads as a genuine, if somewhat naive preview of the nascent sneaker scene that was about to blossom all over the world. However, I still feel the original point remains a good one and it's become the unspoken mantra of everyone who has ever contributed in some way to the magazine. Do it for the love of the game, do it proudly, honestly, with a great sense of humour and the rest will take care of itself.

I hope Sneaker Freaker is regarded as a righteous product. We delve into sneakers at a level most people can't fathom. We represent the soul *and* the conscience of *all* sneaker lovers. That's because we are what we do, and we don't do it for any other reason than our own satisfaction. More than anything, the desire to do 'justice' to my lifelong hobby and to garner the respect of the old heads (by avoiding anything corny) is what has driven me to spend hundreds of hours working on each issue. The more acclaim the project received (thankyou), the more I felt beholden to up the ante next time around. In case you're wondering, that's why there's only ever been two issues produced per year.

Sneakers have always meant more to me than just something I wore on my feet. By creating Sneaker Freaker, I unwittingly set out to prove my point, over and over again. They have had a profound cultural impact on my life and I'm obviously not alone in thinking like this.

In fact, I have often said that every good sneaker is worth at least a thousand words and there are plenty of good ones to talk about. Here's 320 pages of rock-hard sneaker content amassed over the past four years (and six issues of the magazine) and assembled in one place for the very first time. Strange isn't it that a few bits of leather and suede sewn onto a slab of rubber and wrapped up in nylon thread could mean so very much to so very few.

Viva la sneaker!

WOODY

EDITOR SNEAKER FREAKER MAGAZINE
INTERNATIONAL SNEAKER GIGOLO

FOR THE LOVE

Ask almost any Australian over the age of thirty about their first pair of sneakers and they'll be lying if they don't confess to either the Dunlop Volley or its hi-tech sibling, the KT26. There simply wasn't anything else on the market when I grew up. It seems crazy now but I can't visualise what sports stores looked like then without dozens and dozens of shoes arranged down one whole wall.

Memory is a selective thing, I know Converse arrived at some point, Nike too. Somehow I had an original pair of their waffle runners, though I can't remember how I got them. They got their name because the knobbly sole was invented when some dude at Nike put rubber into his waffle machine.

Then adidas kicked the suburbs with 'Rome', which came in white leather with classic blue stripes or if your mother was cruel and vindictive, tan with chocolate stripes. I had the tan and chocolate, bought on sale at Eastland Shopping Centre and I was so devastated I refused to wear them. I guess I must have reverted to the hi-top desert boots during this difficult period of my life.

A little later on, adidas also had another popular running shoe, the Oregon. It was offered in cream with burgundy stripes and had this cool rubber mesh on the midsole. These looked fantastically modern in concert with stretch denim and were a smash hit with the ladies on Saturday night down the Station. The only guys that could afford them had already left high school early to become plumbers.

It is an interesting irony to note that the bung-eyed colourways that seemed so miserable in our youth are now the most highly sought after. Where we once desired camouflage in the suburbs, we now display our individuality through pedantically pursuing styles for their rarity, rather than for their harmony of form and function. Now if only I had hung onto those bloody awful Romes!

As you have probably guessed I think about sneakers quite a bit. Most of us sneaker dudes keep quiet about it - you either get it or you don't. I have spoken to kids who have over 300 pairs, heard rumours of collections in the thousands, though mostly they're based overseas. It certainly helps if you have a size 9 foot, because that's what they make samples in.

Personally I only collect what I can wear, although if I see something special I grab it as potential trade bait. Every weekend there are sneakerfreakers out there hunting thru bargain bins, looking in on garage sales, checking out rural sports stores and scouring the markets looking for gold in amongst the bronze. My best score is a pair of original issue royal blue and yellow Blazer Hi-Tops in canvas. I unexpectedly found them in a Bangkok market and I haggled so much for so long I had to send my patient girlfriend (now wife) back to buy them while I hid around the corner.

Everyone has their heart set on something different so vintage prices are almost impossible to quote because this stuff is only worth what anyone is prepared to pay. First off they have to be original issue to be considered a true classic. Secondly, they should still be in good nick, preferably still unworn, with the box intact. After that you get into the minute detail of it all. Are they limited edition? An unusual colourway? An unreleased model? Do you like them? What is your limit?

Asking true sneakerphiles to name their favourite shoe is like asking Michael Jackson to choose between his children. For me the answer is easy. I am obsessed with Nike Air Force Ones. As far as I am concerned they are the Queen Bee of shoes, the original and still the best. They are a plain looking, solid sort of shoe with a chunky heel, quite rigid support and come in an infinite range of colours and limited editions. I bought my first pair in NYC maybe

ten years ago, black canvas with a yellow swoosh, so sweet looking. I could have bought 30 pairs that day; lows, mid-cuts, hi-tops, orange and blue, navy and white, leather or vinyl, you name it, they were all there sitting on the shelf. I still feel sick and slightly aroused (not in that way!) thinking about it.

The AF1 mid featured a sexy ankle strap that was supposed to protect your ankle. Which I suppose it did, because I never rolled my ankle wearing them, but then again the most radical thing I ever did in mine was trying to catch my tram. The AF1 is also famous as a New York sneaker, and its nickname 'Uptowns' is in honour of the basketball scene in upper Manhattan.

Right now I have over seventy different pairs of AF1s, though the collection will never be complete. My current favourite is the Olympic edition which is made out of red, blue, yellow and green felt with a metallic silver toebox. Of course I haven't actually worn them yet, but it's comforting to know they are boxed in the wardrobe just waiting for me. A while back they released a Year of the Horse LE in white leather with a red swoosh and a mystery Chinese character embroidered on the heel. They look so mysterious I had to buy 3 pairs and put them on the cover of our first issue. You know you need professional help when you start buying in triplicate...

The peculiar thing is that it is easier to collect these sneakers now than it was at the time. The shoe companies have cottoned on to this new wave of interest and all have on-the-money retro reissues planned, so start saving your money now. My big tip is that this summer will belong to the Dunk Lo. They arrived in 1986 in a blaze of sickeningly fabulous colours - hot combinations that matched the trim of the US College basketball uniforms.

The last year or so has seen the Dunk become one of the most collectable sneakers. Stussy, Zoo York and Chocolate Skateboards have all just released limited editions that are now fetching prices over $400US. If you ever want to dream of playing with the big boys, look up those shoes on eBay and you'll get a pretty good snapshot of the hi-roller international trainer market.

The appreciation of old sneakers has changed for me on more than one level over the years, probably to do with the fact that I am paying for them now. In my youth, all new pairs were christened by first mowing the lawn. Then I'd tie them to the back of my BMX and ride around the block a few times. And then I'd have a kick of the footy to finish off the job. I hated the way they looked brand new, so shiny and clean. I much preferred them worn in with the edges taken off. Nowadays, I like to keep them looking fresher, minimise the scuff factor and prolong their lifespan eternally. And I don't ever wear them two days in a row in case they get an attack of the evil stinky sneaker.

So, considering the passion out there, I decided it was about time to start a magazine about sneakers and this is it. It's supposed to be funny and serious, meaningful and pointless, all at the same time. Sneaker Freaker promises to represent the mental and the casual collector alike, but as I said, you'll get it or you won't.

Either way, I hope you get your kicks!

WOODY

ORIGINALS
Superstars
HI RACH
Waffle Racer
SHELLTOES
AIR FORCE ONES
AIR MAX
stansmiths
PRESTOS
UR 80
TRAINER ONE
Dunk lows
JORDANS
cons
air&woven
ZOOM AIR
dunk highs
gazelles
CORTEZ
OREGON
HANDBALL
AIR STAB
BRUINS
Forest Hills
roms
CLYDES
Torsion
SAMBA
KEGLER
mocks
AIR RIFT
CAMPUS

NATALIE WOOD

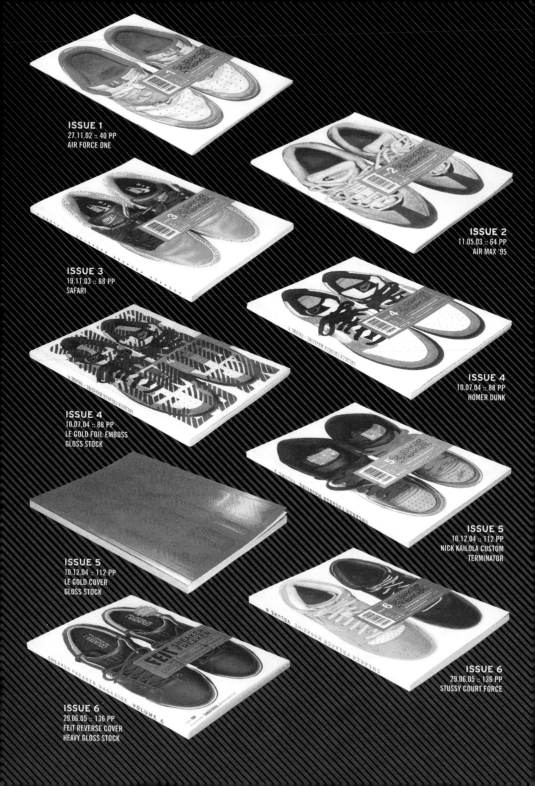

ISSUE 1
27.11.02 :: 40 PP
AIR FORCE ONE

ISSUE 2
11.05.03 :: 64 PP
AIR MAX '95

ISSUE 3
19.11.03 :: 88 PP
SAFARI

ISSUE 4
10.07.04 :: 88 PP
HOMER DUNK

ISSUE 4
10.07.04 :: 88 PP
LE GOLD FOIL EMBOSS
GLOSS STOCK

ISSUE 5
10.12.04 :: 112 PP
NICK KAILOLA CUSTOM
TERMINATOR

ISSUE 5
10.12.04 :: 112 PP
LE GOLD COVER
GLOSS STOCK

ISSUE 6
29.06.05 :: 136 PP
STUSSY COURT FORCE

ISSUE 6
29.06.05 :: 136 PP
FEIT REVERSE COVER
HEAVY GLOSS STOCK

ADIDAS 35

You are looking at possibly the most sought after and beautiful shoe in the world right now - the ultimate 35th model in the 35th Anniversary of the adidas Superstar! Since most of them were given to friends, family and a lucky few competition winners, your chances are slim and none of tracking them down. Unless you have a budget the size of a small pacific island state that is! Seasoned eBay hounds would already know but a pair sold recently for $10,000US. Crikey, is that really what they are worth? Hard to say... The sneaker itself is made almost totally out of Premium Leather (that's right, even the midsole & sole). On top of that you get the Sandalwood Last (to keep 'em smelling rosey and in tip-top shape), the Cleaning Kit and the Gold Shoe Horn, not to mention the Almighty Lockable White Leather Box. If you had to put a hypothetical price on packaging and attention to detail you wouldn't be far off the mark, but as many have said, 'It's only a sneaker for Gawd's sakes!' Yeah right, just try telling that to a freaker who has the first 34 pairs in this series and needs that final pair for a Full House. With adidas having taken it to this ultimate level, it's almost inconceivable to think what might top this package for style and substance. One day that shoe will be here. Scary, isn't it?

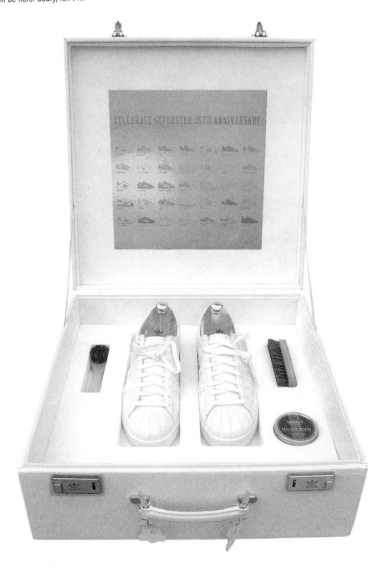

ZX 500 RS

The Forum RS HI

ZX 500 RS

TRAKKYDAKS vs ADIDAS

We're pretty cynical around here and it takes a bit to get our juices flowing. But every so often an idea comes along and you just wish you'd thought of it. Here's one!

The red model is the ZX 500 RS, an early '80s running shoe which was re-introduced several seasons ago. Big deal I hear you say. Well what is so fancy pants is the fact that each one of these shoes is a one-off. Not only that, but the upper material is made out of the chopped up classic adidas redline Great Britain, Japan, Canada and CCCP track-tops from the Sport Heritage Apparel collection. Only 300 pairs will be made, each coming with a special box and hangtag.

Likewise, The Forum RS HI upper material is made from recycled vintage tracksuits found at flea markets around Europe, some dating back as far as the 1972 Munich Olympic Games. Even cooler than that is that each pair comes with a certificate and a picture frame with the 'remnants' of the track-tops as well as before and after pictures. Only 100 pairs of these will be made! Get 'em if you can - good luck!

adidas Forest Hills

adidas Wilhelm Bungert

adidas Forest Hills

La Coste Thrill Croc

Puma Future Cat Lux

Nike Spiridon

Nike Air Stab

Nike Air Stab

Puma Taranis

La Coste Maui Star

Reebok Insta Pump

Nike AF1 Woven

adidas Carlo Gruber

Nike Sweet Lew

Nike Air 2 Strong

DC Azure Mid

DC Lynx 2

DC Griffin

DC Rover

Nike Air 180 (Olympic)

DC Rebound

DC Manteca

DC Striker

DC S-1

Vans Vault

Vans Vault

Vans Vault

Air Max (glow in dark)

Reebok Omni Lite

Reebok Leather CL

Wainscott

NEW YORK COLLECTION

Following on from their successful Artist Projects and Remix Series, DC presents the New York Collection. As you can see, the styles are refined, classy and urban, just like the city... now if only these sneakers didn't sleep! The stand-out model for pizzazz and total WOW factor is the Backstage High which somehow mixes Anaconda, Alligator and Rattlesnake skin textures with classic pinstripes. Yeouch! Then you've got the Kirkman, with its antique brass loops and taslan laces, and the hand-burnished, Oxford-style hybrid of the Wainscott. Go live the American dream with DC...

Backstage High

Kirkman

Work High

STARCK VS PUMA

Renowned international designer, Phillipe Starck, has created a new range of booties and slip-ons with Puma for 2005. As you can see, they're sleek, modern, minimal, sharp, stylish and right outta left field - just what you would expect from a maverick genius! We are told the embroideries are a throwback to the French town of Jovy, known for its lovely jewelled engravings... So there you have it. Dare to be different and snaffle a pair today. You're certain to be simply Starck Struck! (sorry)

PONY CITY WINGS

With the famous chevron on the side and the distinctive circular logo on the ankle and tongue, there is no mistaking the 'City Wings' by Pony. Originally released in 1985, the model became the original street-basketball shoe, coveted by shoe freaks and street heroes alike. From flashy Earl 'Pearl' Monroe (one of the game's OG ballers with uncanny moves to the hoop) to Bob McAdoo, Pony's b-ball tradition is rooted in the seminal days of the pro-game three decades ago. The brand became a staple on the court in the late '70s and continued to be a superior alternative with players like Darryl Dawkins, Spud Webb, Cedric Maxwell, Otis Birdsong and Alex English on the Pony team. Now you can have your own pair - in way more colours than you'll ever need!

ADIDAS CARLO GRUBER

We have tons of shoes living in our office and we always know something's up when peeps are drawn to a certain model like drunks to an ale. You cannot ignore this shoe. It just begs you to pick it up and run your fingers across the luxurious chunky knitted sock liner, so nice and snug to keep your ankles toasty on a chilly slope. And always the same question. What the hell? The correct answer is the Carlo Gruber range from adidas. Two models, same idea. Who the hell is Carlo Gruber? Is he a legendary ski instructor with a penchant for woolly smalls or a fictional creation? We don't know. No one would tell us. Not even Mr Google. But we love him all the same... More please.

Ice Ball Knit Hi

Vulc Knit Lo

REEBOK VENTILATOR

Witness the fitness of the Reebok Ventilator, a curiously named shoe if ever we heard one. There's lots to like about this sucker. Is it the hot pink pops and lime splice hi-lites? Yeah! Is it the grey faux animal print leather? Hell yeah! Kinda '80s, kinda modern, not exactly retro, but possessing a bigger ego than your common garden variety asthmatic gnome. Somebody gimme some air, this Ventilator is totally over-heated! Woohee!

Team Low - Family

Team Low - Team Edition

Dunk Lo - Vapor Mineral

Dunk Hi - White Melvins

Dunk Lo - Diamond Edition

Dunk Lo - Stussy Edition

Dunk Hi - Obsidian & Pink

Air Angus - Baroque Brown

Dunk Hi - Varsity Red, Grey

Dunk - Shanghai Edition

Blazer - German Theme

Dunk Hi - Black Melvins

P-Rod - Birch

Zoom FC - Trifecta

Dunk Hi - Maize, Midnite

AUSSIE DUNK?

This humble Dunk has been nicknamed 'Homer'. Although it's been out a while, there's a little bit of background to this shoe that we thought was worth mentioning...

First off, when SF broke news of this shoe aeons ago it caused a sensation. Was it the natty colours? Partly. Was it the obvious nickname that it earned? Partly. Was it the abstract encryption on the inner sole. Er, no (more on this later). The rumour was that this Dunk was supposed to be an Aussie exclusive. Heads downunder were salivating with the prospect of reselling this little beauty into Europe and the US. But it turned out to be a red herring. Why? No idea. However our enquiries revealed that a total of 3000 pairs were produced, of which 800 were released into the Antipodean market.
As far as we know, Canada, Germany, Spain, Taiwan and London received the rest. Therefore the two biggest markets, Japan and the USA, missed out - tuff titties fellas! Prices went berserk initially but have now settled at around 250-300us.

And now to the inner sole. Why is it so? The little guy appears to have a lightbulb on his head but in actual fact he is Cyclops, he of the one-eyed fable. It's something to do with James Joyce and the film 'O Brother Where Art Thou'. It was a sketch knocked up by the wife of Oz Nike legend, Matt 'Chickenstrips' Jenkinson because he obviously can't draw for peanuts. So now you know. And now you can tell your friends...

AIR 180 BASKETBALL RETRO
(AKA CHARLES BARKLEY)

NIKE - AIR 180

To the untrained eye these come off as just another retro re-release from Nike. However, for anyone with a deep knowledge of hot shit from the Nineties, they are a sight for very sore eyes indeed. Here's a few things we know about them. The term Air 180 actually refers to the cushioning system in the heel, and the fact that the Visible Air can be seen in a 180 degree arc (see pic above). They came in running and b-ball styles, were first released in 1991 and it was claimed then that the 180 Air system provided 50% more performance than previous Airs. Over time, the 180 (especially the Charles Barkley B-ball model) developed a cult status that kept them on the radar of vintage heads everywhere. The fact that all known deadstock supplies dried up years ago had something to do with it, as did Nike's battle with rival brand Avia over the use of a patented 'cantilever system'. We don't know much more about it than that but the legal tussle had many fearing we may never get to see this nuggety little sneaker back on the block again. Not true, as these samples prove!

**Confusingly, not all Air 180 sneakers came with the visible Air unit, as this pair of OG runners below will attest.

** OG AIR 180
(thanks to Harry W).

2004 - 180 RUNNER

RUN ATHLETICS LEGACY

Here's a peek at the brand new shoe from Run Athletics. Designed by Kevin Saer, the Legacy comes from a traditional classic tennis aesthetic, but has a modern twist. It's not revolutionary by any means, but the wise usage of materials and micro design details result in a true vintage hybrid, including laser cut loop labels, cognac vegetable leather wrap and the signature mock-croc eye stays. Retailing at around £65, the first editions of the Run Athletics sneaker will be available initially in the UK, Paris, Germany and Amsterdam. It will be launched late 2005 in the US thru independent boutique retailers.

adidas Barricade III

Nike Shox NZ

DC Sweeper

New Balance 574

Reebok Insta Pump

Nike Shox NZ

New Balance 574

Nike Spiridon

Nike Talaria

New Balance 574

adidas Barricade III

Nike Jordan XX (East)

New Balance 574

Reebok Court Victory

adidas Forest Hills

HUF TRAINER ONE

Here's a definite SF exclusive - the exotic new Trainer One SB put together by Keith at the Huf store in in San Francisco. It's known as 'the 49er' which is a reference to the West Coast Gold Rush way back when. The embroidery of the pitchfork and shovel and the gold lace tips are a nice touch, as is the gold mesh on the toe and heel. And I always love to see a spackle sole! This isn't the first Huf Collab, but I think it's the best they've put together so far. And it's nice to see the Trainer One given a little bit of love as well. Out in late 2005.

STUSSY COURT FORCE

This is not just any old Court Force, this is The Big One! Introducing the Stussy 25th Anniversary model, available in Hot Butter and Basic Black. Premium leathers have been used all over and the addition of the croc skin adds an elegant sheen to the shoe. With distro limited to Stussy hook-ups, this is sure to go gazongas - evil resellers keep your hairy mitts out of it and give us all a chance! At time of writing this was a SNKR FRKR exclusive, so we'll see how long that lasts. And congratulations to Stussy on their silver anniversary!

adidas - Ivan Lendl

Nike - Trainer 1

Puma - 3 Time Leather

K-Swiss - Chemlitt

adidas- Ilie Nastase

tennis kicks!

Fans of the yesteryear of tennis kicks will be positively erect at the thought of these all-court specialists being let loose again. Classically white and a little bit sporty - who could ask for more, especially in Summer, especially just before Wimbledon?

For our money, the Ivan Lendl model is definitely the pick of the bunch. For a guy who played like a heartless robot, Lendl's shoe was one of the raunchiest of all tennis kicks. The pale blue/red accents look startlingly contemporary and it was also the most technically advanced tennis shoe of its time. For the Ladeez we recommend the Steffi Graf. Just look at those poppin colours! Hot pink and fluoro lime, very fancy. Perhaps you also noticed the stars that have been cut into the toebox? Stan Smith fans will also be delighted to see the Supreme model rereleased in the OG colorway, (white with fairway green). And who could forget our man Ilie Nastase? The original bad boy of tennis in the '70s was wearing these as he chucked giant wobblies all over the world. They feature a drawing of his face looking eerily like Andre The Giant on the tongue.

Puma has climbed on board as well, its Match is a very classy model and quite gentlemanly with perforated highlights. Perhaps you will also enjoy the 3 Time Leather. When Puma brings back Martina Navratilova's shoe we will be even happier!

Nike fans will go erotic with the retro of the iconic Tennis Classic which seems like a shit sibling of the Wimbledon. Or you could go for their Trainer 1 in all-white. Don't forget Superbrat himself, Mr John McEnroe, wore them and he kicked ass from here to eternity didn't he? K-Swiss have always been famous for their white sneakers and here are three of their most classis tennis sneakers. The Chemlitt, Powlick and the Classic Mid. These would look the biz with long socks on a grass court on a stonking hot summers day. For a bit of Eurostyle you might be tempted by the Fila Original Tennis. Once a darling of the pro-circuit, this model has been re-released this month and they say it will be very hard to find! And last but not least, Lacoste have a whole series of killer styles just perfect for the French Open. Later Alligator! Love all... ***PANCHO RODRIGUEZ***

K-Swiss - Classic Mid

Fila - Original Tennis

Lacoste - L33

Lacoste Carnaby Croc

K-Swiss - Powlick

adidas - Steffi Graf

Puma - Match

Nike - Tennis Classic

adidas - Stan Smith

RETOUCHING :: WOODY@SNKRFRKR
ORIGINAL PHOTO :: VIRGINIA CUMMINS

BILL MCMULLEN

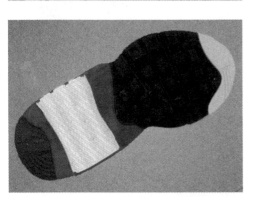

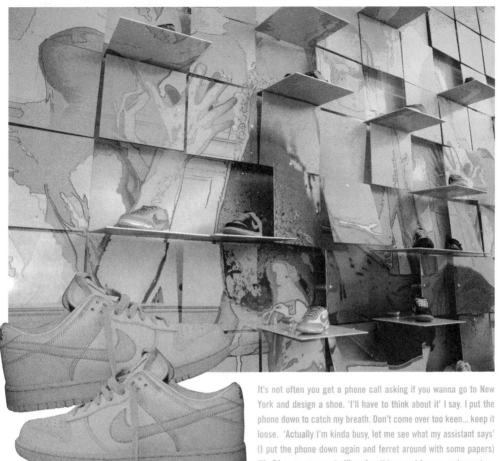

NIKE iD

It's not often you get a phone call asking if you wanna go to New York and design a shoe. 'I'll have to think about it' I say. I put the phone down to catch my breath. Don't come over too keen... keep it loose. 'Actually I'm kinda busy, let me see what my assistant says' (I put the phone down again and ferret around with some papers) 'My PA says we can shuffle a few things and free up a day or two. But, err, she also says I need to bring a few friends along as well.'

The Nike iD program has been running for a while but it's invitation only so I'm quite chuffed by the call. In the meantime, I've already emailed Liverpudlian Dave White and Jor One and asked them to tag along. Most of you will be familiar with Dave's messed out, blobby sneaker paintings. He is a fixture on the Sneaker Pimps Tours with his rock 'n' roll live painting show and he is a cheeky bugger who loves a pint. Jor One is a graff kid and at least a cut above most sneaker customisers. His kicks are supremely detailed, immaculately finished and he's always right on the money. Jor has just relocated from San Francisco to New York and we've never met before.

It's a done deal - we're on our way to the Big Apple to design a sneaker! This is the story more or less of how we got rolling into New York for a few balmy days in Summer and an appointment at the 255 space. It will be interesting to see what these guys come up with.

The heat is on...

This is actually my second trip to the Nike exhibition space at 255 Elizabeth St. The first was some time back for the Laser show with Mark Smith. Since then the space has undergone a complete overhaul. 255 Laser was all blonde wood and über Scando design, which was entirely appropriate for Laser. 255 iD is a total remix, right down to the custom flocking wallpaper, flokati rugs, leather couches, flat screen design pods, pantone colour charts and even a 6 foot high one-off mirror with a deluxe sneaker frame. You gotta hand it to Nike. They aren't afraid to spend money and they know how to treat a lady, right down to the sushi and imported beer.

But raw fish is not why we are here - we have come to see a man about a shoe! The ultimate in the sneaker world. A total one-off. Our colours, our fabrics, our style. What could be better than that? We'd all like our chance to mix it with the best and lay down some choice cuts. Nike iD might just be the only way to prove our point.

There are six Nike kicks up for grabs. The Waffle Racer, Dunk, Air Force One, FREE 5.0, Air180 and the Presto. It's amazing what runs through your mind at a time like this. I had all sorts of ideas before I rocked up for the show but now it's time for hard truth - which ride to choose? Personally, I love the Air Force, but it's a mid and they're a little chunky and the velcro strap has never done me any favours. The FREE is a great shoe and we're down with that but with the upper being predominantly a one piece construction, the colour options are a bit limited. The Dunk is the Dunk, and we won't cop it, so nix to that. The Waffle Racer - nah I don't think so!

So we're left with a choice between the Presto and the 180. The Presto is a great shoe for sure, neat, comfy, sleek as a shark and it's been a while since we made friends with a fresh pair. And there's a nice selection of mesh materials to choose from, so that's tempting. But in the end I decide to go with the 180 runner, mainly because I don't have a pair! Plus, I'm thinking the 180 colours that have been re-released to date are pretty lame-ass. All black and that mucky red? Get out of here. White with lime and royal blue? Not me! The OG all-white with magenta and blue? All that white suede will be killed by death in five seconds. Time to switch it up.

I need to get medieval on this 180's ass - someone get me the blowtorch!

First off, get control of the machine. The Nike iD interface is instantly familiar as it's identical to the online version, albeit with a much better line-up of colours and fabrics. We've also been through this process once before, when we entered the iD Blog Comp. On that occasion, Snkr Frkr writer Hans DC and I created the legendary Golden Brown 180, a brown and gold shoe just like an Aussie meat pie, complete with red ketchup laces riding up front. Unfortunately due to some mysterious Florida-style voting process, the SF crew came in second and the Golden Brown was doomed to live only in our cyberspace memories. RIP!

Now it's time for Round Two. But where to start on a whole new shoe? Here's my only rule. It has to be perfect. And unique. I've got standards to keep. I'm the Editor of a sneaker magazine and you'll all be reading this and cracking my skills. Reality check #1 - we all have to work with the limited colour palette and material swatches that are specific to our model. In the case of the 180s, that means a suede type finish for the upper. The good news is that there's a selection of metallics to work with and the colour range for the rest of the elements is rad.

So I start spazzing off with the machine by choosing some really way out stuff hoping to get lucky like Young Einstein. Unfortunately I keep coming back to black, red and pink. Then if I add some gold? Way to go Kid Robot! I love the Union 180s but there's no Safari print and no vomit cammo to be found in the system. There's no J3 elephant print either as Dave White has just discovered (although he is consoled later when he picks up the black Supremes from Flight Club). When you come to iD you want to go for broke but with as few as 7 or 8 colours to choose from for each element, this is harder than you might think.

Then I get a vision, remember those old Structures? They had a dark frame with a lighter colour underneath, kinda like a skeleton. Black with gold? Looks good but could be hard to match back with other colours. Black with metallic silver! Now we're talking. I spy Dave and Jor who are now both working on shoes that are looking good, except Dave's Dunk is all grey with silver. I haven't got the heart to tell him there are all grey samples of every shoe in the cupboard for everyone to try on to find the right size. He'll find out!

Ok, so we got the black and silver locked down as our base. What to add for colour pops? By this time, Dave has switched to a 180. He has finally worked out the grey thing and Jor is done with his Dunk. Both of them now have mauve in their design. I had already noticed that soft purples have started popping up in new shoes, notably the upcoming Stussy Court Force, Le Bron Air Force and some new Japanese NBs I saw online that morning. Funny how little colour trends happen.

I'm dead keen on this sharp colour called 'Lab Green' that I've seen on the colour chart. It looks great with the silver but I think it needs some grunt so I add a dash of 'Varsity Red'. I fiddle with that combo for a few minutes and somehow a splash of 'Shy Pink' finds its way into the mix. Not wanting to stop, I keep tinkering with the iD machine and I persevere with a variety of different combos. Inevitably though, my eye is drawn back to the same colours. Satisfied, I know my work is done... my very own Mona Lisa is complete!

If you ask me, my newly baked 180 is fresh to death and probably the best shoe ever designed in the whole world. But that's just me. I can't really think of a catchy name for it but that can come later. Right now I am basking in the glow of completing my very own colourway, a proud moment in the life of a semipro-freaker.

We all end up leaving with a little showbag including a printout of our shoe and colour swatches to remind us how it all came together. I fill out some forms and they tell me the sneakers will be delivered to my door in a few weeks, just in time for a cover shoot for this book. How good is this? My own personal sneaker valet delivering door-to-door.

The iD program has been running as a website for several years and has no doubt dispensed thousands of sneakers to happy heads over the years. But experiencing it in the exclusive 255 space simply takes it to the outer reaches of cooldom. You can't help but be schmoozed by Nike's ability to turn on a great show like this. It's a brilliant project and with a little luck, it could be coming soon to a city near you. If I be you, I'd be trying to work your way onto that guestlist right now...

Thanks to to Bridget and Nate for their help!

Hey guys, thanks for coming down to 255 Elizabeth for Nike iD. So how come you chose the Dunk?

Jor One: I chose it just coz it's a classic. The other options they had I liked, but you can't go wrong with the Dunk.

Dave White: I was gonna go with the Dunk, but I've just got a bit of a 180 thing going on. I keep buying a few pairs and I just thought it would be really nice to use that as a blank canvas to play with. I like the classic Dunk shape. I mean, it's timeless but I think the 180, the options they have on offer materials-wise, there's more choice of texture which is important.

Both of you ended up choosing mauve. [laughs] I'm not suggesting anything about your sexuality or anything...

D: Of course not, no.

But why mauve or violet or lilac or whatever you want to call it?

D: To be honest, I've always been a real fan of the greys. My palette as an artist when I was a lot younger was very vibrant. A lot more — I'm not saying Legoland — but it was much more brash and I think the mauve comes across really nice with grey. It's like not mixing it with any other colour, it's just a very neutral colour.

J: I picked the colour because it was the brightest one they had. It wasn't because I'm... [laughs] in love with purple. I had gone in with the intention of making a really bright shoe. What I've done instead is picked purple to add that splash of colour and then left that other section basically white so that I can come in later and put my own colours in.

You're going to customise your custom shoe?

J: Yes, exactly.

And how did you find the experience of actually designing your shoe? Was it harder than you thought?

D: I picked the Dunk straight away and created the shoe in literally, I'd say, about half a minute. It was all very neutral greys.

Ha ha! They had grey versions of every model for you to try on as samples...

D: When Nate opened the cabinet and I saw all those grey shoes in there it was like, 'Fuck, that's what I wanted to do.' So I thought, 'I can't sit there and do that because they'll think I've gone bananas.' It's just one of those things.

You should have taken that grey Dunk all the way home to Liverpool!

D: I wish I had. Yeah, it's weird, man. The thing is, it's just such a nice opportunity. I think it's good that they have the fabrics so you can see and feel them. That's a really nice thing. You could be in there forever. I'm looking at it now and I'm happy with what I've done but I'm thinking, 'Ooh, a bit of yellow to complement the violet'.

Bit of yellow would be nice.

D: It's too late now. It's on the way.

Jor, how did you find it?

J: I hate to knock them, but I was a little disappointed by the colours they had available for the Dunk. They had better colours for the other shoes. But otherwise it was fun. I'm happy with what I decided on, you know, you can't beat it.

Yep. Has it changed the way you think about colours?

D: I think you can be very expressive with colour or you can be very subtle with it. Logically, I found with my shoe that I always came back to the same conclusion. I think that's when you know you're totally satisfied. I loved it. I wanted to get a whole bunch of different materials. Obviously there's some practical problems involved in creating these shoes with a million materials to choose from...

You can't have a million fabrics because they'd go insane trying to make them.

D: I think so. When I actually saw the Big Book I thought, 'Lovely!' You know, imagine just hooking up some mesh for a 180. I thought the possibilities would be there. We've done a great job, but as Jor said, 'I think it'd be amazing if you could start really mucking about with it.' You know, using mesh on a 180 or leather on a Presto.

Geezus, you guys are a tough crowd! What else are you up to at the moment?

J: Same as usual, man. Painting heaps of shoes, hunched over in my little studio in Brooklyn, just trying to make the craziest shoes I can. That's it.

Dave, what's next for you?

D: I've just updated the site with the new collection, the clothing line is dropping in November. I've got a show in Tokyo and, you know, just a few things. Just doing what I'm doing and taking it global and whatever.

Being able to design your own shoe, does it make a mockery of limited editions? You've got your own one-off now... what does it all mean ?

D: It's as much as they want to control it and as much as people want to box you in, you know? What an amazing thing that would be to be able to just sit there and come up with your own concept and production. Personally, what I would love to see are the taboo fabrics: ostrich print, elephant print, being able to play with those options would be my real sort of...

Wetdream? Do you mean just for you? Or for everyone else?

D: Oh no, for everyone else. Don't get me wrong. It's not as if it's just for me in my little placealone. No, definitely. Other fabrics, other textures, other surfaces.

It's good anyway. Jor?

J: What is the question?

That's a good question. I don't know! It's too hot. I need a beer!

J: What does iD mean for limited edition shoes? For the average sneaker layman it's fabulous. They get to go in and get their one of a kind that they've designed. So it's great. For me, it still feels a little limited compared to what I can do. I can pick any colour paints I want, I get to do any graphic I want. If I want to draw middle fingers up saying 'Screw The World!' I can. You can't do that in iD.

D: I think a really good thing that may be the evolution for this place would be, you know, submitting your own design for Laser. That would be hot as you like... watching your drawings burned into a shoe.

Maybe that'll happen. Back to your prior point Dave, I feel a little protective of the cement print. I feel like it's been used too much in a way.

D: Yeah, I know, you're right. For anyone who hasn't got five hundred or a thousand dollars to buy the top end, to be able to go in and pick your own shoe is just amazing. You feel so special and to get a one-on-one consultation, it's like buying a new car, innit? Whatever the weather, we've all walked out with a nice bag, colour swatches and a printout of our work. And a free pair of sneakers! As Jor said, the average Joe goes in to iD and comes out and says, 'Look what I've done!' It's cool man!

It's totally cool. And the best part is they deliver them straight from the oven to our doors - just like the pizza guy! Thanks for tagging along for the day boys...

D: Thankyou - let's go to the pub and celebrate!

From our inaugural launch at Revolver in Melbourne to hosting Nike Speed in a 13th floor Penthouse and releasing Issue 6 in Paris, Snkr Frkr has been involved in some pretty good events & parties over the years. We also had Mark Smith in Sydney, Laser at Loaded in NZ and Huarache 2K at the Aquarium. There's also been two Sneaker Pimps shows in Sydney (one with the Nike SB team), events with Carhartt, General Pants, Dakota 501, Footage, Provider and the first ever Sneaker Swap Meet. Along the way, we've also seen some great product nights including HTM (Air Force and Court Force), Supreme, Haze, Raygun & Heineken Dunks, Lux Air Force, Le Brons, Dunkles, McFetridge Vandals... Thanks to all the die-hard crew who always turn out, night or day, hail or shine, in good times and in bad, to have a party that has something to do with a little magazine about sneakers. Olé!

"Air Wankuss" – By: Woody; Editor of
Sneaker Freaker – Australia

TROOP ORIGINAL

booze and shoes

DUNK R.I.P

Sneaker pundits have been queueing up to pronounce the Dunk DEAD for a while now. Well guess what? They ain't! Most of the SBs have more than held their inflated eBay value and new releases are still causing queues outside skate shops all over the world. Following on the heels of the Shanghai, London, Homer, Heineken, Supreme, Lucky 7, Unlucky 13, California and Jedi models, here's a quick look at some of the recent hot potato Dunks released into the market! Good luck finding them...

THE HUNTER

If you like to get naked in the woods you'll be loving this sneaker! Now, just stop for a minute and look closely at the way this shoe has been put together. Quilted orange satin inner lining. Woodland cammo outer overlocked onto the hessian panels. For sheer imagination you have to hand it to Nike. Actually, this Dunk was designed by a mysterious mob called The Delphi Collective. Unlike the other models pictured here, this Dunk was put together for a member of the Nike skate team - Reese Forbes to be precise.

Aloha!

The Aloha Dunk is a new city collab with ace Honolulu sneaker store Kickshawaii. According to www.fatlace.com, where it was first spotted, the Aloha is a project that has taken some time to get right.

That material on the side of the shoe is called a 'lauhala weave' by Ian G, the owner of the store, and no doubt it would add a level of complexity to production.

Pundits will recognise a similarity with the Bison, in the sense that the toebox is an incredibly vivid colour, backed up with a fairly neutral heel and mid-section. And kids, remember that the Bison was one of the biggest sleepers of the past year, so start saving your shekels now.

More info - www.kickshawaii.com

XIAO LONG

At first we interpreted the tongue logo as some sort of coffee reference but we now know it's all about Chinese dumplings. We investigated a little further and found this info, which was supplied by the guys at Nike China!

"Most of the shoe's color is inspired by the steamers of Xiao Long. Due to the delicious oily juice in Xiao Long, it always gets dirty. We use oily leather to present that effect. The logo on the tongue means the small bowl and the chop sticks. People always eat Xiao Long together with vinegar, which is always put in the little dishes. And always, Chinese people use chopsticks. The stitches on the upper are inspired by the stitches on the steamer."

DUNKLE

No doubt one of the biggest releases of 2004 was the Dunkle, which was a collaboration with James Lavelle (founder of Mowax records, now recording as UNKLE, hence the cute name) and features the distinctive artwork of NYC graff legend Futura, who is known for many things including his spacey artwork for Mowax/Unkle. Lavelle has very close links with Nike and is often deejaying at Nike events from NYC to Paris so I guess it was a good fit for a collab.

Not all shoes deserve the hype but this package was an exception. A while back we got an email from Mike Hernandez who put the shoe together and it gives an insight into how a project like this comes together...

"Sandy Bodecker (head of Nike Skate) let me know that James was interested in doing a shoe. I'm a big fan of Unkle and when I received all the Futura images I started right away. My first thoughts were a pink/black/white story. I wanted to make the design wearable and kinda craze at the same time.

My first comps that went out to James were met with immediate approval. No changes. I used a combination of leathers and nubuck with water-based inks and embroideries to cover the Dunk Hi SB. I kept the vamp black to ground the design and also brought in the patent leather swoosh for a little specialness. Soon after we started to sample the design and I presented a new pink SB shoebox packaging design to tie the whole thing off. The first shoe sample we received was spot on. No changes. Not rocket science, but the project came together quickly as if it was meant to be. The shoe uses 11 screens for printing to make the lateral and medial sides different."

RAYGUN

The Roswell concept was originally created for a 2002 Nike commercial that featured an all-star team (inc. Vince Carter, Baron Davis & Jerry Stackhouse) called the Roswell Rayguns going back in time to 1975 to 'keep the funk alive!' (actually, Bootsy Collins said that - he made a guest appearance).

According to www.5thdimension.com (a fantastic site that features all things super rare Nike) this shoe first appeared at the 2002 ASR show in San Diego. There is also a connection with renowned sneaker customiser Methamphibian and a pair of Air Force Ones but, like a good film reviewer, I'll leave the punchline to be revealed when you go to the site.

It was always thought that these bad boys would probably never see the light of day, which seemed somewhat fitting considering the mysterious goings on at Roswell all those years ago. Fans of the X Files will definitely know what I'm talking about. And if you still don't know, check out the little green martian embroidered into the heel. Considering all the Raygun background and the powerful colour combo, eBay prices for this shoe are sure to go gazongas!

STOP THAT CRAZY PIGEON!

Despite predictions of imminent uncooldom, the Dunk SB just keeps powering on. No other shoe can consistently inspire kids to camp out for days just to land the big one. And they don't come much bigger than this - the New York Pigeon Dunk! With so many kids wanting, and so few shoes available, there was bound to be disappointment. But no-one expected the launch to nearly turn into a New York street riot! We caught up with The Reed Space owner, Jeff Ng, to ask him what went wrong and why it seems reports of the Dunk's death have been greatly exaggerated?

Hey Jeff - how's New York?
NY is culturally dead. And I might add the weather here supremely sucks.

You guys own the store Reed Space, but what else do you get up to?
Staple Design owns and operates The Reed Space. Reed Space is a store and an art gallery and we also do special launches. For example, we launched the Nike Considered line as well as the Pigeon Dunk. Staple Design is primarily a design firm and small independent creative agency. That's our bread and butter. We also do a small clothing line for some stupid reason. Just for shits and giggles I guess.

How did the Pigeon Dunk come about?
My good friend Marcus who used to run things at Nike SB, asked us to create the NYC Dunk that was to be aligned with the White Dunk show. If you remember, there was a Paris, Japan, Cali, London one etc, etc. So he asked us to work on the NYC one. Of course it was a great honor. To be able to bless the seminal shoe, The Dunk, and represent our home town all in one project was just a dream come true. After sitting around and thinking for a while about what represented NY best, the Pigeon kept coming up. It's something very innate to New Yorkers. And something you wouldn't necessarily relate to the city if you didn't in fact live here.

When were they released and how many were there?
Feb 22nd, 2005. 150 for the world. 30 pieces for 5 shops. Rival, Supreme, Recon, KCDC and us. Our 30 had a lasered Staple logo and each was individually numbered.

And tell us the story about the days leading up to their release?
Leading up to the release day was pretty crazy. We had kids sleeping outside in tents about 4 days before the release. There was a snowstorm as well so I was pretty impressed and dumbfounded at the same time. But for the most, the kids were calm and orderly.

At what point did you realise there was a major problem?
I thought it was going to be pretty chill. When I left work the night before, there were maybe 20 kids waiting outside that night. It wasn't until I came to work the next day that I realized there was a problem on our hands. There were about 100-150 kids now. With bodies pressed up against our front gate it looked like there was a Manchester United game going on inside. About a dozen cops were already there. The NYPD was like, 'What the fuck is going on here?'

Did you ever, I mean ever, in your wildest dreams think it would go as crazy as it did?
Never. I was totally shocked.

It sounds funny now but were you scared at all?
I was scared the whole time! There was no way we could satisfy everyone. We had 30 pairs for our allotment! With 150+ people, you knew there was a problem. I had a security team, the NYPD, my staff... nothing could make these people happy. We were seriously, without any exaggeration, on the verge of a full-blown riot scene.

I heard the cops were giving out summonses for trespassing and weapons were found?
About 10-20 arrests were made. I must say the NYPD was so dope about the whole thing. They were very understanding and helpful in fact. After the crowd cleared, we found machetes and baseball bats!

SNEAKER RIOT

Lower E. Side rumble over Nikes

PIGEON POOPED: Cops try to control the crowd of people waiting on line trying to snare a pair of Nike Pigeon (NYC) Dunk sneakers on Orchard Street yesterday after a not broke out. Nike made only 150 pairs of the shoes, which were going for $1,000 on eBay.

SHOE FRENZY: Two sneakerheads get caught up in yesterday's fracas for Nike Pigeons.

By RACHEL SKLAR and LEONARD GREENE

NEW YORK POST
Sneaker frenzy
Hot shoe sparks ruckus
FULL STORY, PHOTOS: SEE PAGE 7
LOST SOULS
1,100 victims of 9/11

25 CENTS

Knife found at scene...

I also heard they made everyone get a cab home, because hoods were waiting for the kids on the other side of your store?
Yeah, the Lower East Side is no joke. There were thugs on all four corners waiting to grab kicks from kids who were waiting in the line. The cops saw this. So they called a fleet of cabs to our back door. Kids would come in thru the front, buy their pair, and then be escorted thru the back right into a cab and off they went. One kid didn't have enough for the cab fare and the cop paid for him. That's the NYPD servicing the community if you ask me!

Does it seem funny to you that anyone would pay 2000 bucks for a Dunk with a pigeon on it?
No. To each his own. That kid who paid 2Gs for a Pigeon probably doesn't understand why someone would pay 3 million for a Picasso. Or $10,000 for a Tiffany watch. Everyone has their fix.

What was Nike's reaction to all this? Were they there for the event?
Love and Hate. Some people loved it, some people hated it. Thing is, some people thought we orchestrated and planned the whole thing. It was on the cover of the New York Post the following day... so I guess people thought we paid for that. Trust me, my life was in danger for most of that day. I don't need press that badly. I just tell people at Nike who were pissed, 'Would you rather that cover have a Reebok on it? That's what I figured.'

What do you think the Pigeon says about sneaker culture in 2005?
It's reaching critical mass. It'll be interesting to see if anyone can top this. I'm not tooting my own horn or anything... I'm just saying I wonder if this is the nail in the coffin for sneaker culture. Or will it continue to be bananas?

It's kinda nice to have peeps go so nuts to get your shoes, but did it make you feel sick as well?
Yeah it did. When those kids were sleeping outside in a snowstorm, I felt bad. I wanted to buy everyone a pizza or something. Then I realized... wait, these guys are waiting here so they can drop $300 on sneakers! They can buy their own damn slice!!

Well it was such a big success, what else have you got planned?
Now you know we can't say. But some cool things are gonna drop in 2006. The Pigeon was only a clue in what's to come. I'm really shocked because some people already figured it out! Sneaker heads are mad observant.

What's the current street price for a pair?
$2000 and up, with fakes running $800 and up.

How long until the fakes appeared? The embroidery is a great copy!
Not sure... but I started seeing them on eBay about 2 months after. The Chinese are very ingenious!

Have you run into anyone who's been rocking fakes?
Yeah... I was art directing a photo shoot for this famous basketball player. His assistant was all amped about the fact that he was getting Pigeons from eBay he just won. He showed me and I didn't have the heart to tell him he just bid on fugazies. Hope he's not reading this.

Can you hook me up with a pair? I know you guys got spare pairs under the table somewhere. C'mon, help a brother out!
I'm disappointed I didn't save one pair on ice. I just have the one I wear. I guess I felt like if I did, I would jinx myself and we would never be able to do another Nike collabo. I'm very superstitious.

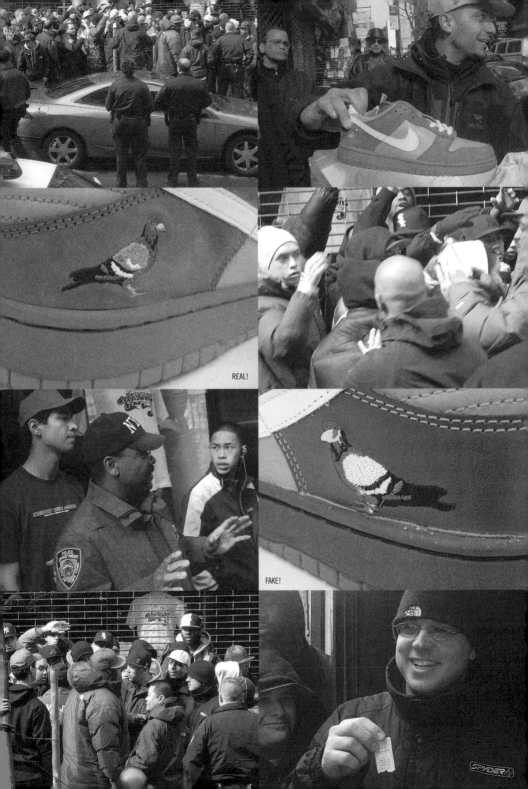

REAL!

FAKE!

HAPPY CAMPERS!

Alright, you've seen the pictures and heard the stories, but what does it actually feel like to line up overnight just to buy a pair of sneakers? When I first started out in the game, people only had to wait for about 5 hours maximum. But now the queueing has quadrupled, in some places 96 hours and more are the norm. Back in January of 2005, I had the opportunity to experience lining up in Hong Kong for the White Raygun Dunk SB. This is a detailed journal of that entertaining, amusing, but exhausting experience. Refer back to this journal whenever you're preparing to camp overnight – some of the tips and advice could come in handy. After all, I've camped out three times in the last 12 months… and boy am I tired!

DAY 1 :: MONDAY, 10/1/2005

6.00pm: Meet up with the kix-files.com crew outside Causeway Place, a small plaza located diagonally from Sogo. The Nike shop is located on the fourth floor in their sports section.

6.15pm: We negotiate how we will be lining up according to the size we want. I end up 12th in line. Since it's only 6pm and still 4 hours away from closing time, there is A LOT (and I mean a lot) of pedestrian traffic. Imagine having thousands of people swarming all over you while you're trying to huddle up in your little corner to eat your dinner – it's like being inside a goldfish bowl.

7-9.00pm: I go home for dinner and pack a few things such as a jacket, bottled water, magazines, a scarf since its still winter in HK, MP3 player and a foldable camping chair.

9.30pm: Arrive back at the campsite and arrange myself. Sneaker Freaker member 'Coolblueflame' happens to walk by so he comes over to show off his newly acquired pickup - a pair of D-Mop Superstars from the 35th range. Lucky fellow!

10.00pm: Finally it's the closing time for the department store! But because we're camping out, the security guards ask us to move to the footpath. We then stand around talking and chatting – sneakers, videogames, even the sexy chicks that walked right past us! One of our friends has copped a pair of Undefeated Superstars so we take pictures because it's probably the closest we'll ever get to another one…

11.00pm: Suddenly my brother pops out of nowhere and brings dessert for us! But then my friend has a strange idea – he decides to go home and get his car so we can take turns sleeping in it instead of surviving the cold and windy weather. Everyone thinks it is a great idea so we catch a bus back to Ho Man Tin to get his car and we also stop to check out the latest posts on the Sneaker Freaker forum!

DAY 2 :: TUESDAY, 11/1/2005

12.30am: Before we head back to Causeway Bay, we en route to Mong Kok to pick our lady friends up. By the time we arrive, some of our group are asleep already.

12.40am: The traffic on the roads and on the footpath has slowed down, and some members are asleep already in their chairs. Then Sneaker Freaker member 'Sir Charles Jr' comes to check us out since he couldn't come and line up with us. We go to a nearby café for supper.

2.15am: The traffic on the road is non-existent, except for a few taxis, a few 24-hour buses and sometimes a few drunken old men shouting insults at us for blocking the passenger walkway. Idiots! The weather has started to get cooler – a chilling wind as cold as 12 degrees is blowing hard, and some of us have no protective clothing. I was woken up from my sleep due to the cold wind since I don't have a sleeping bag.

Lesson 1: A sleeping bag is essential if you line up in winter.
Lesson 2: Sleeping on a chair is harder than you imagine.

2.20-3:20am: 'Sir Charles Jr' suggests we go to an internet café to check up on the latest news on the forum. We ended up wasting our time playing Counter Strike...

3.30am: My first toilet break. A very big moment. The disadvantage of our location is that there are no toilets nearby – the closest one is a 7 minute walk. When we walk in, we ask politely to borrow the crapper, but all we get is a few blank stares.

Lesson 3: Camp somewhere nearby which has a dunny you can access 24/7.

5.49am: Woke up to a big bang! A car accident has happened not far away from us – a mini-van collided with another mini-van delivering newspapers and magazines. Then most of us went back to sleep shortly since there wasn't anything interesting to see. I should have taken a newspaper but they were all crunched up from the accident.

7.30am: Wake for the final time. The sun is getting up and people are flocking from all directions. HK gets busy shortly after dawn coz most people are workaholics who work from 8am to 11pm. Because we're on a rotation system, the guys who didn't stay last night will secure our spots during daytime, while the overnighters go home to get a shower. I head home and go to sleep.

Lesson 4: Organise a system where it's possible for all to get private time. I don't think anyone will want to go near you if you've been sleeping on the street for a week without a shower.

7.30pm: Return to the campsite after refreshing myself at home with a hot shower. The whole group is staying over tonight. We've made an agreement that everyone must stay over on the last night to make it fair. Most people bring blankets and thermal jackets since the news said the weather might dip down to 10 degrees after midnight.

Lesson 5: The weather channel is a happy camper's best friend.

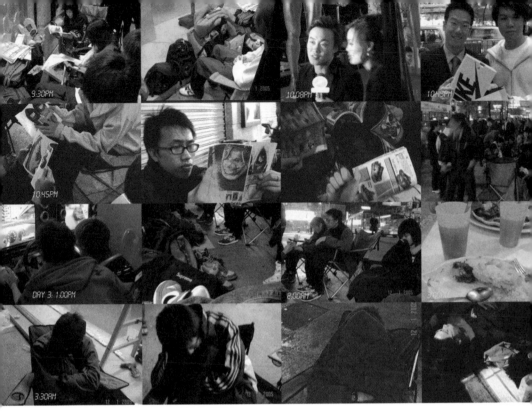

10.08pm: Got a call saying famous Hong Kong singers Joey Yung and Eason Chan are having a press conference at a nearby cinema. A few of us run over to the cinema and take pictures because you don't bump into a famous person that frequently…

10.45pm: Sneaker Freaker member 'Schmarker' drops by to visit me. I give him the Shanghai Dunk Low SB which I helped him trade a few days ago. I can't believe so many people came by to visit me…LOL.

11.30pm: By this time, there are another 5 guys lined up behind our group, which brings the total number of people in the queue to 25. We have nothing to do so I provide issues of Sneaker Freaker for everyone to read. It was a new experience for them to read a sneaker magazine in English…

DAY 3 :: WEDNESDAY. 13/1/2005

1.00pm: Everyone was bored shitless, so we visit the local video arcade. We only stayed for about 45 minutes since arcades close at 2am in HK.

> **Lesson 5:** As well as finding a great toilette, a videogame arcade nearby can be good for morale as well.

2.00am: People in the group start to feel tired so we unpack the mats and sleeping bags. Suddenly a friend of ours rocks up. The chatting starts, and it doesn't stop till much later…

3.00am: Toilet break! But some of us feel hungry so we have supper as well.

3.30am: When I get back from supper, all the guys are asleep.

3.37am: Walk to the famous shopping mall, Times Square. It is the first time I have ever seen NOBODY, not even a single soul hanging out in the plaza. We passed nearby skate store 'Evergreen' to find 3 kids sleeping out to buy shoes as well.

4.30am: A friend suggests we buy some beer since we have nothing to do. The 4 of us (3 guys and 1 girl) walk to the nearest store to buy some snacks to munch on. At this point in time, some people have woken up and start chatting whilst others keep on sleeping. The weather is pretty cold at this moment…

7.00am: Finally, more people come to line up. A few unknowns come and sit down, including a kid who was wearing a pair of Stash AF1 (the one which came with a CD and suitcase)!

7.21am: I get something to eat at McDonalds. Some are still sleeping at this stage and more people have joined the queue.

7.30am: Whilst munching on a hot Sausage and Egg McMuffin, a Nike staffer puts up a poster saying how there's only 28 pairs for sale – enough for every single one of us and a few others who were waiting behind our group. Phew!

8.03am: Out of nowhere come a bunch of people with hoses and pipes and a big pump who start cleaning out the sewerage system beneath us. The pump makes a really, really loud noise while it's running so it wakes everyone up. By this time, there are over 35 people in the line, but no-one took notice of the poster…

9.45am: Because Sogo opens at 10am, we have to pack up our stuff. 15 minutes later a Nike nuffer hands out tickets with our number in the line on it. Only 28 tickets were handed out, so

of course there are a few arguments by the people who came late and don't get one. A person even said he got here at 7am and why on earth he couldn't get one?

Ah yes, shit like this happens in HK all the time.

10:30am: The store still hasn't opened yet, a fire engine comes and the firemen storm into the store. There's a fire on the 4th floor which was also where the Nike shop is located! Oh no! They have no clue when it will open again so all we can do is wait in line till the store re-opens...

Lesson 6: Be prepared and take into account for anything unexpected, even burly firemen.

10.30-1:00pm: All we can do now is wait for the shop to re-open, so we unfold the chairs again and sit down to wait.

1.00pm: The shop finally OPENS! They let us walk into the store in a single file all the way up to the 4th floor.

1.30pm: All our group get the shoes they wanted, therefore the whole operation is successfully accomplished. Everyone else then departs to go to work, school or home for a big sleep...

2.00pm: Finally sit down with my girlfriend for a decent meal and admire my new pickup, but the busy schedule doesn't stop here: I have an interview with another magazine at 3pm...

Lesson 7: Never make any plans after a big campout — you won't have the mood to do anything!

CONCLUSION: Queueing up is hard work and quite possibly dangerous too. If you ask me personally, I think queueing up for a pair of shoes is time wasting. But in the sneaker culture of today where resellers buy up the entire stock in one hit, we have no choice but to do so because of our love of sneakers. Some people may think we are stupid, but it really depends on what kind of angle you're looking at us from — we may think people lining up overnight to get concert tickets to the next Britney Spears concert is stupid too. And it is. But queueing up can be fun if you are going with a bunch of close friends. You could see it as a group of boy scouts going camping — not in the bush, but on a stretch of footpath in front of a store! I just hope one day we will have the chance to buy whatever we want without the need to sleep in cold weather for 72 hours.

So, to the store owners and the big bosses from the big N and 3 stripes, please read this, take note and feel how we are suffering at the hands of your 'limited edition' and 'quickstrike' strategy... See you on the footpath!

STORY BY IORI

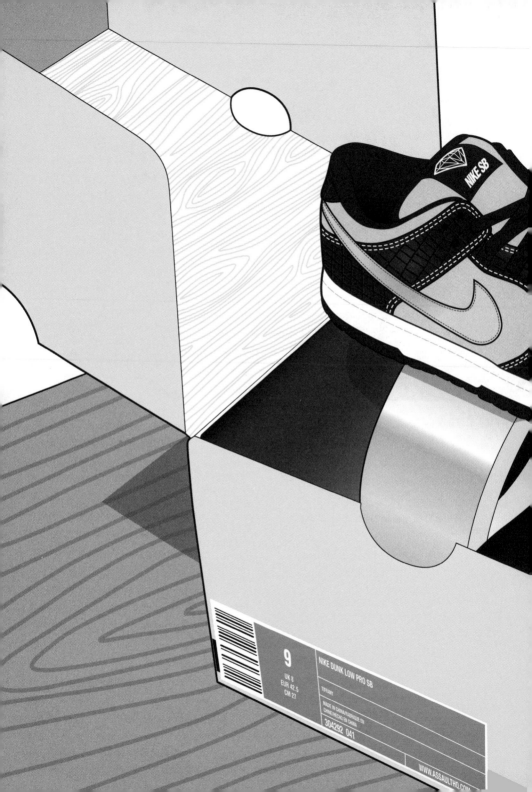

NIKE SB

9

UK 8
EUR 42.5
CM 27

NIKE DUNK LOW PRO SB

TIFFANY

MADE IN CHINA/FABRIQUE EN
CHINE/HECHO EN CHINA

304292 041

WWW.ASSAULTHQ.COM

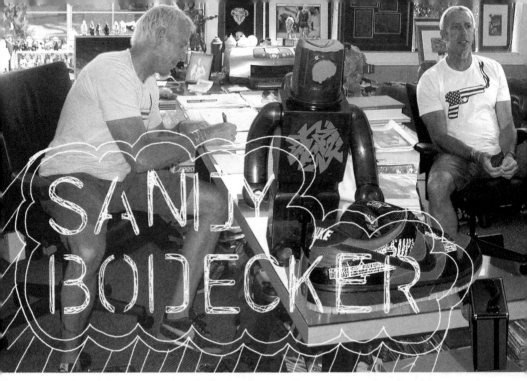

SANDY BODECKER

Meet Sandy Bodecker. Vice-President of Nike, honorary Australian, musclecar enthusiast and the man in charge of Nike's big push into the Skate Park. Under his reign, Nike has reclaimed all the credibility lost during its first ill-fated foray into the world of skateboarding, and then some. With a skate team of superstars at his disposal and prices for many Dunk models stable at around $4-500us, the future looks rosy. But a big question mark remains - can the team make Nike's other skate models (the Angus, EQ and the URL) winners as well?

This is really Nike's second crack at skate isn't it?
Yeah they already had one go but in fairness to the folks that were working on it, it didn't get the support it needed to be successful. Whether they had the right people or not, I don't know. I wasn't involved. This is our first real effort where as a company we have decided we want to get into it in a serious way and not just dabble.

Are you happy so far?
Yeah I think so. It's a really slow process but overall I think we are doing the right thing in trying to get the community to believe that we're here for real. Overall I think the reception has been cautious to date. I think more and more people are respectful and believe that we are doing it the right way.

Is skate a particularly hard area to crack given the nature of skaters' outlook on life?
It's definitely different from what people would classify as traditional team sports. By nature they are more individualistic about their approach to life and they are not as organised as you would find in traditional sports but they love what they do.

As an industry, skate is in bit of a downslide at the moment isn't it?
I wouldn't call it a downslide. I think skate's been up and down before but I don't think the drop-off this time will be anywhere near what it has been in the past. The emergence of the skate park has basically made access to skating much broader than it ever has been and that is especially true in the US. I believe there are over 800 skate parks in the US. Communities believe that skating is not a bad thing - it gets kids out, it's healthy exercise rather than sitting in front of a computer or a TV all day and that's been a big help. The dynamics have all changed, it's less of a rebel type of sport than it was in the past but I think that's true of most of the action sports.

Is it hard operating such a big business under scrutiny of not just your competitors but also extremely opinionated customers? There always seems to be a lot of gossip going on and everyone's always wondering what you are up to...
That's true. We are a big company but one of the things we have always stressed to ourselves is there are benefits to being big. There can be some downside as well but you play to your strengths and we have some power on the creative, the design side, the product side and the communication side and that works for you rather than against you. What we are trying to do within the skate community is to show that we can be a little company and very entrepreneurial within a massive company structure.

Vice-President
x Nike, Skate

Do you look at Niketalk for example?

If you don't then you are a little out of touch with what kids are talking about. You may agree with some of the things or you may not but that's true of just about anything. Just the fact that people are actually somehow scamming line art for the sneakers that you do and submitting colours and getting critiques from their mates, I think it's brilliant. It's a wonderful honour to the product that you're doing that people actually want to spend time discussing it.

How did the Dunk go from being an old basketball shoe to become a huge skate product?

It came along about the same time as this whole retro, cleaner footwear emerged. People looked at skate shoes and they had become way over-designed to the point where people really couldn't skate in them. So we looked back at the product that people skated in back in the day and obviously the Jordan I, the Blazer and then the Dunk came up. What could we do to the Dunk which wouldn't change it but actually offer just a little bit more performance? So we added more cushioning protection with a zoom air sock liner and we added a little more padding to the tongue which didn't take away from the aesthetics or the heritage of the shoe. It actually enhanced it a little bit and you put that back into the marketplace as our first offering and kept it limited to four skate shops cause that's really where we were trying to hit and it just started to resonate.

The older skaters remembered it as a shoe they loved to rock and some of the younger skaters started to see it as pretty fresh. It's just keeping in style with what's happening, kids who know the AF1s more from the urban scene started to pick up on it as well and for us it was a very fortunate entry point.

It allowed us to get some product into the shops, make it easy for a kid to buy into Nike in a skate shop and it also gave us time to start working on developing the next generation of technical shoes which is ultimately what we need to be successful.

Do you mind that Dunks are being worn as fashion product?

You've got to be honest with yourself and we know probably 75% of people that came into the shops initially to buy it were heads. We weren't getting as much in front of skaters as we'd have liked. The heads were picking them up before the shops opened, trying to pre-order and send them overseas. We tried really hard to limit the number of pairs you can sell per customer. We wanted them out on the shelves, we wanted it to be a skate shoe, not just a collector's item.

I think it was the first time we've seen queues in Australia out the front of a shoe shop for sneakers before...

Well that's great, it was a special product because we sold it into only a small number of shops. We brought a little bit extra to it and I think that, credit to our designers for this, some of the stories that we were able to tell with the materials and colours were pretty fresh compared to some of the other product that was out there.

DUNK SB

HEMP DUNK

SUPREME

ZOOM FC

HOMER DUNK

URL

The Supreme is the one with the highest profile, do you agree?

Yeah, obviously the hook up with Supreme was a great one for us. They are an incredibly respected brand and I have a ton of respect for James and his crew. They were *the* iconic skate shop here in New York and they were able to bring together a real diverse group of skaters back in the day and it sort of built off of that. So to be able to hook up with those guys creatively was great for us.

That elephant skin thing hit just at the right time. Was it a great stroke of luck or the work of a true genius?

If you ask James, he is a genius and we'll leave it at that! (laughs) It was great because I remember the Jordan III when it first came out. I worked as a developer on it originally so I was trying to get that stuff to work in the first place. It was really nice to bring it back...

How many pairs of Supremes were there officially?

I think the original order for the Supremes in all the colours was like 2000 pairs. There were just 2 colourways the first time out but these next ones that are coming out, which will drop in October, have three colourways.

How many pairs of those will there be?

We just take orders for the Supreme stores. We don't sell them any place else, which I think is appropriate, they have 5 stores

How did they come to be on the website for just 24 hours?

It was a tease.

It worked...

James is understandably selective, he wants his product to have an impact. He doesn't like to go out there and advertise, so a little tease doesn't hurt and that kind of product will be sold out in a day or two. Everybody wants it.

Does the Dunk stay on the shelf forever or do you see it being retired one day?

I think the Dunk will become a standard. How many models and colours you introduce during the course of the year will vary based on people's sensibilities. We definitely protect it for sure and we will not overdo it, but as long people are still interested in that as a product then I think it's worthwhile for us to do it.

Let me ask it this way, are you sensitive to overplaying it?

We are much better off to underplay it and we will definitely go in that direction hoping that some of our new product like the Angus which we just introduced becomes a staple product. It's basically a good performance product at a reasonable price and its got some style attached to it as well.

Let's talk about your new product, Angus, E-Cue and the URL. Which one will become the classic for the next 10 years?

The E-Cue, especially because it is visually dramatic and it's significantly a higher performance shoe than anything out there. I'm trying to be honest here. We developed it to last specifically for skate and to get maximum protection and still give you as much board feeling as it possibly could. It's a more expensive skate shoe but I think 5 years from now people will look back at that particular shoe and say that it was a benchmark.

JEDI DUNK

BROWN ANGUS

BUCK DUNK

Is retro therefore almost a monkey on your back when trying to get your new product off the ground?

We are very fortunate to have the retro catalogue and it's given us an intro to be able to put other stuff into stores. Slowly, over time, the more people that skate in the new product, the more they realise what a good shoe it is, so our expectations are not so much high volume sales for new product, it's more to get people to understand that Nike is putting the same performance effort into developing skate as we do in track and field or basketball or tennis or any other sport. We love to win, we love challenges.

The Heineken Dunk was a happy coincidence - or was there a deal made with them?

It wasn't specifically designed as the Heineken Dunk - that's just what people called it. We did take inspiration from the colours green, red, black and white with a red accent. People started calling it the Heineken. I think people want stories around the product they buy. There's different kinds of things that you can do that reflect on either a community, a city or a cartoon character and all of a sudden people can relate to that.

Hmmmnh... Well whoever thought of doing that is a genius, I hope they got a decent bonus for Christmas!

Yeah, you have to be much sharper at your game as far as putting product into the market place. It used to be just having maybe a limited number sold in a limited number of stores but nowadays it's not enough.

In terms of Research and Development, what does it cost to create shoes like the E-Cue - I heard it could be $200,000?

Honestly I couldn't tell what the exact cost is because we put everything into our overall R&D. You've seen the operation and how much we invest as a company and you know that's something that a small company just can't do. Even within the skate industry it's been difficult for them to create really technical product because they don't have the same type of resources that a company like Nike has. When you want simple you can get the Troops. Anybody can make a simple retro shoe when there's no technology involved.

How do you define that relationship between Nike and Savier?

It seems to be weird that they would take the Trainer 1 and reissue it without the forefoot strap?

Savier has been essentially an investment on Nike's behalf, so we don't really interact with them. We know the folks down there and we chat from time to time. (note:: Savier has now closed down)

Did you know about it before it came out?

One of the riders, Tim O'Connor, was interested in the shoe and evidently worked on them to develop it. DC also came out with a Trainer 1 but it's the same thing - how many companies have their version of the Dunk? There's 15 of them out here and if I spent all my time worrying about other people knocking us off, it would be silly. The fact is that they are paying homage, essentially honouring the original and we still do the original in the right way and the people who really know, *know*, and that's good enough for me. If people want to focus efforts on bringing back old shoes that they didn't design in the first place then good for them, we'll be onto the next generation.

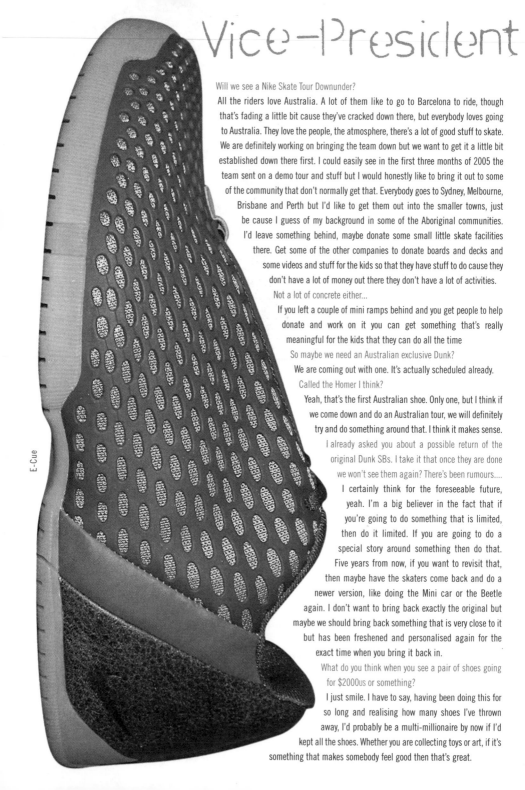

Vice-President

Will we see a Nike Skate Tour Downunder?

All the riders love Australia. A lot of them like to go to Barcelona to ride, though that's fading a little bit cause they've cracked down there, but everybody loves going to Australia. They love the people, the atmosphere, there's a lot of good stuff to skate. We are definitely working on bringing the team down but we want to get it a little bit established down there first. I could easily see in the first three months of 2005 the team sent on a demo tour and stuff but I would honestly like to bring it out to some of the community that don't normally get that. Everybody goes to Sydney, Melbourne, Brisbane and Perth but I'd like to get them out into the smaller towns, just be cause I guess of my background in some of the Aboriginal communities. I'd leave something behind, maybe donate some small little skate facilities there. Get some of the other companies to donate boards and decks and some videos and stuff for the kids so that they have stuff to do cause they don't have a lot of money out there they don't have a lot of activities.

Not a lot of concrete either...

If you left a couple of mini ramps behind and you get people to help donate and work on it you can get something that's really meaningful for the kids that they can do all the time

So maybe we need an Australian exclusive Dunk?

We are coming out with one. It's actually scheduled already.

Called the Homer I think?

Yeah, that's the first Australian shoe. Only one, but I think if we come down and do an Australian tour, we will definitely try and do something around that. I think it makes sense.

I already asked you about a possible return of the original Dunk SBs. I take it that once they are done we won't see them again? There's been rumours....

I certainly think for the foreseeable future, yeah. I'm a big believer in the fact that if you're going to do something that is limited, then do it limited. If you are going to do a special story around something then do that. Five years from now, if you want to revisit that, then maybe have the skaters come back and do a newer version, like doing the Mini car or the Beetle again. I don't want to bring back exactly the original but maybe we should bring back something that is very close to it but has been freshened and personalised again for the exact time when you bring it back in.

What do you think when you see a pair of shoes going for $2000us or something?

I just smile. I have to say, having been doing this for so long and realising how many shoes I've thrown away, I'd probably be a multi-millionaire by now if I'd kept all the shoes. Whether you are collecting toys or art, if it's something that makes somebody feel good then that's great.

E-Cue

x Nike, Skate

What pisses you off?

What I don't like is when product goes into shops and the shops will charge way, way more than they should. It's unfortunate for the kids who can't afford that. I am a bit uncomfortable about that.

Have you ever kicked people out of your distribution network?

We have pretty strict rules with legal boundaries of what people can and can't do and we are definitely less willing to work with retailers that take advantage of consumers. We want kids to have the product.

When the street price is very different from the retail price, temptation must be hard to resist. Nike can't win either because you look like you're charging ripoff prices...

Like all manufacturers, you have a suggested retail price that you ask people to sell the product for. Regardless of what the retailer does we still sell it wholesale for the same price we always do. We are also sensitive of the fact that especially for some of the small shops, sometimes selling this product is what keeps them in business and so you do have to balance it out. What you don't like to see is when you have an order of product that comes in and it never even reaches the shelf - somebody comes in and buys the whole lot and it gets shipped to someplace else. That's just unfair. Those are the retailers we don't want to work with.

What's the fifth series going to be? Can you give us anything at all?

We have a little hemp series which I think people are pretty stoked on. We have some fun stories that are coming up and some great collabs. I really don't want to say right now cause they're not 100%. We are taking the Dunk and using that as a metaphor for a premium product and putting a collection of various products around that and we'll be exploring another iconic product that people skated in back in the day.

Which one would that be?

You'll see! (laughs) It's really interesting. Our riders go out and they come back and ask us to bring this or that out. You have to be a little careful and you don't want to step on toes, you want to have something special and do it the right way. I think there are a few things in the FC product which we are really happy with. It's a really accessible price and it's a good shoe. You'll just have to wait and see...

Thought you might say that, thanks Sandy...

No problem!

URL

FAKERSBITERSPOACHERSWHINGERS SCENESUCKERSRIP-OFFARTISTS ASS CLOWNSPOSERSHYPEMONKEYS NEWBIESILLYWACKERS&CRYBABIES...

With sneakerology gone mainstream, I feel compelled to sit back in my deluxe Eames armchair, light up my jaunty crack pipe and have a fatherly fireside chat with you all. It seems to me there's trouble brewing in the hills. I think we've all heard the rumblings... 'Sneakers are so yesterday!' 'I'm sick of it!' 'Marketing's killed it!' 'Resellers suck balls!' 'Dunks are so passé!' Can it possibly be true?

Not if you ask me. When we started Sneaker Freaker Magazine several years ago, we had no idea how things would unfold. At that point, we were lucky to see more than a few good shoes a year. How things have changed - the market is now flooded with more Limited Editions, vintage brand resurrections, artist collabs, celebrity cock-ups, retro throwbacks and more generic product than you can shake a prosthetic limb at.

There are too many shoes. And when everything is lauded as 'special' it invariably means that almost everything is not. Is it any wonder so much of it ends up in the Sale Bin? Who gives a shit? Buy it for half price. That's what I used to dream of. Not dropping a grand on Consortiums I might be able to flip in HK through a secret hook-up and make 5 bucks on.

As I was saying before I was rudely distracted, everybody wants what nobody else can get. This 'treat 'em mean and keep 'em keen' perversity is something that only the true aficionado can understand, and we all secretly thrive on it. Perhaps we should look to the Steve Irwin school of hunting, ergo, only take what you truly need today because tomorrow you might be starving. Can I also add you don't need to own every trés cool release to be a player on your block. And if I hear one more peckerhead tell me, 'yeah but the packaging is great, have you seen the box?' I'll brain them with the shoe horn from my 35th model SS35s. I don't collect cardboard boxes, I dig sneakers.

And how about a bit more (for want of a better word) retail-regionalism? Nobody wants to see every shoe released in every colour on every high street in every city all over the world. Nobody wants to go overseas and come back to find the pair of kicks you just dropped serious dime on are actually a dime a dozen. Let's get back to our 'Core Values™' from 'Back in the Day™' when hunting really meant something! When you could really stand out and stake your claim as The Real Top Cat on the street.

On another tip, I think there is another subtle battle going on out there. Older heads want props and are feeling a lack or respect from newbies who don't recognise. These metaphorical 'Sneaker Grannies™' need to check into a retirement villa. YES, you remember the old shits first time around, YES you've been around the traps for a while, but so what! Do you really need your egos stroked just for looking like Yoda? Pat yourself on the back by all means, but give the newbies a go - you were young once. Of course they are all a bunch of nitwits. Who wasn't at their age?

This is also a timely juncture to remind you all to support your local stores. If they suffer, we all will suffer. And nobody wants that. Otherwise this whole thrilling sneaker biz will turn into a fad. Don't get me wrong - fads are exciting. Yoyos, ipods, G-Shocks, Pokemon, Yowies, Paris Hilton - fads are fun, fads are for today. But I don't see 'sneakers' like this because it's been going on for 25 years already. It's just that some idiot invented the internet and everybody wants to be cool all of a sudden. It's the scenesters who come and go but they're now secretly wearing their Mostros and I don't see anyone rushing for the Doc Martens in a hurry. If however, you've just dropped 500 large on a Dunkle and expect to cash in bigtime in six months then think again. You're probably better off investing in an Emu farm.

And if you've just decided to start a sneaker website you're a bit bloody late. Don't let me put you off, but please, make it unique (not very unique) and do not call it a variation of these two words. Sneaker and Freak(er). It's not clever. While on the subject of names, I decree that from now on, new stores are hereby banned forthwith from using any of these words in their name: foot, feet, leg, tongue, sole, pimp, sneaker, freaker and kicks! Get over it and just say no to appaling sneaker puns! It was fun for a while but it's time to stop. All existing stores, especially those that stock this book are hereby granted an exemption.

Speaking of names, it's time for Aussies to invent our own parochial terminology. New Yorker's call 'em 'Shits' which is quaintly charming. I believe 'Trainers' may belong to our English brothers in feets. So, how about it Aussie Heads? Dundees? Or Dinkums? I kinda like the idea of 'G'day mate - check out my F#%ks!' but I guess that's a bit risque. I also wanted to start an online shop that sold BBQ accessories and call it Crooked Tongs. Now that's funny (IMHO).

In summary. Boredom is the curse. Honesty is a prerequisite. Originality is the cure. Quality is the outcome. The only way forward is to chuck out the formula, rewrite the cookbook and make the souffle using a different recipe. Otherwise we will all be left with a sour taste in our mouth. Incredible booms in anything have always been followed by corrections because nothing lasts forever. I can only see that as a good thing. The same can also be said for other modern life staples that have been gang-banged to death such as street art, punk rock, raves, breaking etc. Anyone for Australian Idol Beatboxing?? Too late - already happened!

If you ask me, the biggest problem is the constant whingeing that goes on. Stop being crybabies! Let's just get on with it and bring back the purity of love. There are diamonds hidden everywhere, it's just that sometimes you need to look under a rock, not online. And don't be a sheep, be a wolf. It's gotta be more fun eating raw meat than munching on grass.

Am I right? Or am I right?

WOODY

ps. Have you bought something because you thought you might miss out, even though you don't truly love it? Still think you're impervious to marketing?

pps. I am well aware I qualify as a Sneaker Granny™!

¡SNEAK ATTACK!

HIP-HOP

When Bathing Ape's Nigo (infamous for an attention to detail and exclusivity) teamed up with Pharrell Williams (a snappy dresser amid hordes of hip-hoppers in cheap loose denim and oversized tees) to create their own line of kicks, the results would be something special, right? Hmmmm. Well, if what appeared to be a Stan Smith customised by Liberace was your cup of tea, you hastily scraped together 200 bucks! Naturally, the release led to another now-ubiquitous hip hop accessory: the lawsuit. Regardless, the resulting shoe was the perfect embodiment, for better or worse, of the current state of popular hip hop culture: polished, generic and costly.

Given the close ties between Hip Hop and sneakers (some naïve souls might label them the fifth element of this beautiful culture) like the Biz Safari connection, Eazy E in Jordan 3s, The Ultramagnetics' name-checking Troop, iconic fat-laced Pumas…and some rock boxing kids from Queens (more on that later), collaborations are an inevitability. So how come the hit/miss ratio on these kicks is becoming increasingly unbalanced?

Firstly, kudos to the Dassler corporation for keeping it real. adidas hit it on the head with their Run DMC endorsement. The Ultrastar, Eldorado and Broughams that followed were classic kicks that captured the moment and still look fresh 18 years on, with items tailored for the group and its followers rather than forced product placement. Definitely shrewd marketing from all concerned.

On Jam Master Jay's passing, the limited edition JMJ Superstar seemed an equally tasteful tribute, repeated with the recent charity Bad Boy, Rocafella, Run DMC and the Missy shells. Even the afore-mentioned Miss Supadupafly's adidas RespectME range accurately reflected her fetish for garish old school imagery. While Russell Simmons' Phat Farm label recently placed Rev Run in charge of their sports footwear division, the end product looks suspiciously shelltoed, and minus the three stripes, it just isn't on par.

Nike's ultra-limited Wu Tang Dunk in relevant 'killa bee' colours remains a perennial holy grail, and the Rocafella Air Force 1 seems entirely appropriate, yet their artist series has yielded surprisingly shoddy results. Nelly's 'Air Derrty' CB2 looks like salerack fodder, and the 'Shady' Air Burst took the appearance of a particularly uninspired visit to Nike's iD site. By comparison, the N*E*R*D Dunk looks pretty revolutionary. But, as these shoes were sold for charity, who am I to criticise?

Shifting from the big guns for a minute, Rocafella's State Property Pro Keds were more interesting than most, given the true old school legacy of the Court King, but they hardly flew off the shelves. And just to prove the South is still 'bout it bout it', Master P's P Miller range unleashed some remarkably nondescript kicks with playalistic monikers like 'Da Loot'. Check 'em on the shelves of your local TK Maxx (or similar jumble sale megastore) in the near future. Seeing as fellow Down Souther Baby (of Cash Money Records) always seemed like a white AF1 enthusiast in publicity, he cunningly took the opportunity to design 'The Birdman' for Lugz in the style of a particularly cheap looking version of that very shoe. And the Doggfather's Pony range of 'Doggie Biscuitz' are merely custom plimsolls thrown together in a chronic-induced moment of business savvy.

Reebok is hardly a stranger to Hip Hop Culture ("I'm like the peacock on NBC/ Nuttin But Cock, I pump, puuuuuuump pump it up yo/like a Reebok"), but until recently, rookies in a Swoosh and Trefoil dominated game. That is, until the Gucci throwback of Jay-Z's S Carter collection made a 2003 appearance, followed closely by a particularly bland tennis variation and the slurring sensation, 50 Cent's G-Unit range. Despite looking like some unholy union between a Pro Ked and a Rod Laver, the generic nature of this shoe was usurped by the G-Unit XT, which looks more than a little like an eBay AJIV bootleg, bringing us neatly to the Reebok/Pharrell/Nigo 'Ice Cream' range…

Kudos to RBK for green lighting the creation of "all-new" shoes for their artist series rather than merely authorising rehashed colourways of existing kicks, but would the artists be wearing these things if they weren't turning a profit? How about collabos that actually reflect the act? MC Eiht Chuck Taylors? A Jadakiss Air Max/Timberland hybrid? Vegan moccasins for Common Sense? Ghostface Mink Wallabies? Maybe I'm reacting too viciously against the Nigo collab. Lest we forget, the Supreme Dunk Hi's were slow burners. With this in mind, is the 'Ice Cream' a future cult classic, or an LA Gear MJ for the new millennium? We'll let the victims of fashion decide.

GARY WARNETT

YOU ALL PROBABLY THINK THAT YOU'RE THE 'EXPERTS' AT THIS SNEAKER BUSINESS. BUT WHAT IS THIS WHOLE SNEAKER CULTURE THAT WE ARE PART OF? DO WE REALLY KNOW WHAT IT'S ABOUT? IS THE 'WINNER' REALLY THE PERSON WITH THE MOST SNEAKERS? OR IS IT THE PERSON WITH THE MOST KNOWLEDGE? IS IT REALLY A GAME? AND DO YOU HAVE TO 'PAY YOUR DUES' TO BECOME A MEMBER OF THIS EVER GROWING CULT?

Well, I'm not sure if I really know myself. All I know is that it has changed for me. It all began when I started working. I guess I never threw anything out and before I knew it, I had a huge accumulation of sneakers. It then became a habit of buying a new pair of Nike/Puma/Fila/adidas from the local Foot Locker every fortnight. Then I discovered that a few other mates had mad interests as well, mostly through their love of Hip Hop. Pretty soon, I found out that that there was actually a sub-culture out there.

The introduction wasn't actually buying new shoes. The guys would always give me tips on where to go and look for old stuff. Before long, I was a regular at the local Salvation Army stores. It never even occurred to me that I should be saving up and buying up half a store every month, keeping them in a vacuum sealed, climate controlled and airtight locker room.

Mind you, that was 10 years ago. Some might say that a decade is nothing because there are others out there who have been into it since the late '60s, maybe even earlier. Fair enough! But how many of these collectors do you actually know? For someone who has been doing it for a decade, I hardly know anyone. I have met a handful of heads through the years that have been into it for as long as I have or more. But it doesn't compare to the huge number of 'collectors' I meet almost everyday. Or so they say…

To add to that, the knowledge of when, how, where and what is impossible to upkeep. Unless of course, that is your fulltime job. Major companies are releasing reissues and colourways more frequently than terrorist threats arise in this day and age. If it wasn't for the forums and websites that share info, no-one would really be sucked into the hype. But is it a bad thing or is it a wealth of knowledge for the taking? And being part of the 'sneaker collecting' community means being active in one or more of these forums. Which one do you chose? Or is it all of them. Between SF, Instyleshoes, NT, HK-Kicks and the odd secret hideout, sleep might have to come second.

I looked up the definition of 'collect' in the dictionary. Sure enough, it means to 'gather' or 'accumulate'. Which is what our hobby is about. Some say it's a game, why I don't know. Maybe it's a competition to see who can accumulate the largest number of sneakers. All I know is that it's slowly becoming like collecting antiques, except everything's brand new. Ever seen an episode of the 'Antiques Roadshow'? I personally love it, but the entire show is made up of 90 year olds, getting their stuff valued by so-called experts.

In the last three years or so, it seems to me that to be a sneaker collector, one must not only have the correct styles of sneakers, but also the knowledge that comes with it. Drop date, limited edition, collaboration, special colourway, Japan release, deadstock,

quick-strike and on top of all that, an authorative opinion on how many were actually produced. Then you have the customizers and their little army of 'artists' (who isn't these days?). Not forgetting that a true fiend needs a 'hook-up' in every continent of the world. Suddenly it sounds like gambling. Actually more like stamp collecting versus race horses meets the stock market.

Now that's a whole lotta money for most of the collectors that I've met recently. Most of these guys and girls are still in university or have just entered the workforce. And I have seen some of their collections, from the forums and through photos. How does one afford all these new shoes being who they are? Then it suddenly hit me. The shoes are actually currency and a game is played to see who can hustle the other into thinking which is worth more.

I know there are collectors out there who have pretty much every single retro shoe that has been released in the last couple of years. But I never see any of these shoes on the street. Come to think of it, I never see any of these shoes — period! Where the hell have they all gone? Have they been shipped overseas? Or is it because Melbourne is a big place and I can't expect to see everything?

I think it's because all of them are still sitting in their boxes, waiting to ripen in someone's closet.

Maybe I'm a hypocrite in saying that I wear ALL my sneakers, but I don't see the point of having a massive collection of cool shit if I'm not gonna wear them! Sure I have a handful of stuff that I have never touched, and maybe the odd double. But let me assure you that the reason I have stuck to this hobby is because I love having fresh kicks on my feet. I love the reaction you get from people when you pull up your jeans to reveal your sneakers.

It's no good sitting in a box at home.

How excited do you get when you see some cool sneaks walking down the road? Even better when the shoes are treated with respect and worn properly, with according attire and style. Now how often do you get that? Almost never. I for one would like to see much, much more of it. Sneakers have always been a status symbol for me. When I look down on a person's feet, I can normally tell what sort of character he or she is. The fresher the sneakers, the more potential respect I have for the person. There is also much respect for the odd vintage sneaker that has been looked after and still worn today by some cats.

These are the true collectors in my book. A sneaker doesn't actually have a story to tell if it has never been worn. It won't have a soul until you do. So look deep into your collections and pull out a gem, lace them up and walk down the street with pride…

HANS D.C.

BY COREY HAGUE

OP SHOP HOP

Ahh, the countryside. Fresh, clean air, quiet roads, the ability to see the stars in the sky and not a single good shoe store around. After moving back home to the country a little over a year ago I was seriously missing sneakers. Gone were the days of drooling over all the glistening kicks begging for me to give them a good home. I even got a job in a sports store thinking it would make my life easier but I ended up spending most of my time selling cricket bats to guys with no necks. In desperation I turned to my old friend, the op-shop.

They are everywhere, even in the country, and they all smell the same. It's the scent of mothballs mixed with the faintest dash of death. But I've come to love the dank little places and the blue rinsed old ladies that hang out in them because they have landed me some of my best and most treasured kicks. And I haven't paid more than $5 for a single pair of them!

I have a few favorites, but I don't want to boast because my collection is fairly humble. The thrill of the chase is what it's about for me, mainly because my bank account knows I can't afford all the kicks I want. Plus, any fool can go into a store, drop a wad of cash on the counter and walk out in fresh shoes. But how many 'normal' people will go rooting around in stuff that people have thrown away looking for cool shoes? Thankfully for me, not many.

So next time you're fiending but don't want to go hungry, check out an op-shop. You may be pleasantly surprised by what's floating around. They definitely have more crap than gold but the chance to pick up stuff for small change is too hard to resist. Invariably you'll have to give whatever you score a bit of a spruce up, but this all adds to the reward factor. It has been my experience that country op-shops tend to be a little better than city ones because they don't get as many people through them, but who knows? Mostly in the country it tends to be teenage mothers and creepy old men, and I just push them down to get at what I want. Another bonus is even if there are no sneakers, there's still a good chance that there will be some cool clothes, books or hats for next to nothing.

So to all you sneaker freakers, you're more than welcome to come hunting in the country for kicks. Hell, I'll even give you the addresses to some of the better op-shops around if you're not a size 9. But you gotta remember that for every day you score two of your favorites, there will be another three days were you don't pick up a thing. This is the nature of the game we play.

To all the people who couldn't be bothered to check out an op-shop 'cos they figure it won't have anything for them, here's a brief rundown on some of the gold I've dug up:

+ + + + + + + + + + + +

+ TERMINATOR I didn't even know what they were at the time, but I figured they were something special. They were mint and a size 9 (perfect) and they were just so fresh I had to get them.

+ + + + + + + + + + + +

+ REEBOK PUMPS I could never afford these when I was a kid so to see them for $3 was very nice. The pump still works and the black leather looks sweet. They are also surprisingly good to skate in… although looking back I probably shouldn't have.

+ + + + + + + + + + + +

+ ASICS TIGERS I've always loved the look of these. I scored an original pair in excellent condition in a tiny little op-shop for $1. That's less than a can of coke and a whole lot tastier.

+ + + + + + + + + + + +

+ PARIS I've scored two pairs now so I gave one pair to my girl because they were a tad snug. Both pairs were $2.50 (one still has the price written on the sole in black texta) and they are ridiculously nice. Absolutely mint and they are in high rotation now because of how fresh they are. You gotta love gum soles.

+ + + + + + + + + + + +

+ FASTMANS I've never worn these, but I'm tempted. They are black leather with three velcro straps on them. They have the thinnest sole I've ever seen and they look strange, but kinda cool.

+ + + + + + + + + + + +

+ STAN SMITHS These are special occasion shoes and are one of the freshest shoes ever made I think and I love them to death. When I saw them I was blown away with how classic they are, the fat tongue and the dimpled sole just make them perfect. And good old Stan just keeps on smiling no matter where I walk.

+ + + + + + + + + + + +

+ ROMES I dug these when my brother rocked them eons ago. Found an original pair that I think were deadstock for $2 and I was quite pleased. He always gets teary-eyed when I wear them.

SHE'S GOT HI-TOPS!

PART ONE:
The Birth of a Female Sneaker Fiend

How does one become a female sneaker fiend? Maybe these days you're born to a mom who's sporting the latest retro kicks, or your dad thinks it's cool to hook you up with some baby Nikes. Maybe your nursery school buddies tip you off how well shelltoes hold up in the sandbox.

Back in my day, it was nothing like this. My first problem was my parents. With them, style was out, polyester was in, and Value Village was their idea of a mall. So you can imagine their kicks. Oh no. Now, what about my siblings? I have one sister, who's my twin. We're alike in a lot of ways, but not in sneakers. She remembers being only six years old, and all happy about some new sneakers she'd just gotten, and I had to go and tell her they were bubblegums (our lingo for 'they sucked'). So my sneaker sensibility definitely started early.

But maybe my love for sneakers did come from my family. Maybe it was because they were the only things I got to wear that were actually new, and the only things I didn't have to share with my twin. I still remember those annual trips to sneaker stores, where my mom insisted that we jump up and down and run around to make sure the sneakers fit right. It was kind of embarrassing, but kind of important too. Maybe they were growing a sneaker fiend without even realizing it...

In any case, it all crystallized on the playground. I was a regular tomboy, out there playing kickball, dodgeball, whatever was in season. Really, I think my love for high tops started way before I started playing basketball, and I think it had to do with their visual message. To me, I felt like wearing high tops told the boys I was serious. When I was the first girl in my elementary school to have high top Nikes (white canvas with a fat black swoosh), I heard the whispers and comments. 'That girl's got on Nikes.' 'She's got high tops.' The other kickball heads were sweating me on the sly. I loved it. I never looked back, and I've worn high tops almost exclusively every since.

PART TWO:
A Note on Tomboys and Sneaker Fiends

First let me be clear: not all female sneaker fiends are tomboys, and not all tomboys are sneaker fiends. I know some girly girls who rock Air Force Ones very nicely, and some kick ass female ball players who look like they've had the same set since the '80s.

But what exactly is a tomboy? Originally, it just meant girls who liked to roughhouse, play sports, climb trees, and do all those fun things that only boys were supposed to be into. Of course, for many of us, that included having a love for sneakers, the very items that announced our athletic intentions. If tomboys were alleged to grow into lesbians, no-one had told us about it. I didn't hear that twist until college, when a boy in one of my classes said, 'I thought lesbians were just tomboys who didn't grow out of it.' You knew every straight and gay female athlete in the room was offended about being expected to grow out of being a tomboy.

As I said, a female sneaker fiend is not always a tomboy, and a tomboy is not always a sneaker fiend. Maybe this simple equation can expand to: a lesbian is not always a tomboy (hello - lipstick lesbians),

and a tomboy is not always a lesbian. Add the sneaker fiend part, and the possibilities are many, from straight tomboy sneaker fiends, to gay girly-girl sneaker fiends, to bisexual tomboys who wear ugly-ugly sneakers, and so on. So, no assumptions in the world of nice kicks, okay? Being a sneaker fiend means you love your kicks, that's it. If you want to love them with some girly matching bag - cool. If you want to love them with your girlfriend rocking a matching pair - much love. For the rest of the world that doesn't understand, what else is new?

PART THREE:
Joining the Sneaker Fiend "Subculture"

Well, not only was I supposed to grow out of being a tomboy, but I was supposed to grow out of wanting to wear sneakers every day. Yeah, right! I actually changed my idea of my future career when I learned that architects had to dress up a lot to meet with clients. That didn't sound fun at all. So I followed my heart and my feet into being a youth worker. Now I get to wear jeans and sneakers all the time, and my sneakers are actually a plus - a great connection to many a teenage boy, and not just a few girls either. We eye each other across the teen center, and then one or the other sidles up and says, 'I like your sneakers.' It's funny how something little like that can be a great start to a friendship…

It wasn't until two years ago that I realized the depth and breadth of the underground sneaker fiend subculture. When a friend got me *Where'd You Get Those?* by Bobbito Garcia, it opened my eyes. The book was beautiful, full of old pics of my favorite sneakers, not to

mention ball players and b-boys rocking them through the '60s, '70s and early '80s. I loved it! Up to then, I'd kept my sneaker passions local, just seeing it as kind of my own thing. But after that I started to really look around, finding such online sneaker fiend havens as Sneaker Freaker and Crooked Tongues. I surfed and surfed. Wow! I had found my community, and it was worldwide.

The only thing was, I wasn't in it. I didn't see any women in Bobbito's book, and not many on the websites either. So I looked around. Could it just be me? Nah. I knew enough females into sneakers to know that there are PLENTY of us out there. Plus, there are even some really famous ones right now - Ellen Degeneres and Missy Elliot are known not only for their fantastic careers, but also for their love of kicks! So why aren't we more visible in the sneaker subculture?

As I started talking to the female sneaker fiends I knew, I realized that many of them loved their sneakers - always had - but didn't identify as fiends. They were almost scared of the term. 'What do you have to do to be a sneaker fiend?' they'd ask, as if they might not qualify. Most felt like they didn't have enough sneakers to be a real fiend or, if they did, they were somehow embarrassed by their collection. It seemed frivolous, and they didn't talk about it to people. One of my friends called herself a 'closet sneaker fiend', and said she got self-conscious when people noticed her new sneakers. Now, that seemed really sad to me. I love talking about sneakers, and I love it when people notice mine. And I can't say I've ever met a guy who was embarrassed about having too many sneakers!

Check out Lori's website…
www.femalesneakerfiend.com

Not all women like lavender, pink or baby blue!

Most of my interactions with male sneaker fiends are really positive. Total strangers will compliment me on my hard-to-find models, from teens on the subway to dudes working in sneaker stores. Mostly they're open-minded, maybe surprised, but definitely happy to give credit where credit is due. On top of that, I've gotten great support and feedback from some guys who are real leaders in the field (a quick thanks to Woody, Tim and Bobbito who took time to check out my stuff!)

Even though a lot of guys are open to respecting both females and their sneakers, the sexism in the subculture can be pretty daunting sometimes. It starts with invisibility, like having no women in SLAM Magazine's Kicks editions, or Bobbito's book. But it gets worse from there, let me tell you! For example, I was pretty psyched to check out solecollector.com. Now tell me why they have a whole page of models?? Most of them don't even have sneakers on! (And holding them in your teeth DOES NOT count). What the…?!? Then I bought *The Sneaker Book* by Milk Projects. The very opening page, the very opening quote, has some dude named Paul saying: "Both those c#%ts spilt fucking black coffee on my red and gray Air Max 95s." What the…?!?

Keep Rocking
Whatever Feels Right!

PART FIVE:
So What's a Girl
To Do?

Some of the most notorious sexism in the sneaker world comes from advertisers and sneaker companies. You know, I'm happy Vince Carter has a new sneaker out, but why do I have to see it marketed by a picture of him looking like a pimp, strutting with a line of sexy stewardesses in an airport? And I'm happy the Reebok Pumps are back, but do you think I want to buy them cuz they promise to 'fit you like Trina's booty shorts'? Come on now. Beyond marketing, there are the actual products. On the upside, Nike has actually had a few women's basketball players get their own models. I even bought the first Swoopes, in the mid-Nineties, cuz they were the first basketball sneakers named after a woman (Sheryl Swoopes, from the Houston Comets and the USA Olympic team). Even though I usually wear men's sneakers, I'll always ask salespeople if they carry any women's basketball sneakers, just because I want them to know there's a market. It's a shame how often the answer is no! If they do, the selection is pretty small, and the colors…what can I say? Not all women like lavender, pink or baby blue. And even though I love adidas (and give them props for the Missy collection), what am I supposed to think of them when they hardly make any women's b-ball sneakers, and then come out with some high top fuzzy pink things? Come on now…

My advice to female sneaker fiends out there is to recognize you're not alone, but at the same time, keep doing it your own way. Keep rocking whatever feels right, and keep loving sneakers for whatever they do for you. Maybe they're just practical (naw…), maybe you love having what no-one else does, or having the cleanest pair, or the latest, hottest styles. And if guys love it, or hate it, or just don't get it, so be it. Just tell 'em you're a female sneaker fiend, like it's the most normal thing. Pretty soon, it will be. As for me, I'm spreading the word the best way I know. I started a website, www.femalesneakerfiend.com, where I'm hoping to bring together fiends from all over the world - whether they're old school hippies wearing their good ol' Chucks, hip-hop DJs rocking shelltoes, or girly-girls with some crazy pink KangaROOS. Maybe even my sneaker sheroes - Ellen and Missy! I have big plans for sneaker tours, sneaker stores, sneaker books…you name it. As long as I'm wearing high tops and talking sneakers, I'm happy. Peace…

LORI LOBENSTINE
www.femalesneakerfiend.com

You realise you're quite famous don't you?
That's pretty funny, I know a lot of those guys at the sample sales don't know me as a collector and probably thought I was helping out a male friend.

So how long have you been collecting sneakers?
I still have my very first pair of Nikes so I guess you could say I've always collected but in regards to quantity, about 5 years ago. I went to a sale and just got hooked and I just started buying heaps...

You have a pretty wide collection...
Yeah (laughs) I collect anything that's appealing to the eye and a bit different, something I haven't seen before, hence why there's so many different styles... not just old school sneakers. It's a bit of everything and I like bright colours a lot. I do love shoes, I do collect a lot of other stuff, designer shoes, fashion, I've also got a sickness because I'll buy shoes that I don't wear, just because of their aesthetic appeal.

What do your friends think?
They know me as collecting Japanese toys, film posters, records, tee shirts, advertising, passes to '80s clubs, magazines, I collect anything and everything, so they know I'm crazy...

The culture is so blokey...
I know exactly what you mean and people always treat you strange, I had a Sydney guy tell me that he won't sell me stuff because 'Chicks don't collect' but it's funny because when you're up against guys they just never think you're into it...

Do you need to be pushy?
Yeah, you have to be! When they come out with the fresh boxes at sales and give 'em to their friends I have to go up and honestly front them and say, 'Just treat me like everyone else.' Otherwise you just end up with nothing,

Do you have a critical memory of sneakers?
When I was at high school it was all about fat laces and the suede Pumas and I could never work where anyone got them. Old stock found in secret stores, German connections, OS hook-ups... This is pre-internet and email so it was almost impossible... And it wasn't always Nike - Fila, Ellesse, all the old school brands, like I've still got my British Knights (laughs).

Are you proud or embarrassed of 'em?
A bit of both!

What's up with these kids' shoes? They're exactly like those graff character shoes, the way those kids were drawn with the massive feet, super chunky style?
I've got a whole bag of just the Baby Jordans... they're just real cute, what can I say. I also collect the kids' sizes for the same reason, they're in between the baby and the adult. The Cortez are the best, they're really colourful.

With the velcro as well! They'd only last a few months?
At least you know you're not gonna wear them out!

Reebok call their little baby ones Weeboks...
Ha ha...

Tell me about those fancy Jordans with the 45 on the back!
These are a sample, super rare from what I've been told. And they are worth a hell of a lot, I don't think they were ever released. When Jordan came back after his first retirement, they made this but they never released them for production.

Are they for sale?
No. But they could be! Either I'm gonna keep collecting or I sell some because they take up so much room. I have over 500 pairs, including the little ones and like I said, 'I collect so many things…' This just grew from nothing, but now it's OFFICIALLY INSANE.

And there's only one brand here!
I've got a pair of adidas!

Where?
Those Stan Smiths over there…

Oh yeah, I see them… why Nike?
Only because they are innovative, they just do things out of the ordinary, they use strange new materials… that's why they're so copied. Look at all the big new skate shoes. Everyone's copied them, they're 'it' when it comes to the whole design.

Have you got any advice for other sneaker collectors?
Don't do it!

I thought it was 'just do it!'
Yeah… be ruthless, you just gotta collect what you are passionate about, don't do it to make money in the end cause that's not what it's about, you gotta love sneakers. It's not like anyone is gonna wear hundreds of pairs of Nikes… but you get hooked, you gotta buy each style, each colour.
I only buy from sales, otherwise all my money would go on shoes and I collect so many other things. I'd be on the internet trying to buy stuff all the time. I would go completely nuts.

Gimme your top shoes…
The first Jordans I bought in NY - they got a lot of reaction. They're pretty ratty now but that's an original J5, I think this particular colour combo was never released here. For sentimental reasons they are probably the best.
My very first Nikes I still have in the box, they are called Lady Court, from 1982 I think and they were really cheap which is probably why my mum bought them for me. They came in the best box, it had a map of the world on the lid, I'm so glad I kept it. (see above)

You do realise you're probably Australia's most highly decorated lady sneaker collector?
I never went into it to be super competitive and get the most, but in the toy world we say 'He who dies with the most toys wins!' And I guess that's true for shoes as well!

Thanks Zoe…

PROPER VS ASICS

Located in Long Beach, California, PROPER has been supplying the residents of the LBC with the finest in footwear for the past year or so. In July 2004 they released their very own version of the Asics GT-II. It was so hot, we had to find out a little bit more about how the whole thing went down so we asked Tristran to give us his two cents...

Everyone's a sneaker designer. It's funny the first thing anyone will tell you is what they would change. 'Wassup with this color here and where's the mesh and why did they use this material?' From customers and friends alike, this is what we hear all day long at the store. It's not any kind of disrespect, even when people love shoes there is often that one subtle nuance that they would change if given the opportunity.

So when Isaac Alvear from Asics first approached us about working on the GT-II we were excited about the possibilities but a little apprehensive. Not in the sense that we didn't want to work with Asics, just a little concerned about trying to create a shoe that would reflect us, while keeping the shoes functional.

As sneakers are increasingly fashion pieces, we're seeing a drastic departure from the original intention of the shoes, especially when it comes to special make-ups. Exotic leathers and materials are fresh to look at, but in terms of wear and tear they often make the shoes heavy and hot, not to mention expensive and impractical. The way we see it, some materials have no business being used on a sneaker.

With this in mind we wanted our GT-II to be something that we felt looked ill, but would remain durable and functional at the

same time. As we were working on colorways we kept coming back to some old camouflage fatigues that were laying around in the back of the store. We kept telling ourselves the same thing. Namely, camouflage is played. We see the same cammo applied to footwear in countless ways, not to mention its applications in apparel and frankly it's done to death.

Even though we felt that the use of cammo is tired, actual military surplus in its original form is timeless. So what we ended up doing was trying to deconstruct the camouflage fatigues themselves. In the end we based the colorway for the GT-II on standard issue US fatigues, and then utilized the same grade rip-stop and placed it on the upper of the shoe. Added a hit of safety orange to the heel cup, and 3M window in the back to aid with visibility (for all you evening joggers) and essentially we were done.

We worked closely with John Luna at Asics during the whole sampling process and can't thank him enough for his efforts to produce the shoe as we actually envisioned (if at first you don't succeed, send it back until the shit is how you want it). We're pretty certain that Asics got more than they bargained for, but what do you expect when you leave a bunch of two-year-olds alone with a box of crayons and some white walls?

Asics GT-II

We tested John's patience and after three rounds of samples, and too many conversations about mesh and colored mid-soles, what you see is what you get! No crazy screen-prints, no logos embroidered everywhere on the shoe, and no handbag leather... just our take on a classic in materials that will hopefully look better as they become worn and weathered.

With the sample finalized the only thing left to do was to set the production limit and size run. For Proper and Asics, the project was never about money. When you consider that Asics is a global footwear giant, doing something like this isn't exactly going to make the company millions. With that in mind the decision to only produce 144 pairs was less about gouging people on the price, and more about making a shoe that we were into and giving people that are into Asics something a little different.

Judging from the feedback on the samples so far we probably should have made more. But don't worry we're not ones to play some 'limited edition' bullshit with the price. The pricing of the shoe will reflect the charges we incurred in using the rip-stop material in such a limited run and our freight charges. We're not trying to price the shoe out of the reach of the people that want it just because because it is limited edition...

Thinking about the whole thing in retrospect, we feel privileged to have had the opportunity to work with Asics on something like this. To have a company with a history and heritage like Asics give us free reign to tweak one of their shoes was dope. But what we're really looking forward to is July being the month that a lot of people buy their first pair of Asics.

TRISTAN CARUSO
PROPER 425e First St, Long Beach California.

THE ROYAL WE

THE STORY BEHIND THE COLLABORATION BETWEEN VERY COOL SWEDES AND A GERMAN LEGEND.

Interview with *GREGER HAGELIN* from WE Clothing
Written by *JASON LE* (not to be confused with Jason Lee)

For those not down with WE history, tell us about yourself and how the company started?

I am 40 years old and have been a skateboarder most of my life and lived in the United States back in the day (1982-85). I came back home to Sweden and still had great connections with all the skateboarders and distributed a lot of brands. At the time I had a company name G-spot and unfortunately me and my friends had to sell it. That's when we started the company.

Why did you call it WE?

Why we have the name WE is we are always talking about the 'we' thing, people we like and people we would like to work with. WE is really small, we're 4 years old and have a turnover of about $50 million this year. Not too big but we're financially strong and happy.

If you could point to one thing that makes your brand different from others what would it be?

I think the most important thing that makes WE different is that we have the 'Superlative Conspiracy', which is also one of our brand names but is also the whole idea and philosophy behind the company. To have great people working together and everyone can be a part of the superlative conspiracy, distributors, the people working here, our Activists, the consumers, whoever. That's the way we try and do stuff. Its more about good people.

Can you explain a bit more about being a WE Activist? Do you choose people to become one?

We never choose an Activist, most of the Activists contacted us and want to be a part of what we are doing. We have a background in skateboarding and we have been team riders ourselves, but we wanted to reach a larger group of people. A lot of skateboarders growing up became artists and do a lot of other stuff. We didn't really want to call them team riders, it's ridiculous calling an artist a team rider.

How has skateboarding influenced you?

When I got back from the US all my friends and my parents said, 'Oh you have wasted 3 to 4 years of your life.' What I did (in the US) was skateboarding, surfing, hanging out, drinking beer, fucking around with girls. At first I thought I had wasted my life but after a couple of years back in Europe I understood it was the best time of my life because of all the good people I met. We're trying to recreate that feeling with our company, the way we do business and the way we treat people.

How did WE and adidas hook up for this collaboration?

I got a call from Ben Pruess, who is the head of adidas Originals. I've known him since way back. He used to call me once in a while and then one day he said, 'Do you want to come to Munich?' I was a big fan of the Bathing Ape shoes so I said, 'Of course' and we shook hands - lets do it!

Why adidas? Would you have considered working with other brands?

I am a Scandinavian guy and when I grew up I was a soccer player. I remember those guys from the '70s like Gerd Muller and Franz Beckenbauer and I was a big fan of adidas. I remember getting Gerd Muller soccer shoes and sleeping in them. I think adidas, especially for Europeans, means a lot when it comes to feelings like that. adidas have a really, really strong background and history that I like and I think a lot of other people do too.

How did you decide what style of shoes you wanted to do?

We wanted to do something different. We also wanted the shoe to have something to do with skateboarding. adidas told me they had this one shoe. Some adidas designers back in the '70s went to LA to look at trends, way back in '76 and they came up with this shoe that looked pretty much like a Vans hi-top.

adidas didn't really believe in it so they said, 'Ok, forget about it.' They tried to release it in '79 as a basketball shoe but it didn't work. When we saw the shoe, we definitely wanted to do it. There are four different shoes, the hi-top is one but it's female and men's. The style is called Dakota and we are making 1200 units of each one. We are also doing one other shoe, of which there will only be 400. We asked adidas, 'What is the worst shoe you have ever had that did not sell at all?' They came up with this sailing shoe from back in '71. When we saw the shoe we were laughing so hard. We did some small changes to it, it's not a regular sneaker but will be a cool part of what we are doing. The shoe is called the Compas.

I heard a little rumour of an extra special shoe!
We are releasing 200. They're not for sale, we're giving them to our best Activists and people we really like. Inside that shoe and on the sole there's an invitation for a crayfish party somewhere in the world for August 2005.

WE use a very distinctive pattern throughout the collection, what is the inspiration for it?
We do a new pattern for our clothes every six months, use it in our collections, put it on our website and use it in our ads. We were thinking of what pattern we could use for spring and came up with the crayfish pattern. In Sweden, August is crayfish month.

All the Swedes have parties centreing around having crayfish and drinking schnapps. It felt really Swedish, there is beautiful artwork, a good story and we felt doing crayfish parties around the world would be a good idea to bring people together.

Is this a one-off deal or will there be future WE-adidas projects?
It's probably a one-off project but we're thinking about maybe bringing adidas in to do some WE stuff. Turn it the other way.

You recently opened your first US store in LA and debuted the product in a parade at a party. What was the reaction like?
The reaction from them has been amazing. The response from the shops around the world has been amazing too. We're only going to sell this product in 100 stores. We have been trying to tell all the shops buying the product, don't raise the prices like the Bathing Ape shoe. They should definitely sell them at the right price. We want to look after the good friends of WE, that really like what we are doing, that respect the shoe and really want to wear it. It's really boring if we don't see the shoes out on the street.

Last but most importantly when are the shoes available.
The sneakers are released late January, early February 2005. We're really looking forward to it.

Thankyou Greger for you time, it was awesome talking to you.
Thankyou very much.

WWW.WECLOTHING.COM

NOTABLE WE ACTIVISTS...
JERRY HSU - SKATER/PHOTOGRAPHER
JASON LEE - ACTOR/SKATER
ALI BOULALA - SKATER
MICHI ALBIN - SNOWBOARDER
OUTLANDISH - MUSIC
CHAD ROBERTSON - ARTIST
GINO IANNUCCI - SKATER

GREGER HAGELIN

CLOSET KICKS

Very rarely do you come across such a unique pair of sneakers. Designed and made for one very specific purpose within one of the most exclusive industries on the planet - to protect and serve the feet of the McLaren Team's pit crew in Formula 1 motor racing.

Trying to source a pair of these kicks would be near impossible. Well then, how did I get my hairy mitts on these you may ask? Pure fluke really... A few years back when my modest little city hosted the Grand Prix my mum was working in the housekeeping department of the Adelaide Hilton Hotel. Being the best hotel in Adelaide at the time (not hard) that's where most of the teams stayed throughout the racing weekend. The following week, whilst mum was going about her daily job she just stumbled upon them, sitting in the otherwise empty wardrobe. The previous owner had discarded them after just a few days use.

When she arrived home I remember they caused me some preternatural angst. I mean, a bright red pair of Asics? I was into

Hip Hop, so I was rockin my adidas or fresh Nikes (whenever funds would permit, that is). Would a loyal brand conscious head dare turn up to school in these? I remember getting laughed at for running bomber laces in my shelltoes not long before I got these. I wasn't ready to go through that again, I mean it was only petty shit from friends but it was annoying all the same.

Some people just don't get it, and never will. If you were different back then you really stood out, something I always managed to do anyway without even trying. My background is Asian/European, a minority group where I grew up. So imagine the response striding through the schoolyard in these everyday...

"HEY CHECK OUT THE ASIAN KID IN THE BRIGHT RED SNEAKS, LETS CRACK HIS HEAD OPEN LIKE AN EGG"

Yeah, would've been real fun. So I played it safe and stashed them away. I had almost forgotten about them until moving house just recently. Whilst going through all my old gear I was reunited

"TRYING TO SOURCE A PAIR OF THESE KICKS WOULD BE NEAR IMPOSSIBLE. WELL THEN, HOW DID I GET MY HAIRY MITTS ON THESE YOU MAY ASK? PURE FLUKE REALLY..."

with them. It is only now that I realised what I have. These kicks rule! The most unique in my collection by far.

I got them in 1995 which was the last time Adelaide hosted the Grand Prix, and one of the last seasons the team ran this colorway. So what better parting gift could I receive?

The shoe's upper construction quality is second to none and the grip design is unique and works incredibly well. A lot of R&D must've gone into the sole alone. You can really feel and hear the little rubber nobblies gripping to the asphalt when it's most needed (The pit crew would never have slipped up in these bad boys). The incredible light weight is also very noticeable. To sum it up, the shoe personifies all the quality you would expect with anything associated with F1. Especially within one of the richest and most successful teams in the game. See the blackening on the white part of the sole - that's F1 related markings. Fuck yeah! - F1 rules.

It would've been cool to see what the other teams were wearing,

namely Ferrari, Williams/BMW or Jordan. Keep your eyes open this year, and if you know anyone in house-keeping at fancy hotels have them look out. In the wardrobes, that is...

Anyway, another freakish score my mum picked up was a pair of Nikes that 'Pistol' Pete Sampras left behind after playing in Adelaide at Memorial Drive. They were also only one game old. They were two sizes way too big though, so I regrettably sold them not long after I got them for as little as eighty dollars. Oh well, you live and learn I guess.

It does make me wonder why I held onto these for so many years though. Anyway, here they are in post-race condition, well I have worn them around the block a few times. How else would I know how effective the grip design works??

'SUPER' STEVE VARGA

GREEN WITH ENVY

Trying to argue the grace of any shoe that is outside the dominant paradigm of sneaker culture can be a very lonesome existence. Comparisons always return to the simplicity and staying power of sneakers like the Air Force One or the Shelltoe. Fair enough, but spare a thought for the Lone Wolf McQuades of the world! It takes a degree of guts and determination to see beauty where so many others cannot, and to argue about it on the street requires a special kind of crazy that cannot be bought.

The reason I say this is because I have a modern sneaker in my shoe closet that battles for wear-time with the big boys, a sneaker that I covet as being as close to perfect as a sneaker can be. A sneaker that falls properly over any jean line and always reflects well on any outfit you put on!!

I confess. I am obsessed with the New Balance 802.

I should lay some background knowledge before you all turn the page. I only collect what I wear (with the exception of the Air Max '97s) and we all know the rules: no repeats per week and check with the meteorologist for rain and snow reports. Stylewise, I am a fan of the simple runner and trainers: Waffles, AM 95/97s, Dunk Lows, adidas Spezials and the only shoe to call upon imagery of the Minotaur on his hind feet, the Air Rift. All in all, common shoes in the obsessed lives of sneaker freaks.

Also of note - I have no plans for using these shoes for their true purpose and hours of ingenuity in creation: that being active sports wear. I used to sport my OG olive/red Air Terra Humara for most rough activity, but the colourway was just too delicate to damage. A good thing too as Nike eventually reissued the colourway in 2000. As usual, the OG always looks best.

A titan for pain and budget constraints, I was on my last dollars in 1998 when I walked into the local New Balance Outlet in Boston hunting out a shoe to serve one major purpose that my other sneakers simply could not: active rough use; commonly known as 'sports'. Criteria for purchase? A durable runner/hiker that I could avoid becoming obsessed with and that I could sanely allow to become dirty, damaged and soleworn. 'Avoid the love' - that was the plan. Looking back now, I would have been safer entering the clearance section and picking up a pair of children's shoes than I would have been in trying to beat my mind at its own game. The shoe of choice: NB802.

Admit it, you buy a shoe for one of two reasons - the colourway and the way it 'drops' with your jeans. With the 802 I took the opposing stance. I purchased the bottom of the barrel colourway to convince myself that I did not care for the shoe! No connection, no love in the look, all that mattered was the 'sports' factor! Life would be good for a year or two jogging and working out in my new trainer until I discovered that my homely 802 had a gorgeous grey twin sister.

There is nothing more devastating that falling in love with a shoe on someone else's feet, especially when you're wearing the same damn shoe! Case in point was my discovery of a duo tone grey 802 with a lime green 'N', a colorway I had never seen and if I had, I would have stopped my 802 purchase altogether. What is a self-respecting sneaker freak to do in this situation???

My love/hate affair with the grey 802 had now begun - as did the hunt. Unfortunately, a big problem arose. The 802 was over two years past retirement in 2000 and not a single shop carried

deadstock. I had two possible saviors: hoarding NB fans in Japan or eBay. Either way, I was in a bad state: eBay would tended to bring high prices, risky info, and worse, outbidding. Japanese hoarders brought pristine mint product and a very high price. So I chose eBay.

I happened across a pair in my size US9D brand new, full grey with the lime N, no box. In my position, I had no choice. I set my max bid for the 802s at $60us. Praise ye Gods of bargain shopping as it never came close. I was only one of four bidders for that shoe and walked away with my prize for $12us. Twelve dollars for a brand new pair of 802s! Shipping them to Boston cost more than the shoe. Something seemed wrong!

Ding dong, the Champ's arrived! Being a pure jean wearer in any climate, I gave it the 'drop' test across a variety of jeans: Diesels, H&M, Levis. They worked. They simply worked with everything I dropped on them. NB: It's rare for a sneaker to work with anything I toss at it. Most sneaks have a fault. For instance, adidas work best with boot cuts. The AM95/97, Dunks, Escapes, work best with a relaxed/wide leg. Amazingly, the 802 works played friendly across all jean cuts. What I had not noticed was that the 802 was a mid bulge shoe: not too thin and not too bulky, locked in the median. It fit well across all drops, so well, that I immediately got back onto eBay and began to hunt another pair.

Like most freakers, I now needed to share my discovery with the populus. I knew from the start that walking the 802s into a room of b-boys would be as difficult as it could get. And difficult it was - not a soul in the room took notice of my new 'sole.' They went over with a yawn.

So I moved onto the Air Max crowd: a group surely more in tune with the modern sneaker; more open to the color experimentations and unique style of the runners.

This time I made it obvious.

"Yo check out these crazy NBs I just got. This full grey and lime just work. You feeling these cuz I am!"

"Yeah they look good. But they're not AMs," answers the friend.

"Who cares?? They look dope! Check out the drop!"

"Yeah man, They look good, but they ain't me..."

He's right. They're not for him. They're for me. It's almost bitter sweet to realize the potential for a shoe when very few other freakers feel it. Out of the dozens of heads I know in my area, only one other pair has been admitted to, and he wears them to play footie in the grass. How appropriate.

So it is true, beauty is in the eye of the beholder. Maybe one day 10 years from now when kiddies are running high and low for the new school of retros will the full potential of a plain grey trainer like the 802 be seen. A very non-dominating shoe that provides me with hours of pride.

And yes, I am still hunting. In fact, another pair in near mint just popped up on eBay. I assume it's an easy win again. Just don't tell anyone.

JEFF CARVALHO

Jeff Carvalho obsesses about music and sneakers in Boston. Find him at: www.dropform.com

BECAUSE I HAVE A PROBLEM LEAVING THE HOUSE WITHOUT MY T-SHIRT MATCHING THE COLOUR OF MY SHOES I CERTAINLY STARTED GETTING OUT OF THE HOUSE MORE WHEN I CAUGHT ONTO THE FACT THAT ADIDAS MADE THE SAME SHOE, THE SHELLTOE OR SUPER STAR IN A VARIETY OF COLOURS, IT HELPED THAT I REALLY LIKED THE SHOE, ANYWAY I THINK THEY LOOK...

COOL AS FUCK! (my mate Andy Murphy doesn't like them cos he thinks your toes get too hot cos of the rubber shell), but seriously why would you skate in them? They are too good to get those gay as ollie marks, don't get me wrong, Andy's a good bloke I just don't think he has a clue what he's talking about when it comes to shoes. So anyway the first pair I got was white with a green stripe, I got them in Hong Kong and they had a padded tongue and an awesome woven label that said adidas superstar, (see picture) I didn't wear them that much as I only had 2 green t-shirts one of which I wasn't that fussed on. I had a lot of black t-shirts so the next pair I got was white with black stripes, well I didn't really get them because of that sole reason, it was cos that was the only colour available in Australia at the time. I think I got a royal blue colorway next, basically I just bought what was available in Australia, and then often bought my t-shirts to match. All the Australian-bought pairs had the non-padded tongue and had a trefoil printed on them. I think early on in the piece I got a pair of Ultrastars, they are a shelltoe but had a bigger piece at the back and had metal eyelets - anyone who saw the Run DMC shoes released after DMC died will know the shape I am talking about, anyway who gives a shit cos they were ugly as fuck and I think they helped usher in the 'Superstar Metal' which was basically a normal superstar but with metal eyelets. I can't tell you how shit these look (no picture, I don't want to hurt your eyes), and I make no apologies to the fools that bought them, really what do you need metal eyelets for? If you need to pull your laces that tight maybe you should think about buying a smaller size shoe. Other superstars that I have bought and not really enjoyed are the ones that have coloured leather (see photo) but the rubber is still white, so basically you look like a clown. I foolishly bought 2 pairs of these in some deluded quest to get more and more colours, I have worn both of them about 4 times collectively, each time looking down at my feet after about an hour feeling awkward and then going home to change my clown shoes. I have often wondered if you could colour in the rubber with a texta, do you reckon you could? Please send theories care of this magazine. Those shoes would look pretty good then. Does anyone else have trouble typing some times cos you text a lot I was looking for the '?' just then and though I might get it by pressing the number 1 - 4 times just like on my phone. My all-time favourite pair I bought in Nagoya, Japan. (my God what a jetsetter I am) I was stuck just outside of town at some rock venue desperate to buy some shoes and I had to get my Japanese speaking friend to convince 2 local kids to drive me into town and buy some shoes, talk about the most painful 30 minute lift. They spoke no English and all I could say in Japanese was 'really?' and 'fireworks'. That got old in about 2 minutes.

They took me to about 10 stores in town, each time I got the same response when I asked if they had my size, which is Japanese 28.5. NO NO NO NO! The largest size they make is 28. If you love shoes and have big feet don't go to Japan, you see the most awesome shoes in colours you have never seen and none of them fit you. Most stores take you up to the back of the shop where they have a little 28.5+ section which has the worst shoes you have ever seen. It's unbelievably frustrating. Anyway in about the tenth store I saw six colorways I didn't have. I asked for all of them and the guy asked what size I told him, well he wrote it on a piece of paper, instead of saying NO NO NO NO! he gave me a funny look and went out back, he came back with one box and it was dusty (it was kinda surreal like he was bringing me buried treasure or some shit) but in it was a pair of shelltoes with two blues stripes and one red (its a funny shade of blue but I am deliriously happy now as I have a stripey tee with exact matching blue and red stripes) they also had the woven adidas superstar, and the tongue was

made of nylon as well as the sole being a very fine herringbone. I think that you could describe it by saying they had more ridges per inch (like a condom - how is it that we say per inch, even though we have the metric system in Australia and don't use inches at any other time except when describing penises) than a normal pair (see picture). These shelltoes were made in the Philippines, all my other pairs are made in Korea or China or Taiwan (none in Australia for some reason). I was stoked on them, my Japanese guides were stoked on me getting them and hopefully you are stoked about reading about them, so I have included this picture to help with your excitement. As this article is quickly becoming pointless I would like to leave you with: shelltoes are cool, don't skate in them, Superstar metals are not cool, if you have big feet don't go to Japan and don't leave the house without your t-shirt and shoes matching in colour, or alternatively get psychiatric help.

Yours sincerely

SEBBO

STREET SLAM HI

So what's the history of SPX? When did it start, who did it and why?

SPX was started in 1986 by Clive King, who also started Troop at around the same time. SPX was probably the first brand to incorporate technical cushioning, performance systems and windows in the soles, but not for sports purposes. Critically, it was a time for taking sports performance to the streets. At that time, trainers on the market were pretty boring and the kids were screaming for something new, so the plan was to introduce something a bit more in your face - today you would say bling!

Funny, I always thought it was an American brand...

Quite understandable given that SPX doesn't exactly personify the reserved British stereotype. Though it does coincide with the popular misconception that most old skool brands originated from the US when actually Europe was really making much of the running with the likes of Puma and adidas from Germany, and Reebok from England. SPX incorporates the Union Jack within its logo, although designed with the US market in mind, was also an English brand.

Aside from Troop, British Knights comes to mind as well?

As I mentioned, the same company owned Troop back in the day so it's quite likely that they may have used some of the same designers and their similarity is probably not coincidental. I would have to say they were definitely influential as I was involved in the design for BK and therefore am happy to reinforce it as a great brand of the time!! Funnily enough, I fell in love with the brand while I was a 14 year old on holiday with my father in the States, and to his disgust (as he was working for another brand at the time) I bought a head to toe outfit. I ended up convincing him to take on the brand in Europe.

Who was wearing them back in the day?

SPX was loved by the kids that were busy establishing the breakdancing scene and skaters alike. There simply weren't the rigid rules 'You do this so you wear those!' Regardless of who wore them, their home remained on the street.

Were they hard to find?

Finding the original shoes was extremely tough and they definitely weren't cheap as chips! I had to travel the world searching in retro shops and offering lots of people large sums of money to come up with any SPX products. After a year of hunting a friend of mine found the Street Slam in Paris and from memory, we re-created the low version. Six months later at the main shoe show in Europe, I was introduced to an Italian guy and when I gave him my business card with the SPX logo on it, he went that animatedly crazy that only Italians can. It turned out when he set up his company 15 years earlier, it was to distribute SPX. He told me that he had most of the original shoes and catalogues at his office. For once I was lost for words, my two year search for this information was over!

Why did the brand disappear?

The brand disappeared around the same time all of the comparative brands seemed to disappear, as there was a big swing away from the bold trainers towards very basic stuff like the Reebok Classic for instance. At the time even Nike were suffering with their fashion-related products due to this change in direction.

STREET SLAM LO

TO FIND OUT MORE WE CAUGHT UP WITH

ANTONY NATHAN

FROM FRESH FOOTWEAR....

How did you revive the brand?

We spent a lot of time and effort into an overall marketing campaign with the help of a young, creative London agency, which included a website (being updated), a 'bling' exhibition stand, and most significantly a shoe box which was designed as an original ghetto blaster. This activity helped to sum up the brand identity and together with the shoes being so radically different to anything else on the market, we received fantastic coverage in all of the leading fashion magazines.

What's the reaction been so far?

The reaction has been fantastic as the aim was to re-establish the brand with a product that is as loud now as it was then and stays true to the old skool who remember the tunes and the times that influenced a whole new street fashion, while widening its appeal to a younger audience.

Are these sneakers exactly the same as the OG models?

The Street Slam series is 100% authentic and although we had to invest heavily into remaking the shoe, the only difference is that the quality and finish is better. The main reason for this is most of the shoes in the '80s and early '90s were made mostly by hand in Korea, whereas now they are made in larger factories in China using new technical equipment that was simply not available then.

What was the connection with SPX and Lennox Lewis?

While SPX spent more of its time on the streets than in the sports arenas, the brand sponsored the best British boxers of the time, including Gary Mason and Lennox Lewis. Lennox was a promising up-and-coming boxer at the time, and was one of the main figureheads in promoting the brand, appearing at all SPX parties and events. He also wore SPX from head to toe for all of his fights, culminating in the heavyweight title fight with Frank Bruno.

Yeah, I remember Lennox's silky SPX shorts! Was it ever endorsed by any other celebrities/sports people?

There was an SPX Formula 3 motor racing team, though I couldn't see Schumacher in them somehow!

What's the future for the company?

We own the footwear licence worldwide for a big UK fashion brand called Firetrap. We have established ourselves as one of the main fashion footwear brands in the UK and are beginning to roll out across Europe. We will launch in new territories further afield, but we are determined to get it right in Europe first. Regarding taking on any other brands of any kind, we are always on the lookout for an exciting prospect that does not clash with any of our other brands.

Finally, I gotta ask - what does SPX stand for?

It actually stands for Sports Performance eXtreme, but we prefer to refer to it as Shoes that Perform to the eXtreme. **WOW!**

WWW.SPXFOOTWEAR.COM

DISS LO

PRO- EDITION

Whatever happened to... TROOP?

My awesome hi-lite from the first issue of Sneaker Freaker was the original LL Cool J issue Troop jacket (as modelled here by Mr Rekshop) which brought back memories of this mad expensive, crazy brand.

In case you don't know, Troop is an obscure '80s fashion label that also made shoes which were the perfect condiment to the wildstyle era. I have been trying to dig up some other decent photos and info on the origins and demise of Troop but it's hard. When you type 'Troop sneakers' into Google, all you get are links to Scout Troops and hiking shoes. So I have bugger all to tell you except for this one story, but it is a good one.

It concerns an urban myth about the company that blew up so big, it possibly destroyed them. The myth goes like this. The Ku Klux Klan was supposed to own Troop! With its predominantly black clientele, this was very provocative to say the least. Not only that, but the story then spread to include the completely untrue and ridiculous allegation that the sneakers had the words 'Thank you nigger for making us rich' embossed in the pattern on the inner sole. It was also alleged that Troop was an acronym meaning 'To Rule Over our Oppressed People.'

LL Cool J was endorsing the brand and the myth expanded to include an incident where he was reportedly seen stomping on his jacket and denouncing the brand on Oprah Winfrey's show! Not true, it never happened!

No matter what the owners of Troop did, the rumour wouldn't go away. They have publicly denied that the story had an effect but whatever the case, Troop went belly up after only about 5 years in business. How these dirty whispers get started is anybody's guess.

Looking back, I think it's definitely a shame. Imagine what sort of insane world it would be if Troop had kept making clothes and sneakers for the next 20 years!

After disappearing all those years ago, Troop sneakers suddenly made a mysterious comeback two years ago, right out of the blue. The pair shown here on the left were bought new from a tiny little shop on New York's infamous Canal St in 2003. The quality is so-so, the elephant skin is totally ridiculous and they hurt like hell after a few hours of wear. What do you expect? Troop were never known for their good taste. But that's why we like them... if you know what I mean!

FELICITY McCUTCHEON

→ i just had to have a pair of red all stars. they were on the feet of new york breakers alongside low cut pro-keds - rock steady wore them and they had that style of folding down the hi top part of the sneaker so that you had this white cuff at the top. a friend was going os and i made him hunt me down a pair. it sounds weird now talking about hunting down all stars but you just couldn't get them here back then. so i got my pair and folded the top down but it kept folding back up so i hand stitched the sides down. then i got two pairs of thin white laces and used my mom's sewing machine to join them to make fat laces. i got some weird looks walking around in those people hadn't seen anything like it. remember those puma canvas low cut plain sneakers we used to have? what were they called?

→ they were 'tennis' i think - all the kicks were canvas then, rubber ball front nike and converse. perfect for writing on the side and deluxe customisation.

→ yeh that's them - i hand painted mine a grass green colour to try and make them look like the sought after suede pumas we'd seen in beat street (clydes). i think i made some more fat laces for those too. actually - i remember sewing 3 pairs of normal laces together once - i wanted the fattest laces ever but i couldn't get them to go through the holes in the sneakers!

→ i went the enamel paint and couldn't stop at 2 coats, i had the glossiest shoes around but was discouraged to find them cracking especially when i rocked a little floorwork - you know like kuriaki at the roxy. laces were hard to find, I remember how excited we were at getting the hookup from proball - the only place that had

nylon fatlaces. you knew who was down at the writers bench by who had what. that source was kept secret and the business was selling laces to those not smart enough to track them down. my first pair were the famous hot pink and grey pattern - very miami vice.

→ they had so many colours and combos that it was so hard choosing - we'd spend a long time in that store. did you ever wonder what this crazy b-boy fashion item was doing in this little basketball store in a small tucked away suburb? i kind of imagined these games of basketball with all the players wearing fat laces and breakin in between dunks..

→ the shoe products have always played a role in writing - we dominated the pinnacle of fashion with some serious colourway lacework and we used shoe spray paint for bombing pieces, the raven oil dye to top up $67 markers for tags and used shoe polish bottles for round markers.

→ ahh - remember discovering those weird pumas in that clearance store upstairs in that arcade in the city? - they were exactly like clydes except imitation suede. nice colours too - deep blue and black and the toe was a different colour to the shoe. they were like $20?

→ i think they were a version of puma states. when i visited interstate i met a lot of cool writers from wearing those shoes on the train, just hanging out.

→ everybody that visited from interstate that were in the know left with a pair of those. i wish i'd never thrown mine away - they were the biz, but i think they were falling apart so badly and growing weird mould like a high school science experiment. they

looked real fine with navy laces.

→ i personally liked the felt baby blue laced arrow style not straight across. Also known as plait style.

→ that's the only way to lace your kicks. my favourite pairs around that time were those and that pair of short-ass little blue canvas adidas with the white rubber toe and the white stripes which i wore with crazy grey and bright yellow laces. i loved those coz i think i was the only one with a pair. i found a box-fresh pair recently and got so excited after not seeing them for about 15 years - i bought them even though they're too small for me and hurt my feet after 3 steps. maybe i'll use them as book ends or something.

→ i had the nike penetrator high cut with neutral suede stripe, customised by cutting them into lowcuts, slicing the side of the lacing rack down 1cm and restitching the leather, providing extra lace expansion for maximum width, combined with a hand painted black stripe. 6 months later they released a low cut with black stripes...

I'M THE PACKMAN (EAT EVERYTHING I CAN): THE PACKMAN
JAM ON REVENGE (THE WIKKI-WIKKI SONG) : NEWCLEUS
BREAK DANCIN' - ELECTRIC BOOGIE : WEST STREET MOB
GET WET : C-BANK
DOG TALK : K-9 CORP FEATURING PRETTY C
FEEL THE FORCE : G-FORCE FEATURING GEE & CAPTAIN CEE
RAY GUN - OMICS : PROJECT FUTURE
THE RETURN OF CAPTAIN ROCK : CAPTAIN ROCK

excerpt from a conversation between Kab 101 & Kano 172 November 2002

sneaker wars

Sometimes I think we all forget that cammo is designed with a purpose, namely so soldiers and equipment could hide in the jungle, snow, desert or urban terrain and not get popped so easy. It's become ubiquitous now, almost a permanent aspect of modern life. But camouflage and other military themes didn't just become cool overnight. It was an underground movement for a really long time before it became a fashion thing.

It probably began as a fashion movement in the late '70s when punkers like The Clash and The Sex Pistols goaded the media by dressing as cartoon IRA/Sth American/revolutionary guerillas. In fact, it was so shocking it got them on the news and has since been copied over and over.

You might also remember that in the Eighties, rap groups like Public Enemy and their bodyguards (codenamed SW-1) had an image based on a militant look, mostly as a reference to the Black Panther movement. Unfortunately it ran so deep it is still with us today today (e.g 50-cent and his G-Unit rubbish).

Brands like Bape have also used their own versions of cammo on just about every product known to mankind, including shoe collabs with adidas and even pepsi cans. So, military themes have co-existed with music, fashion and sneakers as staples of street culture for over 20 years.

The sneaks that have been getting all the press lately are the Stash AFI's. Stash has a rep as a 'NYC graffiti legend' and has done a few commercial camouflage patterns in his career. He is also obsessed with barb wire, weapons and urban warfare. This made him the perfect collaborator for Nike on the AF1, considering that 20 years ago the LA SWAT team wore a special mock-up.

Stash chose to give the Nike AF1's a wintry-white brushstroke camouflage panels and a reinforced toe. The 'brushstroke' style cammo-patterns are the coolest patterns at the moment. There are also some nice 'daub' patterns that are a little rarer still which are made using paintbrushes and have heaps of nice detail around the edges when you look up close.

Futura has a similar reputation to Stash as a fan of military themes. He was in the Navy once, so it I guess he knows all about it first hand. I once saw him in a magazine showing off all the military stuff in his crib and it was a really nice collection.

Anyway, Futura designed a Nike Blazer Mid in Suede with numbered boxes, and chose a green and beige colourway as a camouflage reference. Sometimes the colours say it all. Have you ever noticed how shoes are sometimes promoted in colour-ways like with names like 'cadet blue', 'steel grey', 'stealth grey', 'khaki', 'dirty brown', 'bomber green', 'petrol' and even 'blood red?'

I admire Futura's choice to keep the design clean because not everyone wants extreme styling. I like basic canvas sneakers with brass eyelets. These are made using the same materials and methods used to make heavy-duty canvas military tents. To me that makes more sense than commercially-driven styling and ultra-performance gimmicks.

A few of the great simple sneaks are being re-issued in colour-ways that are outright militant. I've seen Vans done in Olive Drab No. 9, which is the same green that everyone in M*A*S*H wore. Elsewhere in this issue you'll find the new Asics running shoe done by the boys from Proper featuring ripstop canvas and so on.

You may be surprised to know that several of the companies that make your sneakers also make new generation military boots, which are now quieter, lighter and more comfortable

The Adidas GSG9 Tactical boots look mighty mean. They're used by the crack teams like SWAT, the US Army and the German anti-terrorist group. They're made in the home of hardcore, Germany, and are made in 'tactical black'. Nike has a shoe called the Air Assault and Oakley has released an SI Assault Boot which is extremely tough.

Just remember, if trouble is brewing, the best way to use your shoes is to help you escape! One Love!

DENNIS HURLEY

How do you define your job?
95% of it is taking product out of the vault and individualising them for someone like a collector. I focus on the sneaker heads!

How does Limited Edition fit in?
Well, back a couple of years ago when Drew Greer started it, it was real small and focused on the East Coast, kinda New York. It's spread out now, we still have team sports and colours, that kind of thing. When I came in it was kind of like, 'Well those are cool, but I'd like to see some other colours and materials and shoes that didn't make sense for the traditional market'. That's how this started out 3 or 4 years ago as just a little side thing. Now the Indie line covers off a global standpoint, whereas Limited Edition is more focused on hardcore, especially New York.

How did you end up at Nike doing this?
It's real funny, my roommate from college - his Mom worked here so I had an 'in'. I started off picking up phones doing customer service and then I landed in Development and Cross Training and then became Tech Rep and then I was an Ekin down in South Cal. I loved being an Ekin.

I see you've got Terminators on, are they the new Dunk?
I dunno, we'll see what the heads think. Maybe? I think it's just giving people out there another option cause I don't think the Dunk is going anywhere, it's one of my all-time favourites. Everything's not just Dunk and AF1, we have other sneakers that we've never brought back.

Man, that's an understatement.
Yeah... for me it's like working in a candy store when we open up the vault.

You DO have a vault, I knew it!
We have a great archival vault of every catalogue.

Oh, not like one of every shoe in every colour in a huge aircraft hanger or something? (deflated)
No, not like that. Just catalogues, but it is pretty accurate up til 2001. After that there's so many make-ups from so many countries, we can't document them all. But from a true heritage point of view in the '70s and '80s - we have it all.

Is it hard to do something that stands out now? The market is getting saturated now, all the old brands are back...
This building is filled with so many talented people, and our performance guys are pushing the envelope so fast that if we can just draft a little off them it's cool. I'm always wondering what they're doing and how can I re-interpret it for a retro. We can never catch up to the end line guys. That's the chase, as mad as it sounds. If we can create some crazy stuff that makes b-ball and Running guys go 'damn!' that's the chase...

There are a lot of websites that relentlessly pursue information and gossip, do you watch what the kids are saying?
Yeah, the first thing I do in the morning is check the sports page. Then I check the sneaker sites. Then at lunchtime I check again and before I leave I check again (laughs) and then just before bed I have another look. Not so much to see what other people have done but to see what we've done, what worked, what didn't.

Nike
Footwear
Product
Manager
"INDIE"

JESSE
LEYVA

Ever wondered who makes all those supercool shoes we get the fiending pains for? Meet **Jesse Leyva** from Nike, Beaverton. Jesse has been responsible for the Haze Dunks, the Undefeateds, Alphanumerics and the Grunge series amongst others. Has he got the coolest job in the world? Has he what!

The feedback is usually pretty quick and decisive isn't it! Now, what's your favourite project?
Crazy as it sounds, it was the first shoe that got sold. The Dunks we did for Alphanumeric. I think they could have been better but at the time I didn't really have more than one shot at it. Maybe we could have made more of a go at it, but we might have freaked it. It turned out really cool though. We were going for the whole baseball hat thing and it didn't come back as clean as we wanted but it's still one of my favourites.

It was just for the Alphanumeric staff wasn't it?
Yeah, for his Ali and his crew but then we had a few for the Nikeheads, we had a promo deal.

Do you know what the Alpha Dunks are worth these days? I can't remember seeing any for sale for some time...
I don't think anyone is selling right now. A lot of people ask me about the crazy prices and I explain it like this. In 20 or 30 years time when people think of this time and the biggest things happening in the art world, well this is one of them.

Yeah, how much would you pay for a print by Haze? At least a shoe is functional and I guess you could hang it on the wall...
Yeah! All those people who are into art, would you spend $50,000 on a print? No! But would I spend a couple of hundred on a sneaker? Hell yeah!

Is it a sign of a really healthy scene or complete madness?
It's both. I think it will come back.

Any other favourites?
The Haze Dunks are up there as well.

To settle a few arguments, how were they done?
It was literally an airbrush. I was into graff and looking at the whole '80s scene, like who was bombing trains way back so we looked at Haze, it was a cool collaboration. The guy is so talented. It was so much fun working with him.

HAZE DUNK

JESSE LEYVA

I noticed a lot of variation in pics I saw, were they that different, I mean, did the painter get a bit carried away or something?
Yeah! (laughs) There were big differences - when they first hit Hong Kong I remember the guys there were saying 'those are knock offs'. You might hear that a lot but that's the whole idea behind them, we didn't want them to have any pattern. They wanted a stencil and we were like 'no stencils' just literally airbrush it like you would do it on the street.

What others have you been involved with?
I did the Michael Lau deal for the toy show in HK last winter. I also did the Undefeated Dunks and um...

Did you do the Grunge series?
Yeah, it was cool. I was happy because it was a big challenge, our factories are all about making things clean and precise and the same. Because when you buy a shoe for sports that's what you want. And to have them start thinking in a random fashion was hard, but they're used to it now. The first project we did was the paint splats and that was the first to introduce the notion of every shoe being different.

Looks like you buffed them with an orbital sander, true or false?
Yeah! (laughs) That's EXACTLY how it was done. We looked at growing up as a kid and having your shoes beat and we thought why not have that right from the jump?

In terms of design, how do you go about your job?
I look for ideas, we travel a lot round the globe and we're not really looking at things only from a sneakers point of view, but more from pop culture in general. If we see something cool, music or a band or something... about 3 weeks ago we landed a Deftones Dunk. We're not releasing it, we just did it for their tour and that was ill because I love them. They wanted a Dunk and they were down with it.

How does it look?
It's black with green and has Deftones on it. They launched it at the show in LA. Only 48 pairs, enough so they could wear them.

OK, what else have you got on the go?
We're always pushing against the competition, but I think 2004 is better than 2003, we have a couple of collabs coming down the line.

Nike
Footwear
Product
Manager
"INDIE"

GRUNGE DUNK

GRUNGE TERMINATOR

Do you get calls all the time interested in hooking up with you?
We do get calls but we're getting away from collabs because so many people do them. From my perspective I'm only curious if somebody wants to do something no-one has ever done before.

Does working in the industry take the romance outta sneakers?
Not really, its almost like the exact opposite. Everyday I'm like, 'I can't believe I'm getting paid to do something like this!' I remember when I was a kid my mom would be like, 'They're just shoes, get rid of them, what are you doing?' I never thought that this is what I would be doing.

It's funny, a lot of people I interview mention their mom in relation to their sneakers... what does she think now?
She thinks it's dope. She's like 'Aw man, you told me!' We'll meet for lunch and she's like, 'You're in a tee shirt and shorts and a ball cap' and I'm like, 'Yeah, it's my corporate look!'

You must have some rare air in your closet now?
Yeah, working here I'm into one-of-a-kinds - not even things we sample on purpose but like things that were mistakes, I like to keep those. So now it's like the first round of AF1 camouflages that came back all messed up.

They're cool, you know the AF1 is my shoe? (hint hint)
Yeah I noticed!

What about cammo? It just wont quit will it?
People asked me why I did cammo and personally it's a staple for me. Cammo is timeless, it's like a white tee shirt or grey sox.

You have a cool job, what's the coolest thing about it?
As crazy as it sounds the coolest thing is working with such creative people, Mike Aveni, Bruce Kilgore, John Barbour, Tinker - those guys are like legends now.

Do they know how influential they have been?
They know it now but the coolest part is that they don't care less. It was so in the past to them. When we brought back the Safari, I got to talk to Tinker. Man, he was so far ahead, that shoe didn't do well when it first came out, it was done in the '80s but should have been released in 2003. Can you believe that? A lot of the shoes that we brought back, Tinker did first time around, Safari, Escape, that was Mark Parker, the Raid, they are just stoked to see them come back.

THE pump IT

Reebok's great moment in the sun was in the '80s when they served it up to Nike.
One of the principal reasons was the birth of the aerobics boom and another was the Pump series. Regarded by some as a crappy gimmick and by others as a stroke of genius, the Pump nevertheless deserves its chapter in the history of sneakers.

To set the scene, you have to go back to 1982 when Nike's Air system blew up with the launch of the Air Force One (the first actual Air soles were in the Tailwind in 1978). By 1987 Nike had introduced visible air. With pressure mounting (shocking pun intended) Reebok needed something to give them an edge so they bought the Pump patent off designer Harry West and incorporated it into their tongues.

In a technical sense, the Pump system is far more diverse than Nike's Air system. Instead of merely cushioning the user's foot, the Pump system offers a custom fit while protecting the heel, the ankle and the collar area of the foot. Different models of the shoe had different Pump systems, which were integrated into the tongue of the shoe. The lining of the shoe contains a bladder which houses the air chambers which inflate, making them like air bags for the feet. With all that pumping you'll also need a way to release the pressure so there's a little valve to let air out of the chambers!

In 1989, the first Pump was released into the market. It was called the Pump ERS, and was a hi-top intended for b-ballers at a record price for its time of $400AUS. Their advertising campaigns focused on the slogan 'Pump Up and Air Out' and although it made quite an impact, only a limited amount of pairs were sold of the original and it wasn't until Reebok expanded the Pump family into other categories that the concept took off. Reebok also took aim at the Ladies' market in this era. Two specific models were released for the feminine market – the AXT Pump and the Aerobic Lite Pump mid. With a cheaper price tag and super ladylike colours these flew off the shelf.

In 1990, Reebok signed NBA star Dee Brown to wear its Pump basketball shoes. They released the Omnizone Pump and the Twilight Zone Pump. These were lighter and smaller than the first b-ball shoe Reebok produced. Omnizone Pump has since become regarded as one of the best basketball shoes ever. You might also remember that Dee Brown wore the Omni Lite Pump in his infamous 'Pump It Up' ads and again pumped his shoes on court before winning the 1991 Slam Dunk Contest during the NBA All-Star Weekend with a blind or 'no-look' slam dunk. By this time the Pump technology had also made its way into tennis shoes that Michael Chang wore.

Reebok rolled out other Pump b-ball styles like Pump II Hi, Battleground Pump, Transit Zone Pump and the Double Pump. In 1992, Reebok endorsed Shaquille O'Neal, the year's first pick in the NBA Draft. They gave him his own signature model, the Shaq One Pump, the first to use Graphlite technology. The shoe was praised at the time for its light weight and ultra-responsiveness. By this time, Reebok had made serious

UP!

advances into the sneaker market and were challenging Nike who had seemingly lost their sense of direction. But they didn't hold the lead for too long: Nike bounced back from the shadows with their new Air Max and popularity of Jordan and Pippen (thanks to their first back-to-back 3-peat of the NBA championships).

To counter, Reebok signed up Shawn Kemp who was with the Seattle Supersonics then. They released the Kamikaze series (I think a lot of people forget about this, but I can't because I used to love the ad on Channel 10's NBA show) but it didn't have the killer punch.

In 1994, Reebok decided to give the Pump system another shot. They released the InstaPump Fury which was different to the old Pump system - it was lighter, more compact and substantially better than the old system. Designed to be a laceless running shoe, it relied on inflating the bladder to pack any empty spaces inside the shoe. The design was quite radical at the time — it looked nothing like the old Pumps and must have seemed quite odd compared to anything else released during that year. The InstaPump Fury was a big hit in Japan thanks to its nutty looks, crazy colour combos and a hi-performance reputation. In 1995, Reebok released a variant called the InstaPump Fury Road. The design and the colour chosen was slightly different to the InstaPump Fury but sales never kicked in.

In 1996, Reebok dropped the words Insta in front of the shoes to become simply the Pump Fury. Also in the same year, Reebok incorporated the Graphlite and the Hexalite technology into the shoe. In 1997, they started releasing limited edition colours for the shoe, which include the Jackie Chan model.

In 2000, they revised the Pump Fury again, now incorporating DMX technology which contains jelly-like chambers in the sole and air chambers on the outside of the upper. Limited editions kept on rolling out, including collabs with Size?, T6M (Gruv), Keanan Duffty (KD) and Chanel.

In keeping the modern obsession with retro styles, Reebok re-released the Pump Omni-Lite in 2004 which were pretty successful, especially in Japan. In 2005 Reebok also rereleased extremely limited pairs of other models as well, including the massively oversize Pump Bringback and Court Victory.

Funnily enough, the Pump system has also been appropriated by other corporations. Seiko have made a pump watch and Wonderbra put out 'AirWonder' which pumps up your cleavage using two air bags inserted in the cups. And let's not forget that Nike made 3 attempts at imitating the Pumps, namely the '89 Air Pressure (as featured in Issue 2 of Sneaker Freaker), the Air Command Force and the Air Force 180 high.

Like 'em or loathe 'em Reebok have contributed a lot to sneaker culture. They were the first to promote shoes solely to the women's sports market, the first to collaborate with movie stars and a big posh brand and they didn't mind developing innovations in sports footwear. The Pumps were also the first shoes that could entertain you when you're bored (I had a lot of fun Pumping and deflating when I was bored in class).

One thing is for sure, I'll always treasure my only pair of Shaq 2s which are stuffed under my bed because I doubt we'll ever see a retro of these.

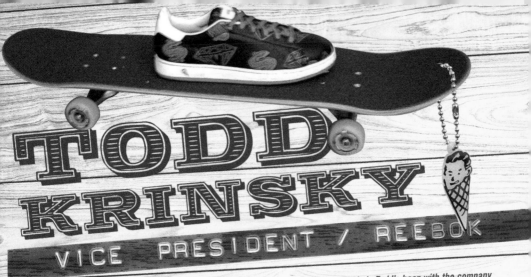

TODD KRINSKY

VICE PRESIDENT / REEBOK

Ladies and gentlemen, meet Todd Krinsky, also known as the Vice President of Reebok. Todd's been with the company for over a decade and knows the joint from the ground up. His current job is signing heavyweights like Fifty Cent and Yao Ming and then developing successful products that bear their name. In some ways, his job is akin to that of a conventional A&R guy at a record label, except that Todd is a hardcore shoe head and has been since he was knee high to a grasshopper. Todd is also pretty forthright and dedicated to the cause. Read on as we discuss the evolution of Pump, the demise of Ice Cream and a bunch of other stuff as well...

So how's Reebok these days?

Well, it's good. We're entering into a whole new world now with this fusion of sports and entertainment. There's a lot of new opportunities and new consumers and it's kind of a different era for us right now than where we've been.

You've been at Reebok for more than ten years, how did you progress through the company?

Originally I started in the Mail Room, but I grew up selling sneakers since I was sixteen. I was a basketballer, an avid shoe collector, and so I ended up getting a job in Development building shoes. Then I moved to Asia and learned about Manufacturing. But I always wanted to get into marketing and in 1999, I moved back. In 2001 Paul Fireman came back and we really started to strategise Youth Culture, so they put me in charge of that: music, basketball and the whole RBK thing. I brought in some new people and started to sign artists and become more relevant to Youth Culture globally. And that's where we are today.

Well it's good to see you can still make it up the corporate ladder with loyalty and persistence. You've obviously got an innate understanding of the business from the bottom up.

Yeah, absolutely. Reebok is a bit of an entrepreneur environment because of Paul and the way he started the company so it allows for young people to have ideas and move within the company.

Do you think your program has changed the general perception of Reebok?

I think with young people we have. A lot of athletic brands have flirted with hip-hop culture, but nobody really wanted to embrace it and give back to it. So I think by doing the Jay-Z deal, we made a statement that we understood Youth Culture and we're not just gonna use and manipulate it, we're gonna invest in it. So we did deals with Jay-Z, and Fifty Cent, now there's a whole load of artists who wanna deal with us. Youth Culture is all about sports, music and entertainment, so if that's where young people are, then that's where we wanna be.

How did you assess Jay-Z and Fifty Cent as partners for Reebok endorsements?

We do a lot of focus groups. We ask kids, 'Who do you listen to?' and, 'Who do you like for fashion?' But it's more about analysing these guys. Some people sell records, but they don't drive fashion. You want that guy that sells records, but you're really listening to what he's saying. If you watch their video, see how they carry themselves, that's a very powerful thing. A guy like Jay-Z is so powerful in Pop Culture because young people watch what he says and they go out and buy that shoe and shirt. So it's about cultural influence. But we don't have a criteria and the reason we haven't done ten deals up til now is because we're really scrutinizing who we do business with.

So how's Fifty Cent these days? Is he staying out of trouble?

Ah, yeah... He's in Toronto shooting a movie that will come out around Thanksgiving. His album is up to four million (G) Units already.

Sounds like he's following in LL Cool J's footsteps?

Kinda like Eminem, actually, with the Eight Mile thing. It's loosely based on his life.

OK, and will there be new G-Unit product to coincide with that?

Yeah, we have a new launch with new footwear and apparel to launch with the movie. There's a soundtrack and a video game as well, so the holidays will be a big period for Fifty.

Sounds like he needs his own Fifty Cent Theme Park!

Yeah, after you got video games, movie, soundtrack, your own sneaker and apparel, I mean there's not much left.

G UNIT

DJ SHOE

S. CARTER

S. CARTER

You're not really a star unless you've got your own shoe in hip-hop right now!

That's the blueprint that's been created by these guys. Get a platinum record, create your own label, your own apparel company, and now the new thing is to merge with bigger corporate partners. Hip-hop just gets more mainstream and there's just tremendous opportunities for these guys from an endorsement perspective. And the more fashionable, the cooler you are, the better your records sell.

So how do you assess the success of these deals? Is it just about raw sales or is it about the perception that reflects on the brand?

Well, the first thing is we do not sign artists and say, 'Here is the shoe'. We're trying to create a diverse portfolio and the way to do that is to get involved with different personalities to help drive the design process. We signed Jay who is a little bit older, he's the CEO of DEF JAM records, he's got a different lifestyle, he vacates in the South of France. He is amazing. He is a retired rapper, so he takes on a more sophisticated style. You know, Fifty Cent is more street, so he has the gangster image. As we're signing artists they bring their own style to the process and our goal is for RBK Entertainment to be a very diverse array of product that reflects the individuals.

And what we get out of it, outside of revenue, is that we continue to be part of the intrinsic fabric of Youth Culture. Young people look at us as being in bed with all these hot stars and the key for us is to keep being on the cutting edge of who's next, who's hot nine months or a year from now. We know all the new records and so we're at the forefront of creating partnerships with artists that are going to be hot. And that's the tricky part because we create product 12-18 months out, so it's not as easy as it seems.

So who is gonna be hot in 12 months time?

(laughs) I can't tell you!

You guys always say that!

There's probably two or three people that we're looking at. The other fallacy is that we're looking for the next Fifty but that's not the case.

He is a phenomenon, so we're not in this fantasy world that we're gonna sign the new G Unit. They need to be relevant to Youth Culture. Maybe they're regional? From a music perspective, guys in Houston, Texas, everyone loves their music, but kids from New York don't even know what they're saying. The slang is getting crazy...

And what about rock and roll? Or are you just fixated on Hip Hop?

Well, I mean clearly there's more to Youth Culture than just rap, but the easiest thing about hip-hop is that it's synonymous with sneakers. They are closely linked, so it is very easy to sell product through that genre. We are looking at other genres, but we haven't figured out how we can leverage the product.

I read somewhere that you had a long term goal of knocking Nike off Number One? Is that still possible?

I think it is if we stay the course. Meaning, we can't get caught up trying to do what Nike does. We have to create our own space on the highway. We need to be very, very consistent and stay on the fusion on Sports and Music to help drive our business. It's a long-term process, but we've finally got the brand straight and now it's about The Message. We've also got a lot of technology coming out. We are still an athletics footwear brand, and so we have new Pump shoes coming out. We have affiliations with the NFL, the NBA, the NHL.

The one thing people always associate with Reebok is the Pump. It was such a massive hit in the late Eighties that it became a very hard act to follow. Has it been a monkey on your back all those years?

Well I think that when we did Pump, it got too big. It got away from us. We made too many models, we even had golf shoes. I think that the models we brought back that sold well were the key models that were very limited and really meant something. It created heat for the brand for sure, and it's been really cool but all of it is to set up the new Revolution of Pump. Because starting next year, the Pump will not have to be self-pumped, there'll be a dial on the shoe and it will self-inflate so the athlete can control how much air they want in their shoe.

PUMP ATR

PUMP 2.0

PUMP BRINGBACK

COURT VICTORY

Are you talking about Pump 2.0?

Even further than that. I'm talking about the new Allen Iverson shoe for next year. I can't go too far into it because the shoe will launch soon but the point of it is the same - you can control the air cushioning. We'll all be able to modify how our soles fit and the reason why it works so well is because kids are so used to cutomizing everything in their world right now. Music, TV, everything. On the basketball court, every kid wants to look different. So kids are getting tattoos, wrist bands, armbands, and haircuts. We're coming in with a technology that allows the athlete to do that.

Does everyone want to look different so they can get a deal?

Ah, no. I think its just this new generation of kids. I'm not talking about superstars, just high school kids. I think the reason they all do it is because they think differently. Not arrogant, but they're very confident, they wanna stand out. You ask them who they admire and they say, 'I wanna be the next me.' So I think customisation in their world, like with their iPods, is everything they do.

Have you been involved much in basketball?

Yeah, I do all that.

Was it hard to get Iverson and those guys to believe in Reebok?

Ah, not really. Before we had a Grassroots program, a lot of young people didn't have experience with Reebok but that's changed now. It's much easier to negotiate with young athletes now, because they've grown up with Reebok, so we're in a different place right now.

Who do you think will sign Andrew Bogut to a shoe deal? He gets a lot of press down here because he's Australian...

Yeah, I don't know. (laughs) He probably will be the Number One pick. The thing about being first is that it's about potential. So he may be the most sound player right now, but there's some 18 year old high school kids who haven't even finished growing yet. The whole draft has changed because it's about potential.

Has Yao Ming finished growing? Is he 7 foot 5?

Yeah, he has. He's big.

From our point of view, we were very interested in the deal you made with Ice Cream.

With who?

With Ice Cream. (laughs nervously)

Oh. Yeah.

We all read the press releases that explained the collapse of the deal, do you have any comment on that?

That's something we can't talk about. We enjoyed working with Pharrell, it was great. I personally worked very closely with him and was just amazed at his creativity and the way his mind works, but as far as the business arrangement, we leave it to the press release.

OK. My only comment was, and I appreciate this is sensitive, was that it seemed like we all forgot that Nigo from Bathing Ape was involved. Do you think you might work with those guys again?

Ah. We may. there's a possibility we could. We worked with Nigo and he was very creative, it was interesting the way he approaches projects. We thought he was pretty cool so there's a possibility, we talked about that at one time.

Do you think he might bring out his own version of the Pump? Bape are known for copying shelltoes and Air Force Ones...

Yeah, it has been mentioned, that would be one of the key projects.

I think it would be big in Japan!

Yeah absolutley. Even in Europe, London, places like that.

Is Reebok planning a full blown skate team?

Well yeah. We signed Stevie Williams, one of the most famous skaters in these parts, a young African American kid from Philadelphia who used to be with DC. He has skate shoes with RBK coming out next year and he has a team, so that's our entry to skate.

Will Pump be involved in Skate?

It could eventually, but right now we created a simpler shoe... but in the future, yeah it could be. That would be an interesting fusion...

You mentioned you're a collector, tell us about your shoes.

I sold shoes since I was sixteen, so back then I used to get 12 pairs of everything and I'd keep one for myself. I had the OG Pumps, new Avias, the Jordans. I've given away my non-Reeboks now. (laughs) So I don't have all the Jordans but in my basement I have all the old original Pumps. Over the years I gave away all the competitors stuff.

Was that hard to do?

Yeah. You know I live and breathe the brand and I've worked here for years so I'm a passionate believer in Reebok, I really am. But you know, I'm a collector, I remember the first Forums... I actually gave those to a friend of mine. So yeah, I ended up parting ways with a lot of it. My basement now is only Reebok and Allen Iverson. I just started with my son who is 3 years old.

He's just grown out of Weeboks!

Yeah... we do the G-Unit stuff, Jay-Z, some Iverson, who is his best friend now.

Well that's gotta be cool right?

Yeah. He's at the point now where he still doesn't really realise, he goes to the games and hangs in the locker room, he doesn't know any different. He's only 3. It's not cool yet...

Just normal.

Yeah.

Have you got any other surprises for us?

The biggest thing is the Evolution of Pump, not as we know it on the tongue where you pump it up. All our guys in the league like Allen, Baron Davis - that's what they'll be wearing. There will be different prices, different looks and the testing that has gone on the actual product is phenomenal. It's gonna fit different and look different. So we're very excited about bringing this new technology to kids. It will also apply to football, soccer, everything.

And then, on the music side, you will see the hottest stars in a few years time wearing Reebok. What's exciting about that is that we don't even know what that product is yet. We have talented designers here, but the collaboration is what is exciting. We're a brand that is born on creativity. So the artists, when they come in here, they get to live out their dreams. A lot of these kids were sneaker collectors so when I got with Jay-Z the first time, the first half hour was spent just talking old shoes, remembering the old tennis sneakers, the Gucci shoe, because we are the same age. So the whole thing will go to a new level.

We look forward to it. I'd love to see those new Pumps.

I gotta see if we're allowed to show you. The Iverson shoe may be a possibility. Somehow it got on the internet and some kids got hold of it. Which is bad, but all these kids said how cool it was...

So you didn't want it to get out.

No, it won't be released til November. So it was a bit early. We were a bit upset.

Thanks Todd.

OK, thankyou.

"THE TASK: SIX PEOPLE, TWO FLIGHTS, ONE BUS, A HELICOPTER, ONE HOUR AND A MILLION COMBINATIONS TO MAKE SIX ONE-OFF PAIRS OF SNEAKERS!"

"ROAD TRIP NEW BALANCE"

This is the story of six sneaker-heads put on a plane - and then another plane and then on a bus for three hours afterwards - to have their trip memory-sticked and photographed to find out what happens when one sneaker company is so generous as to invite them over to create their very own masterpiece.

If there are those among you who work in the production of any given goods, would you please raise your hand? OK, that's what we thought - an irrelevant number. Except for the few, most of us have no clue about how things are actually manufactured. To us, they just miraculously 'appear' in the stores out of nowhere - and no, UPS does not make anything. They only deliver. But where from? We can only speculate, we can only imagine what these places look like and what is going on inside them...

Since the production of sneakers has almost been completely moved from Europe to the Far East, one would literally have to go a long way if one wanted to do on-site research for the subject. 'Almost' is the keyword in the preceding sentence - because there are a handful of production facilities still operating within Europe. New Balance is one of them, located in the idyllic town of Flimby, three hours north of Manchester at the coast of the Irish Sea. The setting for our 'Road Trip - New Balance'.

The assignment came at short notice with only little information given: 'Go to London, catch a flight to Manchester, meet the crew on the plane, get further instructions, and make your way to New

Balance for the final showdown. Six people heeded the call and were accompanied by a NB rep, who kept order and the participants on their feet to carry out their mission. The first included a bus, several cases of beer and only a limited number of in-between stops. The task: to expand the drive to the night quarters at Armathwaite Hall to a maximum, to consume the highest amount of ale possible (driver excluded, of course), with a minimum of loo-stops (failed miserably at that one), and to entertain one another with the most exaggerated 'sex-drugs-and-rock-and-roll' anecdotes. Two names stood out at this exercise - they took the title easily and there are not enough Xs to define how their stories would have to be rated.

The final test - a six course dinner - had some struggle with the high numbers and difficult arrangement of the silverware but all made it through and found themselves gathered around the fireplace to resume the day's struggles in the end.

While the night passed quick and uneventful, plenty of obstacles and the final round lay ahead of the group the next day. The English breakfast appeared to be the easiest hurdle to take. However, due to the lack of technical skills and flight experience, the crew was unable to shorten the trip by taking advantage of the helicopter parked outside the hotel. This delay would later turn out to have been a costly one - precious time needed for the grand finale...

The arrival of the contestants at the NB headquarters took no-one there by surprise. All arrangements had been made, the instructors were assembled, and all information was prepared to get the team on the way through the NB factory with its numerous production sectors. Memory skills were challenged here for the crew had to gather valuable information and hints regarding shoe production. 'Name all outer panels of the NB 576 and 1500', 'State all areas suitable for embroidery', 'How many types of mesh are available?' and 'What material is suede?' - were just some of the questions that

had to be answered. With the end of the instructional period, the crew was given only a short break to gear up at the local shop.

Then they were confronted with their last, yet biggest task. They were to apply their freshly acquired knowledge to master the complexities of sneaker production, to defy the professionals at NB and succeed at assembling an instant classic. The crew set about picking their own materials, colorways, and choosing the most significant spots for their embroideries. All within a limit of 60 minutes (damned be that helicopter) and using only one's own imagination to visualise the results.

If these terms don't sound too demanding, the dozens and dozens of fabric rolls and boxes with hundreds of materials sure do. Six people, one hour, and a million combinations can only make matters worse. Only with the helping hands of the fine people at New Balance, could this onerous task be finally completed.

Six individual pairs of sneakers are currently in production. Thanks to NB in Germany and over in Flimby - you were great sports and your patience and energy is yet to be matched. Cheers!

JÖRG HAAS
www.beinghunted.com

CUSTOM SHOES FOR
MICHAEL JORDAN

*Shoes custom built & airtained
for Michael Jordan*

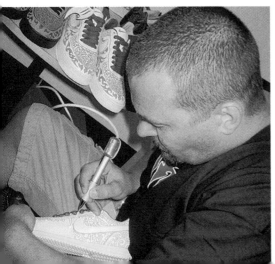

LASER AMAZER

AN INTERVIEW WITH MARK SMITH

With all our obsessiveness about shoes, it's easy to forget that behind every great sneaker is a creative person struggling with inspiration to come up with something completely new. With that in mind, meet Mark Smith, curator of the Laser Project. How does the laser part work? Simply put, the beam of light follows instructions from a computer program to burn the leather in insanely intricate patterns. We're talking about fractions of millimetres here. These shoes really have to be seen up close to truly appreciate the fine detail. If it sounds hi-tech, it is. If it sounds space age, it isn't. Laser technology is used in many everyday applications, from eye surgery to signwriting. When used in footwear though, it has many other performance applications beyond the merely cosmetic. As in music, where the spaces between the notes are the most important, the genius of the Laser project is not what is burned away, but rather what is left. Confused? Read on and all will be revealed. We were part of a select bunch of players granted access to the Elizabeth Gallery in New York to hear Mark take us through the project step by step. Afterwards I spoke to him about his work...

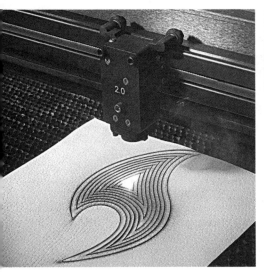

How did you come to be working at Nike?

Well, I have a degree in Advertising. With a minor in Psychology, I thought I'd be an ad guy back in the '80s. Then I earned a degree in Graphics/Packaging from Art Center College of Design. After graduation, I designed tees at Maui and Sons Surf in California. Then a bunch of friends moved to Oregon and started work at Nike. I figured if they could... (also my future wife was one of them, so, naturally, I followed). I was hired by Mark Parker and ended up in apparel until Tinker Hatfield hired me into footwear.

Shoe design seems to be bit of a glamour occupation at the moment, you guys are like rockstars! Kids are dreaming of designing Jordans rather than becoming firemen these days....

Yeah! Except rockstars get those funny colored M&Ms...

What other projects have you worked on at Nike?

Most of my work has been on concept stuff that never sees the light of day. Special projects and promos for specific athletes. I collaborated with Tinker on Jordans IX thru XV. Air Raid, Jordan

Vindicate, Jordan Ultralite, those were mine. This year I did shoes for LeBron and a pair for Kobe. Most recently, I've been working on HTM, SWO and University of Oregon football uniforms. Tinker and I have also begun work on the Air Jordan XX. I really never know from one week to the next what projects are coming down the road for me. That's one of the best aspects of this place.

The most obvious reference is tattooing, are you deep into that?

I love the commitment it takes to permanently mark oneself. It also feels good and I enjoy the cultural significance. I like any true story telling that goes on in many personally designed pieces. It's just a fascinating medium to work in - skin is a truly special canvas.

Laser technology has a wide-ranging series of applications, how did the Nike experiment with shoes originate?

Jay Meschter in the innovation kitchen was investigating the use of laser cutting on some very cool concept shoes. He was looking into some very interesting ways of slicing materials. I just saw another way of using this tool.

Chris Lundy Dunk

So, did you just call up Phil and ask for a laser machine?

Well, kinda… our group is tasked with innovation on many levels. We are fortunate enough to have access to tools that allow us to look into future applications and processes. Along that road, the laser became a natural tool for us to look into.

So, how does the process work?

We start with the flat pattern pieces. Design the graphic around the architecture of the shoe and its parts, and watch the tiny little sun burn its way into your retina for a while. Then we stitch them together. There are some slight differences between the samples made here in Beaverton and the factory built pairs. We consider the Beaverton pairs to be artists' proofs, where we are working out the technical specifics. Each pair is unique, and has slightly different characteristics from which we pull certain details, compile them into the 'best of' and send to the factory to complete the process into a full run. The laser we are using is an R&D machine, a little bit different than the factory machines. We are learning every step of the way on this one because this is the first time for us.

I really dug your talk introducing your shoes at the exhibition.

Thanks. It was a lot of fun to tell the story of this project. It was the first time meeting most of the people in the room. Everyone was really cool and I had some wonderful conversations with people from all around the world.

Giving a pair to Michael for his 40th birthday must have been an occasion and a half. Were you nervous shipping them out?

The fact that they were the first round of that particular pattern and process meant that we had to be on our toes all the way through. Chanmy is an expert stitcher, and she really made the difference on the craftsmanship. I had a lot of help on the pattern work from Mike Friton in the kitchen, as well. A real team effort. It was a lot of fun hitting the deadline and coming through… We had about 4 days to actually pull it off.

Did he send you any feedback?

Yeah, he was very positive about them, and in turn he very kindly reciprocated for my 40th birthday. He also asked me to design him a motorcycle racing suit, based on the design cues from the shoes. He is on the track and very serious about the speed. Very serious.

Nice work bringing your mates in to the game! Tell us about them as individuals and why you chose them for this project?

I first asked Mike Desmond to play around with some pattern pieces as a canvas. I was introduced to Mike by a mutual friend, Aaron Cooper and we immediately struck up a deep friendship. He has a dual life, something I can relate to personally. Mike directs a concept car design crew for a major auto manufacturer during the day and he does hot rods with his brothers, and custom motorcycle stuff with Jesse James at nite. Custom culture is in his blood.

I met Chris Lundy on the first day at Art Center. We were in the back of class leering at everyone, and I knew we'd get along. Chris was into big wave surfing on the north shore of Oahu. He had completely blown his knee in a serious accident. After rehab he turned his life over to painting. Flow is at the root of all his endeavours. Surfing, painting, boarding, guitar, and creative dialogue through the English language.

Maze Air Force

Tom Luedecke came to the innovation kitchen in February and I asked him to tap into his heritage as a German. With a keen eye for detail and a wonderful graphic sense, he dropped the Celtic bomb on the Cortez. Tom paints at night and has a serious background in the martial arts. His sense of humour was key to his success in interviewing for his position at Nike.

Around May, I called Maze to help out on the Air Force One. I had met him on a completely different project with Nike and immediately connected with his approach to creativity, humour and overall exuberance. He has an infectious laugh and has done everything from movie set design to directing and graphics. He is a bit of a legend in the graffiti world as well. And he's a hell of a drummer.

I knew that when I asked them to become involved, they would give way more than I could expect. It wasn't about finding the biggest names and blowing this thing out. it was all about doing something very personal with some very personal friends.

Congratulations on a major breakthrough. I'm thinking not so much about the decorative aspect but the way you can sculpt leather. You showed me an Air Force One made out of one piece of leather!

Thanks very much. The one piece upper was a direct result of looking for the largest canvas available within the particular shoe pattern. This tool allowed us to explore this aspect fully. It also led to re-engineering the inside of the shoe completely from a pattern standpoint. I have to say it is fun seeing the moment when people see how the one piece construction was achieved.

You also told me to wear mine with no socks! Sounds dangerous...

I selfishly wanted the inside of the shoes to be as comfortable as possible because I rarely wear socks myself. The pigskin feels better than cotton or lycra. I wore a pair for 60 days straight with no socks and was actually able to remove them, in public, within a confined space, without incident or injury...

Is it just comfort or is there a performance aspect to this concept? Comfort is key to performance.

Tell us about some of the performance applications you envisage? Will we see laser used in running or soccer boots for example? We're trying a lot of things with the laser.

You guys never give anything away! The laser product rolls out over the next few months - can you fill us in on the range? Some kids are gonna want the whole set!

There are 6 designs. We used the Air Force One, Cortez, and Dunk as platforms. Maze's AF1 is standard construction with overlays. My AF1 is a one piece construction, as is Lundy's dunk. Desmond's Dunk is normal construction. Luedecke's Cortez is one piece and my Cortez is normal construction. There will be 3 colorways. Pigskin linings, and slow recovery, collar foam packages. Plush Poron, pigskin covered sockliners. And the packaging is pretty sweet. We just wanted to keep them special so there won't be millions of these floating around the world.

Thanks for your time Mark, good luck with your laser beam...
No, thankyou!

WORLD EXCLUSIVE PREMIERE

COUNTER 1
FIRST INSTALLMENT 040405

COUNTER 1
FIRST INSTALLMENT 040405

FEIT | **SNEAKER FREAKER**

TM

ISSUE 6

MADE IN MELBOURNE

29.06.05

THIS PRODUCT IS BUILT USING

SPECIALIZED **FEIT** KOMPONENTRY™

*join **FEIT***

Please enter **SNKRFRKR6** @ www.joinfeit.com

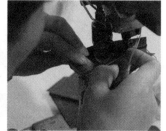

FEIꟾ

FEIT; (fight)

Why FEIT?

Laying down to die would be boring. Challenge is the key - it's what keeps us inspired and entertained. In this over-popularized, over-saturated and over-exposed world dominated by large corporations and a few fat wallets, the little guy needs to stand up and say, 'Fuck it!' Democracy is being eroded.

It gets harder and harder to be the small guy out on your own challenging the big guys. Besides, what else are we going to do? This is what we enjoy.

So we liquidate everything we own, get Rodney and Ashley to peddle their arses out on the street. Roll the dice, work fucking hard and see what happens. It's far better than working for someone else.

What do you stand for?
What do you stand against?

For the underdog, for a colour-blind society, peace in the world. Reduction in pollution, especially in China. Save the pandas, save the whales, save the elephants, save the trees, save yourselves.

More sexy chicks on the street. Better music, better movies. More change. The rise of the Orient (just to piss off the West). A return to real democracy and the realization that capitalism is just the biggest mousetrap of all used to control our minds to keep us occupied, fat, dull and unaware of what the fucks really what. And I think I mentioned what I stand against.

What makes Feit different?

The product. First of all we don't make our product in a one-stop-shop like other footwear brands. We've taken the best people we have known over the years that specialise in different areas of product design, development and manufacturing. The owners of the company are completely hands on, it's a personalized service from go to woe.

The first thing we noticed about your shoes was the prominent chiselled toe or bumper bar. That's a nice tweak, will it become the signature FEIT element?

I'm glad you noticed that. The toebar really influences the look and feel of the shoe. It is, literally, directional. And it provides a very modern, futuristic element to a classic shoe. It is one of the key design features, and it will be a signature FEIT element.

The second thing we noticed was the tag on the box which says your shoes are made using 'Specialized FEIT Komponentry.' What is all that about?

As you know, shoes are made up of a number of different parts. Each part, or 'Komponent' of all the Feit products have been separately developed and manufactured. We focus on the last, the sole unit, the footbed, the pull loops and the hard wear as individual pieces, then we bring each FEIT Komponent together via precision assembly.

The innersole makes for a nice comfortable ride, what's hiding down there?

The innersole, or footbed, is a fusion of those used in modern military footwear. It has been specifically developed for support and comfort, with dual heel and toe cushioning, as well as an anti-bacterial top sheet to reduce heat and odour. Then there is the sole by Vibram.

You mentioned you had a master craftsman work on the FEIT last, what's the benefit of going to those lengths?

It comes down to quality. We wanted to ensure our product looks good and is high quality. The only way to achieve that is by using the best materials and craftsmen available.

Six years ago I was in a small town called Civitanova Marche in Italy, the home of traditional Italian shoe making. During my stay I met a 74-year-old last maker named Verdiccio Paderone. His father was a last maker/cobbler and over the years he has made lasts for just about every high-end men's dress shoe brand you could imagine.

His work was, and still is, amazing. All that knowledge and experience, along with his fantastic attention to detail and tradition shines through. Very few people in the world today employ traditional last making techniques, because very few are capable.

We wanted every Komponent of every FEIT shoe to meet the standards set by Master Craftsmen like Verdiccio.

Can you explain a bit more about Vibram? The sole unit has a very prominent logo on it, what's up with that?

Vibram is the world's leading outdoor sole manufacturer. It's an Italian company with a history of innovation and quality from 1936.

Usually they develop and manufacture their own soles and sell them to other footwear brands. We decided to approach Vibram about the possibility of re-working an existing design. They agreed, and together we developed the 3-piece sole unit on the shoe that you see on the FEIT range.

How important is the last?

To some degree it's the most important Komponent of the shoe, if the last is wrong, you're basically screwed. It provides the shoe with its shape, look and feel. It impacts everything from visual design, through to comfort and wearability. That is the reason we went to such lengths developing and producing the last. We desired a look that was a fusion between your basic court sneaker shape, which we all love and are comfortable with, combined with a more tailored, more upscale shape. VC was the perfect guy, he gave us a more straight and tailored look, which we were after, and his magical hands had blessed the product we were about to make.

I also really like the thumb straps, they're pretty neat....

The loops were first on a project I collaborated on many years ago but they never reached the market. We decided to reintroduce them for both practical and design reasons. They help you put the shoe on and position the tongue. Designwise they provide another exclusive element that we call FEIT.

Is FEIT a semi-formal sneaker or a sporty kind of shoe? Are you designing for work or play?

It's a tailored shoe inspired by Seventies court shoes. I suppose it is a fusion. Hopefully, people don't have to change between work and play.

To what extent did research play a role in evolution of the brand?

The brand is more reaction than research. Reaction to mass-produced, mass-marketed product. That is why the first line is called Counter 1. The product, however, is all research. All I do is look at shoes. I'm beginning to forget what people's faces look like. Look shoes, think shoes, eat shoes, piss shoes. I'm on the road constantly observing.

As consumers, have our notions of quality been eroded when it comes to footwear?

Yes. We have become used to our shoes falling apart after a certain amount of wear. This occurs far too soon, and can be avoided. I also noticed that little information regarding production and development is passed on to the consumer. This is true of many products. I feel that you should know what you're getting. I suppose they tell you when you buy a Rolex, but not when you buy a Seiko.

So how do you convey a sense of quality without resorting to cliché?

By producing product that is, without question, a high quality product. The proof is in the pudding.

Oh good, I like pudding! I also noticed you call your hard polished leather models 'Standard FEIT Issue'. Is that bit of a potshot at all the brands overusing the term 'premium'?

Yes and no. In the footwear industry it is not only words that are overused and unoriginal. We decided to call it 'Standard Issue' because it is our basic, one colour, all leather standard style. To us 'Standard Issue' should be premium. It is the most durable and utilised piece, therefore high quality is completely necessary. Highest quality should be standard in footwear.

FEIT broadly seems to fit with some of the new independent brands like Callous, RTFT and Visvim, is that how you see yourselves?

We are an independent brand like those mentioned, and we are coming up at a similar time. There is some good product being developed by some of these new, independent brands, which is great, particularly for the consumer. In the same breath I believe FEIT is as able to stand out from these brands as it is to fit in.

Are we seeing a style shift to a more formal kind of streetwear? Do we all have to start dressing up again?

We don't HAVE to do anything. Dress how you wanna. Our products fuse technical, tailored and classic influences. They're as versatile as streetwear is.

And where can we find the shoes?

Undefeated ~ Los Angeles	Union ~ NYC
Rivington Club ~ NYC	Clientelle ~ NYC
Nom De Guerre ~ NYC	Offspring ~ London
Gloria's ~ London	Aspecto ~ Manchester
Norse Projects ~ Copenhagen	Wallace ~ Copenhagen
Boutique Sportif ~ Stockholm	Carharrt ~ Melbourne
Footage ~ Sydney	First in Flight ~ Adelaide

Wow! OK that's nearly every cool store in the world. That can't be easy, how did you manage that?

Dog Adler, Dog Bierman.

With the first range dusted... what's the 5 year plan? Do you take over the world?

Take it a day at a time. Keep FEITing the fight.

The FEIT style has certainly grown on me in more ways than one. I'm not sure how you have managed to make such a clean, simple shoe so interesting. You've also bridged the gap between smart casual and a proper shoe.... not always an easy thing to do. Good luck with your projects....

Amen brother.

Cesario Low

One of the new breed is Creative Recreation, straight outta Orange County. Each of their shoes is handmade with quality leather and are limited to 500 pairs worldwide. They are definitely a kick for the mature collector who isn't afraid to buy something upmarket, and also for sneaker freakers who want to dress to impress. You could say they put the smart back into smart casual! (but we wouldn't) Snkr Frkr caught up with Brandon Brubaker, Rich Cofinco and Robert Nand...

When and how did you find your passion for sneakers?
It all started with custom Vans in southern California. When we were growing up you could walk into any Vans store and custom make your own shoes. It was all about showing up to the first day at school with the illest pair of shoes on the block. After that, Jordan came on the scene and it was over with, we were hooked.

Where are you guys located?
We are located in Newport Beach, California. It's about a 45 minute drive south of LA. We actually shot our last ad down the street from our office (the image of the yacht on the back bay).

You guys have designed for some fairly large companies, give us some background info...
We have been doing a ton of freelance work in the past few years to help get Creative Rec off the ground. The way we look at it, the more freelance work we do right now, the more limited we can keep Creative Rec. In the past we have done shoes for VonDutch, Vans, Gravis and Quiksilver. There are some other companies that we are currently working with on projects that should come out in 2005.

What made you branch out to do your own thing?
The three of us were working at Vans (we were responsible for about 90% of the skate shoes and 100% of the snowboard boots). We'd been working there for about 6 years and we just got tired of people not letting us do what we wanted. We had all these great ideas and all of our managers were like, 'Nope, we need shoes for the masses.' So one day we had enough and we went out on our own

Is it hard to come up with new concepts in every range?
We just design shoes for us to wear. We don't pay much attention to trends, because by the time a shoe hits the market, chances are that trend is already old news. We're all about designing shoes for us to rock personally.

What do you draw most of your inspiration from to design your kicks?
We get most of our inspiration from the lack of innovation in the footwear game right now. We're trying to set the bar and raise the standards. Oh and we can't forget trees!

How many pairs of each style of shoe do you make?
That's a funny question to us. Everyone is always talking about limited edition this and limited edition that. Some companies claim there are only 2,000 pairs made world wide. That shit makes us laugh! We've never even made 2,000 pairs of any of our shoes. On average, we make about 500 pairs of each color, world-wide. If you want to talk about limited, Creative Rec is some of the most limited footwear you can buy.

Where can kids find your shoes?
Right now we're trying to keep distribution as tight as possible. We are sold in the USA, UK, Canada, Germany, Australia and also in very limited numbers in Japan. We are in some of the best boutiques and footwear specialties shops in all of these regions.

Cesario High

★CREATIVE★ REC

Yo product has been put into a lifestyle category, would you agree with this?

We don't really care what category people put us in. As a matter of fact, we don't want to be in any category. We want people to know us as a footwear company. We make fresh shoes for people with style - period. If people see us as a lifestyle or streetwear company then so be it. As long as people understand what we're trying to do over here and they're feeling what we bring to the market, then we're doing a good job.

Customised shoes have become quite popular. Have you guys done collaborations with other artists/designers before?

Do you find that you have to design some plain shoes in each of your collections to facilitate this?

The recent custom craze was a good thing for the footwear game. It really made people take notice of shoes and look at them as more of an art piece rather than just an afterthought for your feet. We've actually done some custom Creative Rec for ourselves.

Do you guys have any other hobbies or passions?

We live and work in Newport Beach so needless to say we like to surf. We also like soccer, basketball, fishing, snowboarding and occasionally you'll catch one of us on a skateboard.

Who has the biggest sneaker collection? What does it consist of?

Robert has six pair of the most exclusive hard to find handwoven sandals straight from the Fiji Islands delivered in a bottle from coast to coast. They date back to the days of Jesus.

What sort of people have you found supporting the brand?

We're happy to see that it's a pretty diverse crowd of people that have been supporting our brand. We don't ever want to get categorised into one specific group. For the most part the people we see rocking our shoes are those who see that we're doing something different and even though they don't yet recognize the name they appreciate the design. At the end of the day we're just happy to be doing our own thing. The three of us have been friends for a long time and we hope that people are feeling what we're doing. We've been working on Creative Recreation for three years now and the name is finally getting out there. We know that it will take us a while to 'make it' due to us trying to pioneer our own path, but we really believe in what we're doing and hope we pick up some fans along the way.

MARTI MCFLY

For more info go to www.cr8rec.com

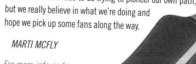

FIDEL

STASH RECON 12"
figure sporting Stash AF1s.
Photo :: Simon/Concept Shop HK

SNEAKERSVISION SNEAKERS
for 1:6 scale figures.
Photo :: RTHQ

BY NIKOLAI @ WWW.RTHQ.COM

Towards the end of the Nineties, collectable toys based on urban street culture began to emerge from Hong Kong and Japan. The toys formed a new genre, comprising characters that were reflective of urban fashions and subcultures, and others that brought characters from various artists' walls and canvases into the third dimension.

The trend has grown rapidly with collectors literally worldwide. For those unfamiliar with these collectables, there are three broad categories of urban toy: vinyl, 1:6 scale and minifigures. Vinyl figures tend to be made from a rotocast technique, which gives the figures a more cartoon-like feel to them. Whilst some are very detailed, the rotocast figures tend to lack fine detail, whereas the 1:6 (or twelve inch) figures tend to be detailed to a level of intricate detail. Finally, the minifigures vary between Lego-like block figures to single piece plastic moulded figures - some even dispensed by vending machines.

Early players in the game, and those credited for creating this collectable (and artistic) hobby, are Hong Kong artists Michael Lau and Eric So, and in Japan the fashion and toy companies Bounty Hunter, A Bathing Ape and Medicom. These people and companies have produced the quintessential urban toys - many of which are exceedingly difficult to now get hold of - and

where available, the price reflects their scarcity and demand. The involvement of the Japanese companies saw the urban toy spread to the West via the record company Mo Wax and the clothing company Silas. The internet however must also be credited for bringing this hobby to people's attention on a global level, through fan sites and of course eBay.

Collaborations with contemporary artists, double-names and limited editions, different colourways, bootlegs, fakes and high prices by resellers are all familiar to both the urban toy and modern sneaker collector, but the similarities don't end there. In reflecting urban styles, it is only proper that the sneaker, the ubiquitous part of almost all urban subcultures, is embraced. Whilst many figure makers have either sculpted their figure's shoes in the style (or directly replicated) of their favoured kicks, some have taken it to the next step and teamed up with the shoe companies.

Both Nike and adidas have seen the marketing opportunity urban toys affords them. Their association with these hip collectables adds to their 'cool' factor and gives the collector a new item to hunt down. Some of the artists who have designed figures have also designed or suggested colourways for the shoe companies. In some cases, Nike have not only lent their swoosh

RAY THE AEROSOL (adidas version)
Photo :: Plastic Particles

TOY FREAKERS

and approval to the figures - but real sneakers as sported by the figures were actually made, including those designed by Stash (AF1s), Michael Lau & Fiberops (Wildwoods) and ThreeZero (Premium Dunks). Nike have also collaborated with Medicom to produce several Kubricks and Be@rbricks. These have encompassed Nike products including Air Force Ones, the HTM series and Nike Soccer.

   adidas have proven to be strong supporters of the urban toy scene. In July of 2004, they hosted an exhibition of urban vinyl toys at their adidas Originals store in Berlin. Organised by German-based Plastic Particles, the exhibition showcased the work of designers from Germany, Japan and the UK. All the artists gave some of their figures an adidas twist - and 150 collectors were given the opportunity to buy Headlock Studio's Ray The Aerosol figure replete in shelltoes.

   Whilst the urban toy scene continues to grow, the close connection with some of the sneaker companies is expected to strengthen. This will hopefully see more imaginative sneakers as the toy makers complete the circle of not only making plastic replicas of their sneakers of choice, but inventing entirely new colourways and designs.

BOY D (Maharishi variant)
Michael Lau x Fiberops x Nike
Photo :: www.DPMHI.com

For more info on urban toys, check the following websites:

NINGYOUSHI
www.ningyoushi.com

STRANGECO
www.strangeco.com

PLASTIC PARTICLES
www.plasticparticles.de

DPMHI
www.dpmhi.com

KID ROBOT
www.kidrobot.com

CONCEPT SHOP
www.conceptshop.com.hk

In my opinion, Gravis captured the zeitgeist of sneaker culture in 2001 with its Superhero Footbed Project. For those unfamiliar with this product, let me explain. Five contemporary/urban/graffiti artists were brought together to design artwork for Gravis' Perimeter Support Footbeds.

Perimeter Support Footbeds are what most people call innersoles. Perhaps not the most inspiring part of a shoe. It's covered by the foot, and all the wearer asks of it is functionality. At the same time, it is the largest and most uniformly level component of a shoe (after the sole): a perfect canvas. Of course, the question does arise, why would you need artwork on your innersole? And, of course, you don't. But the pretence of sneakers being made purely for sport has long since been dropped, as reinforced by continued retro models, numerous colourways and endless limited quickstrikes. If you want to create interest in your product you need to capture your potential market's audience.

Anne-Marie Dacyshyn and Ricardo Camargo from Gravis, working with Stash, called upon Futura, SSUR, Kostas Seremetis and Phil Frost to provide artwork for the Footbeds. Each artist contributed work which was easily identifiable as theirs for those familiar with them. Dripping spraycaps and military figures made up Stash and Futura's designs respectively. Kostas provided his Assassin comic book character and Phil Frost did faces in his instantly recognisable style. Whilst well known for his Che Ape design, SSUR's work is also heavily influenced by pop art and culture alike, and his design was a '70s style photo of a glamour model.

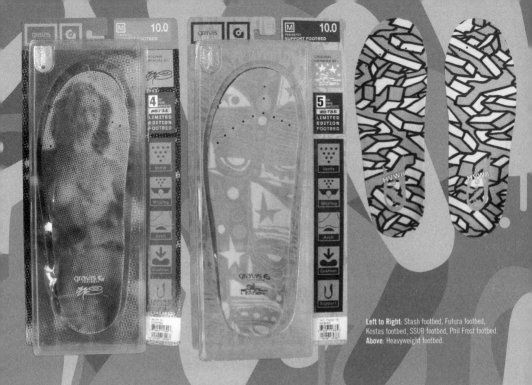

Left to Right: Stash footbed, Futura footbed, Kostas footbed, SSUR footbed, Phil Frost footbed. **Above**: Heavyweight footbed.

The choice of this group of artists represented a core US group that had established themselves as commercially successful in retail garment and product design especially in the Japanese street wear scene. Any issue of Boon (or similar) around this time featured one or more of their items (from Ts to toys to latest shop opening) without fail. I would go as far as saying they were being revered in certain parts of the Japanese press like pop stars. Gravis' copy in the Japanese magazine Kick Style explained the choice of artists as follows: "These individuals possess the qualities of creativity, progressive thought and the unique ability to make an impact on their environment."

Collaborative efforts with these artists and various companies have almost become commonplace. Both Stash and Futura have worked with Nike on several shoe projects and their efforts are always embraced by the sneaker-buying public. However, a mere four years ago many of these projects were yet to happen. It was Gravis that harnessed their talents for the sneaker game. Interestingly Gravis has continued in this fashion, calling upon outside talent to add that something to its product line. In 2005, it's Marok (from Lodown Magazine), Peter Huyn (Uxa), Japanese Snow boarder Rei and LA graf writer Aero. It would seem Gravis is dedicated to this side of things rather than it being a case of flavour of the month.

Thank you to Dominick Volini at Gravis and Tyler Gibney at Heavyweight Production House. Photos of Gravis Superhero Footbeds courtesy of Gravis.

The artwork on the footbeds is only part of the story. It is the whole package that makes this product a wonderful piece of (relatively) affordable pop art. The footbeds come within plastic blister packs on a card, just like action figures. When the collectable toy scene was really starting to blow up, whether it was Spawn, Star Wars or the (then-fresh) Hong Kong vinyl scene, Gravis was presenting this collectable (and limited/individually numbered) product in an instantly recognisable form to an audience who has grown up with toys coming this way. And many are still buying them with the express intent of never taking them out of their package.

Whilst I don't doubt a few people would have opened the packs, this is one collectable where the full effect is only gained when it is kept intact and unopened. It is admittedly an absurd product, but it is this barminess of selling a limited edition innersole as artwork packaged like an action figure that attracts me so much to them. As already stated, I view these as an item of pop art. They beautifully capture a moment when elements of pop culture ('80s nostalgia, toy collecting, graf artists and sneakers) were intersecting and excitement was growing. Now, if you would do me the courtesy of not outbidding me until I have the set...

NIKOLAI :: www.rrthq.com

p.s: Gravis has continued to use various artists to design footbed artwork. In 2003, the Heavyweight crew, Diskah and P-Nut Gallinsky also contributed designs. The Heavyweight footbeds came with the Comets.

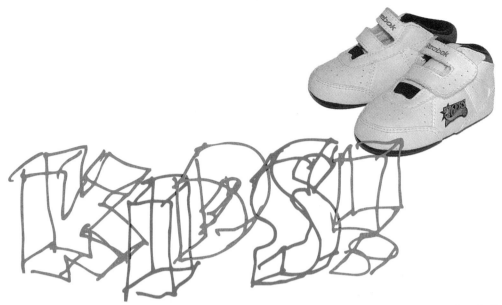

As my wife's waters broke, it was go time. The bags were packed, the car full of petrol and I had my sneakers ready to rock. I had given it some thought. When it comes to labour it can go for some time. Guys, you have to be comfortable standing around during that time! Also, these are going to be the first sneakers your child ever sees, so the old saying 'first impressions count' couldn't be truer. A third variable I had to consider was the potential for rain and mud in the UK.

Like matching a wine to a meal, the choice quickly whittled itself down to a few obvious candidates. Anything with suede was out, due to both the aforementioned mud and various fluids that come with birth. Yeah, it had to be the Air Safaris in khaki/dragon red/brown. A killer colourway with distinct detailing which is easily wiped clean. They proved themselves worthy...

A week later and I have a healthy baby boy. I was never fussed whether it was a boy or a girl, as long as it was healthy. Now I have a boy, it has dawned on me all the things we can look forward to... Lego, playing with cars, action films and, of course, guiding my little one in the art of sneaker freaking.

I hadn't even thought about footwear sized below a US13 until now. So imagine my excitement when I realise that my son has a whole world of sizes to come. From newborn, to children's, size US 9 (sample size!), sizes within the Japanese releases and perhaps up to his father's size (he already has big feet - I'm hopeful).

But hang on there. I need to think clearly. Is it right dressing your son in Weeboks or Wovens before he can talk? Despite my passion for sneakers I'm a conservative guy with old-fashioned beliefs. I can't believe I am saying this, but I think babies should dress like babies - not adults. So no Weeboks or Wovens (as tempting as they are).

Once he outgrows the booties, things will be reconsidered. Double names in sneakers don't just have to be between exclusive Harajuku labels and Nike. Sure the adults might want those hard-to-get urban toy tie-ins (Medicom Dunks, Lau Wildwoods) - but how about Lego Bionicle sneakers? Insane! Then there was the superhero pack of Dunks, with rumours of small footed-sneaker heads snapping up the denim Hulks!

When it comes to school I'm going to have to approach things carefully. Sure it is important he has good kicks, but they can't be too flash - that breeds resentment rather than respect amongst some unpleasant children. At the same time, I have to be able to have them in my house under the same roof as my collection. I am also going to have to teach him how to look after them. How to lace. How to team them with his threads. Now I know what people mean when they say being a parent is a full-time job!

As for my collection, its time to think of the future generation. Can I wear sneakers for much longer? I'm thirty now, but what about in five or ten years time? Will it be cool or will I look a bit sad rocking sneakers in an attempt to grasp onto my lost youth? Should I go hell for leather now snapping up sneakers and enjoying them while I can? Should I wear out what I have or should I now think about preserving what could be a potentially awesome vintage collection in great condition in eighteen years time? Or will he say, 'Daddy, Dunks are so played out!' Should I be buying sneakers now and keeping them on ice for my little one when he is old enough? I can't give an answer yet; this requires some thinking.

The birth of a child brings excitement, anticipation, questions and responsibility. I look forward to the challenge!

NIKOLAI :: www.rrthq.com

In New York, they wear Air Force Ones. In Asia, all the kids go crazy for Jordans. Londoners dig adidas and everyone knows the Eskimos are just nuts about snow boots.

In Australia however, the humble thong (aka flip-flops, double pluggers, jandals etc) is regarded as the best and most comfortable form of footwear ever made, especially during summer when the tarmac could torch the skin off your toots in 10 seconds flat!

If you don't believe me, think about this then - can you name someone you know that has never worn a thong?

No, I bet you can't. (For all those non-Aussies, I'm not talking about the 'thong' that Sisqo sang about, though it would be funny if you mixed the two of them up).

I for one, being a sneaker enthusiast, can claim to speak on behalf of the entire Australian population who are crying out for a pair of super thongs with a level of cushioning, comfort and breathability like no other. It is for this reason that I present to you my latest creation, the world's highest performance thong (drumroll) - the Airwin!

Just think about this. A thong made with visible zoom air for quick and responsive cushioning. Combine that with an AirMax '95 midsole. So simple, yet so comfortable... it's the shit!

Just the thought of the Airwin sends shivers down my spine!!! Like the Air Jordan and Air Force One, the Airwin will go down in history as another historical moment in the history of sneaker evolution. Or something like that. Viva La Airwin!

DARREN LIM

ENGINEERED TO
LAST FOR 100km
OF RUNNING

ATTENTION CONSTRUIT POUR
COURIR 100kms MAXIMUM

May Fly Journal
AMY CONNELL

$4.95

MADE IN MELBOURNE

SNEAKER FREAKER

THE CONCEPT

A while back a man in a van came by the S.F. office and dropped off a box. There was a press release attached extolling the virtues of the new Nike running shoe - the Mayfly. Big deal we thought, running shoes are boring and to date we haven't really seen any point in including them in Sneaker Freaker. However, when we picked up the package we couldn't believe it - it felt like an empty box - was there really two sneakers inside? The answer was yes. The Mayfly weighs a staggering 135 grams...

Intrigued, we opened the box and pulled the two bright yellow shoes out. The outer material is made from a very fine ripstop parachute material and has a felt toe and tongue. The midsole is made from a very light phylon which has minimal rubber pads for grip and strength. Although it might sound flimsy, it actually feels surprisingly strong. And it is light, insanely so.

Why would you make a shoe so light? Well, the press release said "For every extra 100g on your feet, you use roughly 1% more energy to perform at the same level." So this is a shoe for serious runners only, the sort that would appreciate a very minor increase in performance, perhaps as little as a few minutes over the course of a marathon or a few seconds over a 5km fun run. Therefore it is built to suit lightly framed distance oriented runners rather than those with heavy builds.

Another limitation is that it won't last forever. In fact, Nike says the shoe is designed to disintegrate after as few as 100 kilometres! And in keeping with this planned obsolescence, Mayfly owners can send the shoes back to Nike in a self-addressed stamped envelope. The remains are then made into new rubber athletic courts. With a concept as hi-falutin' as that, we couldn't resist checking these claims out. Otherwise how would we truly know if it was bullshit? Not being inclined to jogging ourselves (plus the simple fact that the sample pair we were sent was a Women's size 6), we asked Amy Connell to take our pair of Mayflys and roadtest them around the streets of Melbourne. This is her report...

After 10 Km

Day 1. Monday April 6 - 10 km's
Distance: 10km • Time: 45 mins
Location: Ran a hilly 10km route on road
and paved paths. No grass.
Weather: Sunny and hot 27ºC
Comments: Felt fast, very lightweight. Amazing.
Felt like I was running in bare feet...

After 20 Km

After 30 Km

Day 3.
Friday April 9th
- 30 km's
Distance: 10km • Time: 8km fun run
in 33 minutes and ran another
2km as warmup/cool down
Location: Ran on a combination of
road and gravel around the botanical
gardens and behind Fed Square
Weather: Sunny and warm: 20ºC
Comments: Once again I did not
notice the ground – the shoes feel
totally amazing!

Day 2. Wednesday April 7th - 20 km's
Distance: 10km • Time: 5-minute kilometres
with one lap of the Tan (3.85km) in 15:30 mins
Location: Bitumen over to the Botanical Gardens and then one
lap of the Tan on soft gravel Weather: Sunny and warm 25ºC
Comments: Felt super fast once again.
Shoes still look perfect...

After 40 Km

Day 4.
Sunday April 11th - 40 km's
Distance: 10km • Time: 47 minutes
Location: Sidewalks around my house
Weather: Sunny: 22ºC
Comments: Shoes felt light and fine.
I am very surprised that my feet aren't sorer.

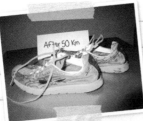

After 50 Km

Day 5. Monday April - 12th
Distance: 10km - Time: 45 minutes • Location: Sidewalks and around a park.
Weather: Sunny: 20ºC - Comments: Shoes felt very light still.
Not feeling any different from when I first ran on them.

Day 6. Tuesday April 13th - 60 km's.
Distance: 10km • Time: 50 minutes
Location: Soft path and gravel around work Weather: Cool morning: 15ºC
Comments: I have worn these shoes now three days in a row!
If I was going to feel any thing strange - it would be now – still fine!

After 60 Km

Day 7. Friday April 16th - 70 km's.
Distance: 10km • Time: 53 mins
Location: Roads & sidewalks around work Weather: Sunny 22ºC
Comments: Shoes are still rocking - feeling great!
Shins do not feel sore at all...

After 70 Km

Day 8. Saturday April 17th - 80 km's.
Distance: 10km • Time: 50 mins
Location: Roads and sidewalks Weather: Cool, rainy 15ºC
Comments: Felt fine – the coldest and windiest
morning yet but the shoes held up well.

After 80 Km

After 90 Km

Day 9. Monday April 19th - 90 km's
Distance: 10km • Time: 46 mins
Location: Roads and sidewalks Weather: Cool morning: 17ºC
Comments: Shins hurting slightly today,
shoes may be starting to give way...

Day 10. Tuesday April 20th - 100 km's
Distance: 10km • Time: 42 minutes
Location: Roads and sidewalks around work Weather: Warm 22ºC
Comments: Felt better than yesterday. 100km is up and they
did not feel all that much different from when I started

After 100 Km

THE VERDICT

I was really keen to try out the Mayfly. The idea of the shoe certainly sounded interesting and I was determined to really give it a workout. I'm not Kenyan, but I guess the best way to describe the Mayfly is that it's like running in bare feet but with the added benefit of padding.

I was genuinely surprised at how well the shoe performed. I don't think I would buy the Mayfly and train in it, but if I was preparing for a big race I would wear them for sure. Perhaps I could shave a few seconds off a PB? Who wouldn't want that?

One thing that surprised me was how strong the shoe was. I weigh less than 50 kilos so I probably didn't stress the foam or the parachute material as much as some other heavier people might. Towards the end I did notice that the foam had started to lose its ability to absorb shock, but it was only very slight.

So, in hindsight, I guess I thought the Mayfly would literally fall apart after 100 kms, kinda like the police car at the end of The Blues Brothers. It didn't work out like that, they became a little discoloured and worn-out looking, but that was about it. I'm not sending them back though, these are keepers!

AMY CONNELL

FREE

"FREE IS A 'WELLNESS PROGRAM' THAT GETS AT THE HEART OF WHY WE ALL EXERCISE. NO ONE HAS FUN WHILE INJURED. EVERYONE HAS FUN WHEN THEY'RE PERFORMING AT THEIR UTMOST" :: TOBIE HATFIELD

In a previous issue of Snkr Frkr, we roadtested a super lightweight running shoe made from parachute material known as the Mayfly which was designed to fall apart after about 100 kilometres. As far as concepts go it was a pretty cool shoe. A great story in fact. Anyway, it got us thinking about how we should be receptive to new ideas and how everyone says they are so over retro and asks why don't we write about new school stuff? Fair enough, we will. So we are. A while back we came across some research that Nike has been doing into a new story for athletes. The idea is known as FREE, and here's our report.

Strange to say, but FREE is probably the ultimate Nike shoe, in the sense that it harks back to the primal days of Bowerman and his mad training schemes. But in doing so, it defies convention and runs diametric to the current crop of well-cushioned, over-tech, heavy training sneakers. In fact, you could call FREE 5.0 an uprising against AIR, a jihad on inflatable systems, a war on padding, a coup d'état for the barefoot.

For a mega-corp, Nike staffers pride themselves on taking maverick positions. It is a trait that seems an endemic part of the culture. Consider then, FREE to be the embodiment of this notion. In this case, the concept was developed by Eric Avar, Jeff Pisciotta and Tobie Hatfield, who have nearly 40 years of experience at Nike in different fields.

So, where's the gimmick with FREE? Well, there is and there isn't one. There is no massive visible Air in the heel. No hi-falutin' foamposite, neo-nanotech, boing-boing, heavy-duty, mega-pump, sensory overload, push a thousand buttons rocketship. Which is not to say that it hasn't been designed with thought and bio-mechanic super-duper computer modelling. It's just that there's so very little between you and the road.

FREE is designed to be like running in barefeet. Only better. FREE chucks out everything you have ever thought about comfort and performance in a shoe. FREE knows that we have all grown soft, mollycoddled and weak.

If you've ever wondered why the Kenyans run so well sans shoes, this will explain it. Look at the sole. FREE allows the body to roll with the punches, letting your feet take the load, strengthening the toes, ankles and tendons, building muscle and toughening the whole foot, aiding both durability and longevity. FREE will literally make your foot more robust and minimise such bugbears as chronic shin soreness.

The lack of structure in FREE doesn't mean you should go tear arsing around in flip-flops. Far from it in fact. FREE has an astounding level of complexity in such a simple package. Sometimes the simplest answer *is* the best and FREE is as simple as it gets.

Look a little closer and you'll notice the micro details. The little nicks in the seamless upper fabric which allow the foot to breath and the sidewalls to stretch. The heel, which has a surprisingly tough mesh pocket, allows the foot to move back in a dynamic fashion. And check the way the sole has segmented chunks and curves from side-to-side as well as rotates from toe to heel.

OK, enough of the mumbo jumbo. Does it work? Hell yeah! I'm certainly not using the shoe as a part-time training tool, but as a casual shoe, FREE gives you an amazing sense of poise and balance that has to be felt to be believed. It's not my normal bag and I didn't expect to love it, but I do. It feels so radically unlike any other shoe that it has changed my cynical attitude towards the concept of performance in footwear.

And it's true! By the end of the day, you can feel it... a slight soreness, a vague sensation, a subtle feeling in your joints that you've been doing something good for your body. We can only imagine how the benefits of that workout could be extrapolated after an extended and correctly applied physical program. Remember, FREE is not to be worn straight up in heavy duty traffic. Your feet need time to adjust to this new sensation.

From an aesthetic point of view, FREE definitely has a lot more crossover potential than Mayfly (and it won't disintegrate after a few laps around the block). It fits both men and women and also comes in a hot cross trainer model featuring the forefoot strap and an outrigger styled off a Huarache/Trainer One. It's a pretty low slung kinda shoe and would sit well with both heads (heresy I know), fashionistas and trendsetters on the go. It might even supersede flip-flops for the ultimate summer shoe. Either way, it certainly looks the biz without socks. Socks are the Antichrist when it comes to FREE!

The most obvious Nike design reference is the Presto, with its stretchy sock-like construction and lightweight, casual, man-about-lounge feel. I loved the Presto and when I first saw it in the flesh, I flipped. Sleek like a cat, simple and ultra-stylish like a mako shark. There's one major difference with the Presto though. It was never a performance shoe, and this feeling is even more poignant after you've worn the FREE.

Will FREE become one of the truly modern designs that goes down as a classic? I think it might... Anyway, that's my homework assignment completed. Genius! All you retro lovers, are you still with me? Brilliant!

WOODY

FREE 5.0

PRESTO

FREE

TOBIE HATFIELD INTERVIEW

*In Issue 5 we roadtested a super sneaker known as Nike FREE. As time has gone on, we have developed very fond feelings for this shoe. It might be a hardcore athlete training tool, it might be unusual looking, and it might be the antithesis of a clunky old Air Force, but we love it. In fact, FREE has altered our perception of sneaker technology in general. First we were simply afraid, now we are excited. In light of all this we nabbed designer **Tobie Hatfield** for a brief chat to discuss his latest creation: Nike FREE 4.0 - one step closer to barefoot running.*

When you came out to Australia for the FREE launch I read your bio - I didn't know you were a very serious pole-vaulter in College.
(Laughs) Yeah I did a fair bit. I started when I was six years old, it was pretty much the whole of my life up 'til... I think I retired when I was 28. So I was on that stick a long time.

That's gotta be one of the more individual, difficult and obscure sports to take up.
As far as track and field goes, it's certainly one of the more technical events. With all the other extreme sports going on, there are more dangerous ones, but it has its thrills and spills so you have to be a little bit careful and a bit crazy. But, all in all, it was fun for me.

After your athletics career, how did you come to join Nike?
Well, basically I was coaching at Wichita State University in Kansas. I grew up around Nike, I knew Coach Bowerman and a lot of the other notables that helped start Nike. We were all jocksters, we were into trying to make athletes better and we all knew about Coach Bowerman and his innovative ways back then. When I finally decided to give Nike a go in 1990, I decided it was a good continuation of what I was doing with athletics. Especially when some of the athletes started competing in the products I helped create. It was a good match for me and an easy transition.

The ideas in FREE seem so obvious, why hasn't it happened sooner?
I think it has actually been in a lot of people's minds, certainly around Nike for some time. The idea of helping to strengthen athletes' feet and their lower leg extremities is not a new idea. Bowerman was doing this in the early days, making shoes that were so flexible that you could bend them from the tip to the heel. They gained that flexibility by not having very much foam underneath the shoe. In a sense it was very much like you were barefoot, but you had to be very conditioned to be able to use them. I think the great thing about FREE is that we are able to give the athlete the cushioning along with flexibility. That is the breakthrough: enjoying the best of both worlds.

I want to talk a little bit about the way the shoe looks. You worked on the Presto, which was very successful, do you see any relationship between the two products? Is FREE the son of Presto?
I can honestly say that Nike FREE is really a continuation of what we started with the Presto. Earlier on, with the Presto, we said that we wanted the foot to be more in control and not the shoe. And so some people say, 'If you designed a Presto 2, what would it be?' And I say, 'Well Nike FREE would be it.' So yes, I think there is a large connection between the two shoes. There are a lot of other influences that go into it as well. And the barefoot training gave us the impetus to take that to the next level.

The function always has to be at the forefront of everything we do. And then we definitely make the aesthetics match the character of the shoe as well. We knew the shoe would be unique and it would break paradigms. It should also somewhat look that way, but you don't want to scare people too much.

You mentioned not scaring people, what's the reaction been?

It has been fantastic, I just got a report yesterday. To date there's been over 25,000 trials at events. We have vans going around trying on the shoe and the response has been fantastic. It's a very information-intensive product. It's not just another shoe on the wall, it's a tool, a weight room for the feet. We have to explain ourselves, but once we do that they are selling really well...

So did FREE start with an idea or did it develop out of research you were doing? How long did it take to come together?

Well, we really started back in 2001 when we trying to research a lightweight training shoe. And so, as we typically do here in the Innovation Kitchen, we go to our experts: the athletes, the coaches and the physios. We ask them because we wanted to see what was going on. We talked to Coach Linana about what he was doing with barefoot training and that's when we knew there was something missing, but we didn't quite know where the shoes fitted into that.

But before we could ever think about designing a prototype we needed to know more about the foot itself because what we were trying to do was celebrate the foot, to help athletes be more aware of the importance of having a stronger and more flexible leg extremity. So we tried to figure out how the foot worked by studying it in motion. We had a lot of data while the foot was sedentary, or even in a shoe, but we had practically nothing while it was in motion.

One of the things that really surprised me about the shoe was that I felt I had a renewed sense of balance. It made me think that we have lost touch with our feet to pick up information...

Yeah! After we started to make prototypes, the feedback was that people felt more aware of their surroundings, that what was under their foot was more obvious. We didn't see that as a negative, but as a positive. At first we thought maybe they were feeling too much pressure... but they were saying the opposite, they liked the sense of balance so that you can grab and grip with your feet and be at one with the terrain. But at the same time being protected too. That was kind of secondary to what we were doing at first.

One of the other things I noticed about FREE was that it has an almost silent impact. Other running shoes tend to pound, but FREE makes almost no sound at all. Was that something you anticipated?

Ah, no. I can't say I was expecting it but it didn't surprise me either. I was told by runners they would come up behind other guys and get ready to pass them and surprise the guy in front because they hadn't heard them coming. But again, as you look at it and you visually slow it down with the hi-speed video that we looked at, you'll see the articulation happening and you see every single segment of the shoe contacting with the ground. Much like if you saw piano keys going from one to the next. One goes down and the next one goes up, so it was a very smooth transition and it was corroborated by athletes when they got into it, the feeling of smoothness from heel to toe. The lack of sound was a pleasant surprise...

The less pounding, the less impact on all your joints and tendons, knees and so on. Have you been able to prove FREE is able to minimise injuries?

Well, we can't really say that because there are too many variables that go into why someone gets injured. What we can say is that the Nike FREE, through our studies and scientific evidence, allows your foot to become between 10-20 per cent stronger and 5-10 per cent more flexible, and we do know that added strength is a great deterrence to injury. At the very beginning, Coach Linana said, 'You know I can't scientifically prove it, but I just know that when my athletes do more barefoot training they are less injured.' With consumers it is ultimately their decision on how they will use the shoe. Whether they use it correctly or not is something that we can't monitor.

4.0

Well I can tell you a friend of mine who has had a recurring tissue injury over the years finally managed to run a marathon wearing FREE, and he is adamant that the shoe helped him finish the race. That's really encouraging! You know I could say almost everyday I am hearing testimony from people who are getting back into running after wearing the FREE. It seems to help with particular people. Some people are not wearing orthotics anymore after wearing FREE. So we have a lot of testimony - and again I really want to emphasise that yes, the FREE is a good shoe - but we're celebrating the foot more than anything. So FREE just goes along for the ride and helps protect you and make sure you can run on multiple surfaces. It's really your foot and ankle joints that are being encouraged to work through the full range of motion and that's more normal. And when it's more normal things go better for you.

The most obvious difference between FREE 5.0 and 4.0 is that there's no laces. The heel looks a little thinner as well. Are they the only changes?
We've always felt that for true athletic activity it is really hard to have a shoe that has no adjustment at all because there are so many different foot types and people's perceptions of how they like to wear their shoes. We hoped it didn't need much and that's why the velcro strap is still there. And we think it works very well.

As you know, the 5.0 is the first iteration and on a continuum going to zero, with barefoot being zero, the next is obviously 4.0. Based on our measurements, the 5.0 was exactly where we wanted to be, not too close to barefoot but enough to get people started in this first phase. And we're excited with 4.0 being released this summer that we have taken another step down towards barefoot. 4.0 is not an improvement over 5.0, it is just the next step towards barefoot.

Does that mean there is a 3.0?
We'll take a look at it. All along we said we'll never promise to get to 1.0 or even zero because at some point we have to be realistic. There may be a point of diminishing returns, where you go too far and start to do more damage than good. We want to find out where that point is... honestly we don't know.

I noticed that the sole unit from FREE has ended up on the new Considered range, how did that come about?
We knew with FREE that we were looking at many new paradigms and we always wondered how much could translate to other categories. I wanted to sprinkle some of the pixie dust from FREE across other Nike products, so when Active Life came to us and said they were interested in FREE, we felt like the sole would would be perfect. The FREE sole doesn't have quite the same angle and articulation as Considered, so we fine tuned it to their needs as a very comfortable walking shoe, rather than as an advanced barefoot running tool.

I have to admit I was always a bit sceptical of shoe technology, but after wearing FREE I have become a true believer. It has changed the way I think about footwear and I'm sure Coach Bowerman would be very proud looking down on some of these projects you have developed, especially FREE.
Well thank you, that's exactly what the late Arthur Liddiard said as well when he saw FREE. And I am so glad he saw it before he passed on. We're never satisfied here at Nike, we will continue to make better shoes, to be healthy and thus perform even better.

ALL THINGS

GEN.1

GEN.1

You gotta hand it to the guys at Beaverton. So many new projects, so many new ideas, it's almost a full-time occupation keeping track of all of them. This latest effort is called *Considered*, and it has been cleverly designed to create minimal impact. The shoes are constructed from as few individual components as possible, have almost no lining, use recycled rubber, hemp laces and Vege-tan leather and can be easily disassembled.

All things *Considered*, we think they've done an outstanding job. The final result appears defiantly un-Nike, but at this point we are interested in ideas over aesthetics, though we are eager to see the next incarnations of *Considered* as they are released.

Putting out a project tagged with a 'green' reputation like this is a political gamble for a megalopolis like Nike, who are an easy and predictable target for activists. We're not here to defend their track record on human rights and environmental policy, but we do think they should be applauded for their efforts in this instance.

At least Nike have had the balls to ask some hard questions that generally get swept under the carpet. Namely, how do companies alter their work practices to produce consumer goods with minimal waste, use less raw materials and eliminate toxic byproducts like solvents and PVC, not to mention making them eminently recyclable. We caught up with the Designer, *Andreas Harlow* for a chat about this unusual looking project...

Hey Andreas, how's Beaverton?

It's good actually. We're pretty busy. As you can imagine we're working hard, but it's a nice time of year.

We know that you're originally from New Zealand and studied in Wellington, how did you end up at Nike USA designing shoes?

Good question... I'll give you the short story. I originally came over to the US to snowboard and I decided to stay. I got into footwear by accident and did that for a few years before Nike gave me a call and here I am.

That was brief!

Oh you want more than that?

Well I know a lot of our readers are very interested in shoe design as a career...

OK, I can tell you about that. I went to a school for general product design, there's not really a shoe design school as such... and then I got into different products, architecture a little bit, furniture, lighting, computer products... But, to me, I'm a pretty outdoorsy kind of guy and it wasn't really grabbing me the way I'd hoped so that led me to sporting goods. So I followed my passion to some degree...

Well that's always a good thing to do. Tell us about Considered in your own words, it's obviously a project that you are passionate about. How do you describe it?

Well you've probably seen the website and seen a bit of press, but my description in a few short words keeps three things in mind: innovation, sport culture and the environment. I guess the environment is a new addition to that equation, but those three things cover

CONSIDERED

GEN : 2 - BB LOW

GEN : 2 - BB HIGH

it pretty well. Innovation at Nike has been about making people jump higher and run faster. We still do that pretty well I'd say, but this environmental issue is something that is becoming more important.

Have you found people to be cynical about a massive company like Nike putting out a product tagged as 'environment friendly'? What's the reaction been like?

Well, when you do something new there's always gonna be haters, doubters who are mistrustful. We've encountered a few of those. But on the flipside of that, I'd say no-one's perfect, we're trying to do the right thing with the knowledge that we have, so you can look at it two ways. People say to me, 'How can you work there when Nike does this and that?' And I say, 'Well you can stand there and whine about it and form a picket line, or you get involved and try and change something for the better.' And that's my personal perspective on it.

I would totally agree, why attack someone for doing something good! Considered raises some interesting questions about the way we consume products and also the way things are made.

Was it a hard project to get through the Nike system?

It was definitely a challenge, I'll say that. (laughs) I think a few people didn't quite understand what we were doing but now that we have some product it has helped that situation. Also, there was a lot of support and a lot of people that were working on this project for the last ten years, to my knowledge have been adding ingredients to this solution. So we had good support at the same time.

Really? So this has taken ten years to get the product to market?

Yeah, well I mean, it depends on how you look at it. If you look way, way back at some of the sustainability work being done at Nike, it would go back a long way. The guys in The Kitchen, Mike Aveni being one, have been working on this for some time. There were a bunch of raw ingredients lying around, we've augmented it, added to it and made a cake out of it.

Who else helped bake the cake with you?

The core group that I work with was Richard Clarke who is Creative Director in Active Life, Jesse Leyva was also involved in the marketing, Brad Long who is a developer and works with the factory to get the shoes made, Steven Ploem in Thailand was also instrumental and not to forget the guys at The Kitchen, Tobie Hatfield and Eric Avar, they had did a lot of work on the FREE aspect to it.

That was probably the first thing I noticed in Generation 2 of Considered, the new FREE sole unit. Why did you use that sole?

In Gen 1 we were talking about the craftsmanship of yesterday with the technology of today. That led us to think about natural things. So when we went down to The Kitchen and talked to them, the work on FREE was well underway and it just seemed like a good fit. It helped the shoe to flex, to seem more like a part of your foot. So it feels good and it's better for you. We like to say this shoe is good for the environment but also good for your feet.

The fact you have used as few steps as possible in manufacturing, there's no lining, the stitching is on the outside of the shoe, there's no reinforcements internally... there's a lot of constraints in terms of design. Did that make it difficult to control the final outcome?

Yeah that's right, your question shows design thinking at work. I totally agree, we tried to look at it really more like the glass is half-full than half-empty. For example, when you do a normal athletic shoe, there are a huge amount of things available to you and that can drive the end result a certain way. With this project we just tried to be really honest about the things we could and couldn't use and let that drive the result. That's one of the reasons the shoes look and feel unique.

Speaking of which, the overall look has a rustic, almost woody feel to it. If you're making something like this with an environmental edge to it, does the product have to look like that to convey the message as well?

The short answer is no, they don't have to... but when we started Considered we made a conscious decision to make the shoes in a way that people could understand them. You may see in the future that our new shoes take a completely new aesthetic because we've chosen a new mix of ingredients to attack that problem. With Gen 1 and 2 we took a more natural approach and we think it makes sense, and people who are looking for that kind of product would understand it.

I agree totally. I suppose I was hypothesising if you made the shoes silver and red would anyone understand the project? The texture and the colour implies the nature of the shoe.

You hit the nail on the head. But it's not to say it couldn't go other places and we've been working on that for the last year or so. There's a limit as to how far you can push people before they drop off and we didn't want this to be a cerebral, self-congratulatory effort, we wanted to get shoes on feet and also do the right thing.

Why did you choose to make these shoes in Thailand?

There were a lot of reasons, the primary one would be the ability of people in those factories to execute the product. The second major one was the materials were available locally so we went with ecologically sound leathers from a local tannery which was a major focus.

I often get enquiries from people who like sneakers but have political views opposed to leather... did you ever consider using a synthetic upper?

Yeah we did, we've been working on that for a little while, and I empathise with anyone who doesn't wear leather products, but these shoes are not for them. Hopefully in the near future we will have something for them. It's a complicated issue. From a pure design point of view, leather really is, especially with this project, the best material to make this shoe from, if you take away the emotional aspect. It's long lasting, it has good handle, it breathes well, it doesn't require lining or oil to make it per se. So there's a bunch of factors.

That raises an interesting point. Which is, how do you assess products in a holistic way environmentally? In case of leather versus synthetic material, the by-products of synthetics aren't great. Then you throw in transport pollution, energy usage, recycling potential and so on, and you've got a very complex equation.

That's right, especially when you start adding glues in there, they become quite hard to biodegrade and recycle. It's a pretty complicated issue and I've gotta say we spent a lot of time as a team strategy-planning about what we were and weren't gonna do, which materials we would use and so on. And I think to some degree we are still in a learning process on that because some stuff you just have to try to find out, there's really not a lot of information about it.

FREE INSPIRED SOLE UNIT

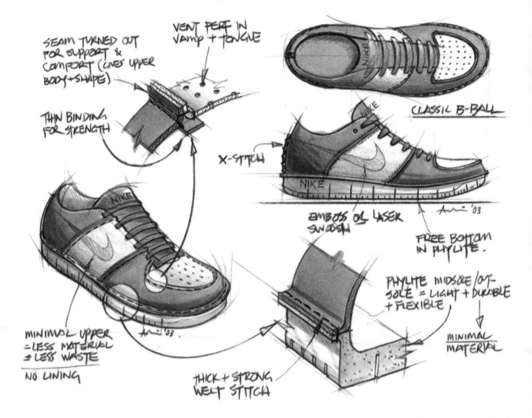

SEAM TURNED OUT FOR SUPPORT & COMFORT (GIVES UPPER BODY + SHAPE)

VENT PERF IN VAMP + TONGUE

THIN BINDING FOR STRENGTH

X-STITCH

CLASSIC B-BALL

EMBOSS OR LASER SWOOSH

FREE BOTTOM IN PHYLITE.

PHYLITE MIDSOLE / OUT-SOLE = LIGHT + DURABLE + FLEXIBLE

MINIMAL UPPER = LESS MATERIAL = LESS WASTE
NO LINING

THICK + STRONG WELT STITCH

MINIMAL MATERIAL

The project also has a recycling element. Will it be like Mayfly, for example, where you post them back to head office?

I wish! That didn't happen with this project unfortunately. The recycling issue is one that I think our sustainability group has been championing. So, in all honesty, my expertise and my sphere of influence has been limited to the design and production of the shoe. They're the experts on the other side of the coin.

There's also an aspect of Considered which uses recycled materials as well isn't there?

Yeah, correct. In Gen 1 we used Nike Grind on the rubber outsole as an example. In Gen 2 we got rid of the outsole altogether. So, again, we're just reducing the amount of material we use as a result. The idea with the bottom of Gen 2 is that the whole piece could be cut off as a single polymer unit and can be ground up and made into another product.

Have you calculated how much energy it takes to make a Considered shoe, as opposed to a normal sneaker?

I don't have that info. Our sustainability group have done a bunch of research on the prototyping and the actual production. Hopefully we will have some hard facts soon.

How do you see Considered evolving? Will it take on a life of its own at Nike?

That's a good question, it kind of has. To give you some idea, we are in the process of designing Gen 5 right now so it has grown a little bit and it is having an impact on other products at Nike. To gauge that impact you'll have to look in a lot of different places.

Does that mean we will see existing Nike shoes re-considered or re-engineered?

Yes. It's definitely one of our strategic goals and we have a policy on that, it's just a question of when. One of the other projects I am working on will take the notions of Considered and, how shall I put this, in a different material palette and for a different consumer... I don't want to give too much away but that's a big one and we hope that will be a bit more mass market.

You mentioned Gen 3 and 4 before, have you finished sampling on those ranges?

Yes we have. I think people will be pleasantly surprised at the different approach we have taken. I think it is exciting looking at the same problems in different ways, in the same way that a song can be remixed as a dub or a reggae version or whatever. The same thing applies with Considered, although it's not so much a stylistic thing, it's more about solving problems in a different way. Projects like this take quite a bit of trial and error so it keeps things fresh, we learn things along the way and we try and incorporate them as we go along, so in that sense it keeps everything fun.

Thanks Andreas and good luck with your projects.

According to the Nike Sustainability Group, *Considered* creates 63% less waste than a comparable Nike light hiking shoe, creates 33% less waste than conventional production, reduces solvent use by 80% compared with typical Nike products, primarily uses materials found close to the factory, requires less energy to construct, uses vegetable dyes and leather tanned using recycled wastewater. And in case you're wondering, 95.6% of Nike shoes now use water-based solvents.

Just For Kicks is the debut film for French sneaker freak and director, Thibaut de Longeville. Although it has yet to be officially released, the film has already gathered praise from mainstream film buffs and major heat from the inner sanctum of the kicks community. Three years in the making, and with maybe a few more surprises in store, Just For Kicks is set to surf the sneaker culture wave into the mainstream.

Congratulations on the impending release of your film Thibaut....
I'm sure a lot of shit happened to you along the way.
Oh boy!

Lot of big egos, lot of people with interests and stuff.
All of that stuff. All of that stuff.

And I'm sure you're not going to tell me about it, are you? [laughs]
I love to tell people about it! Honestly, I love talking about such a big experience in my life, you know? I'm like, 'Jesus Christ! All this happened over a shoe flick!' What is that?

What's your background?
Myself, I started caring about sneakers since I was 15 or 16 years old and now I'm 31, that's a lot of time. It's a lot of time fucking taking airplane tickets to New York just to find shoes. It's a very particular habit, and the history behind it, buying the books, it's a little manic if you want to think about it for a minute. Basically, my background is skateboarding, street basketball and obviously, hip-hop. My culture is street culture.

Professionnally, I've been running a communications firm in Paris called 360 for 10 years, doing a lot of youth culture consulting and producing creative content for clients like Nike, MTV, Virgin, Sony Music, Universal Records, etc.

There's been films about breakdancing, scratching... but really it's the first time anyone's put effort into making a film about sneakers. It seems like JFK is more about the New York kind of thing, right?
I was raised in Senegal, West Africa, but I've spent a lot of time in Paris and I've spent a little time in New York. I was just like other kids from outside the United States who've been looking passionately at little details on album covers, or how such-and-such behaved. You read sometimes that stuff about how kids in Japan got into the whole sneaker thing and very often you see Yo! MTV Raps is a part of it. And my whole film is biased in that sense, that what really got us into the whole sneaker thing, my generation was very far from athletics.

And that's reflected in the film?
It's really an identity thing, you know, and I think that's the interesting part. The relationship with commerce and marketing and all that stuff is an interesting subject, but I wanted to make my film about culture and about identity, you know? I say I'm a reformed sneaker addict, but I'm still not cured from my little addiction. I still care about fucking sports shoes, I can't help it. I stopped by to look at a store and look at the shoes before I came here. I'm somebody that doesn't stop.

And it's going well?
It's a huge thrill for me. It's my first film as a director. There's a potential theatrical interest for the film, so we're now talking about that. When it comes out it's probably only going to be in digital theatres. Not that I expect that it would be something like a Mike Moore film or The Matrix, but we have interest for it, you know. The majority of people compared it to Style Wars or Wildstyle when we showed it.

What happened at the premiere?
The premiere was probably the highlight of my professional career. It felt like a true blessing to interview a lot of people for the film and I think 80% of people who were in the film were at the premiere. Having people like Charlie Ahearn [Wild Style] and Henry Chalfant [Style Wars] there, you know, and the sort of kudos they gave. Bobbito Garcia stood up when the film was done and said, 'My name is Bobbito Garcia, I'm the author of Where'd You Get Those and this is my passion in life. I'd have to say I have to give this film the stamp of approval. This is the official film about sneaker culture'. He gave a whole speech about it. I had to call him up and say, 'You didn't have to do all of that, man'. It's a big thing, you know?

How did you get started?
The way I started working on the film was by doing research, I wanted to write a book because it's just nerdy guys like us and we have these conversations all the time saying we should try to do a book about this stupid culture that we all share. While writing all these things, it was like, 'There's really material there for a film,' you know?

This is a documentary about hip-hop culture more than anything else. But it's also the first that I know of that speaks about youth culture and their relationship with product.

JUST FOR KICKS!

So, do you touch on the modern scene at all?

People say, 'Oh, you're doing a film about sneakers!' They assume it's going to be about what you see in the press: limited edition stuff, Alife, Supreme and that sort of stuff. We do mention that, but it's a very, very biased story.

People have said Just for Kicks is the Dogtown and the Z Boys of sneaker culture. That's obviously a big reference when you hear it but, in a sense, it's obviously what I was aiming for. And it's very strange when you think about, say, you're talking about these films that are true icons of skateboarding culture or hip-hop culture, but this particular subject is just as important, you know? That idea to me is an odd fact. Something about shoes that there is such a big culture related to it, and it touches on so many things.

How long has it taken?

I started three and a half years ago, you know, just researching the content and stuff. I knew that archives that would be the biggest thing. We shot for six months on and off starting in July last year, but I'm still editing and I'm still changing a couple of things, so it's a year. It's a good year of your life and it's a lot more preparing it.

What sort of stories are you covering in the film?

Stories about brands when they were nothing, you know, like in 1985 when they made the particular decision to bank on a guy named Michael Jordan who did not play in the NBA at that time to say, 'You know what? We're shitty right now. We have a shitty image. We're not going anywhere. We might even close the company.' Which was serious talk at that time.

He turned down adidas. Amazing stroke of luck for Nike!

Yeah, but Michael did not like Nike. He did not like the image that Nike had as a company: it was the runner's shoe company. Michael's passion as a kid was adidas, that was his #1 pick. His second deal was Converse. He got turned down by both companies. Unfortunately I wasn't able to put the name of the person who turned him down at adidas in the film.

That'll go down in history as one of the biggest fuck-ups!

[laughs] You can't always be right.

Well, it's not a war or famine, but that's still a significant moment...

Yeah, definitely. It's a case study in sports marketing, you know? The interesting fact is, and this is also related to not being from America, when we first heard of Jordans we didn't know who Michael Jordan was. I saw the sneakers before I saw Michael Jordan play. And that, to me, is very significant.

Jordans were beyond having the best athlete in history and having the best commercials. My point is that what made them so legendary is that it was the first time a b-boy character was put in a commercial background with a big commercial pitch. Michael Jordan, *Winner of Everything*, you know? You could have made this guy into a true blue American Hero with a very clean image, but they used this homeboy from Brooklyn, typical New York sort of guy. And who was Spike Lee at the time? It's not as if you're calling Steven Spielberg today to do a commercial, but it was an odd choice to do that, and really was a sign of marketing genius from Nike.

But one of the other reasons why the Air Jordan I caught fire to that level, that very little people know about, is that Michael won the hearts of the streets the day he wore that shoe for the first time when he literally humiliated the Boston Celtics, then an all-white team that surely didn't have the favor in the ghetto. That shoe then became the 'bad boy' shoe and a symbol of black pride in America's inner cities, which was amplified when the NBA banned them because they didn't have enough white! They reached social phenomenon status when David Letterman made his classic 'no whites in the NBA' joke when he invited Mike for the first time on his TV show... all these stories are so interesting.

Did you try and get Jordan? I presume he's not in the film, is he?

No, he's not in the film at this point. We're still working on it. We have a 65-minute version, that's what we showed at Tribeca Film Festival, that's the Festivals & TV networks version. But there's chances now, because of the interest that we've gained, to get other stuff in there for the feature length. I'm very happy with the film the way it is now.

But there's always more you could do right?

Yeah, you can't say no to Michael Jordan, can you?

You were saying about the Tribeca Film Festival...

The way the Tribeca Film Festival thing happened was really a blessing for us. I was so into it I had no idea that people would be interested in this kind of thing. One of our producers, Alex Stapleton, submitted the cut to the Tribeca Film Festival jury and I was like, 'Yeah, right, go ahead!' This is three weeks after the deadline to close the festival. They told us we can't do anything about it, you know, too late, we've got 250 films! Sure enough, they watched the film on the Friday and then, on the Monday at nine in the morning they say, 'There's going to be 251 films.' And it was really cool. It was the best avenue we could have had to launch the film. Just for me to meet Robert DeNiro and have him say, 'Hey, I like your film.' You know? I don't know if that will ever happen again in my life.

JUST FOR KICKS!

It's always nice to hear praise. Did you tell your mum?

I had to. I had to. A lot of the film is about New York and I'm a New Yorker at heart. And I'm always amazed by the mixed nature of who is there and what that creates. It really completely blows up before you know it. And it's a very, very big buzz to have people who, to me, are giants, you know, in general American and global youth pop culture embrace the film.

You must have done an insane amount of digging?

There's a pretty big book about the adidas story which you guys may or may not have. This thing that tells you the whole Dassler family story and whatever, and you get to 1986 and there's this little pop-up thing that says, 'Hey! Oddly enough, these guys named Run DMC made a song called 'My Adidas'. Next!' That's all you get, and I always found that outrageously hypocritical. Run DMC, and '80s Hip-Hop as a whole put adidas on the map in the US, and for a long time, they didn't get the props for that. That's one of the reasons why we chose to document that story so thoroughly, the other reasons being that the true story behind the song 'My Adidas' is to me one of the greatest stories in music history. We just happened to get lucky with never-seen-before archive material on that topic. So we went bazerk with it, decided we were gonna create a music video to 'My Adidas' just for the film. To me, that story is a million times more important in modern pop culture than Michael Jackson's gloves, Madonna's Brooklyn Queens style, or Elvis' Blue Suede Shoes.

RUN DMC then recorded 'Walk This Way' with Aerosmith and joined hip-hop and rock together for the first time, which evolved into all sorts of things in terms of music and style.

Yep. And that shoe and that particular brand embody something to this day that's still somewhere in your psyche no matter who you are. It's like when I showed the first rough cut of the film to my mother, when that song came on she's like, 'Ooh, I remember that!' She's seen stupid kids around, dressing stupid with no laces, all that.

The interesting fact which we've really tried to bring to the forefront in the film is that, that song, if you listen closely to the lyrics, it was not particularly about shoes. It was a cultural statement and a social statement. What very few people know is that it was written as a reaction to an existing song called 'Felon Sneakers' that was describing the general b-boy look as criminal attire.

What RUN DMC meant when they said, 'My adidas walked through concert doors and walked all over coliseum floors, we stepped on stage at Live Aid, all the people gave and the poor got paid,' is that, 'We are not criminals'. They were invited on Live Aid and they could have got onstage in a military outfit that said, 'Hey, we're going to save the world with Michael Jackson!' But they went on stage in the pure 'Tougher than Leather' b-boy look.

You know, RUN DMC were basically devotees of hip-hop culture. Their icons were Rocksteady and breakdancers and they were in complete conflict with other rappers at the time. Other rappers were dressing in Parliament-Funkadelic style but RUN DMC were pulling their style from the streets. Them and Russell Simmons. You know, 'Fuck that, we're not going to create a sort of Michael Jackson sort of poppy image, we're gonna be all about the streets.' And, to me, it's such an important symbolic thing that that frame of mind is ultimately what blew up a German sports soccer brand in America.

How did that happen?

We were fortunate enough to interview a gentleman by the name of Angelo Anastasio, who you'll see in the film. He was the marketing director for adidas from 1984 to 1991. This is a guy who was doing sports marketing who was playing soccer with Pele and these guys who was sent to America and told, 'You're good with people, you're good with marketing, you go ahead and try and market our brand over there.' He came to the United States and started promoting the brand through soccer, but he wasn't really going anywhere with it.

And then, because he was in LA, he started hanging out with movie producers, movie stars and rock bands, like Rod Stewart and Chevy Chase and people like that, who all shared an interest in soccer. He realized by giving product to these guys, particularly Rod Stewart, that he was getting more exposure than what he was trying to do with soccer. This is when adidas invented entertainment marketing.

Before that there was no idea of a watch in a James Bond film that has influence and drives people to buy a product. He said that if it wasn't for RUN DMC and that song being popular, that adidas would probably not exist in America.

And it was to do with culture, not athletics.

It really was a culture thing, it was a style thing. It's odd to think that there's a culture about a consumer product of that nature. I guess one of the things that stands out in the film is the idea that it's not very much about the brands, it's about the people. It's a lot about the street people who basically determine that this is cool, not necessarily because such-and-such-a-guy told you. Now, that's the hot shit, you know what I mean?

I certainly do Thibaut - good luck with your projects!

ARE YOU

NICK & JEN AT CLASSICKICKS

Dave Ortiz

We get tonnes of emails from kids who wanna open their own store so we asked **DOM SMITH** to look into it and this is what he came back with...

Dom's **HOW-TO GUIDE** has been compiled after extensive interviews with the owners of Classic Kicks, Alife Rivington, Premium Goods, Goliath and Dave's Quality Meat. That's five of New York's most excellent sneaker shops (because of course, if you can make it in NYC, you can make it anywhere!!)

We also checked in with Motive807 from Texas, just in case you are considering breaking into an area that is not already flooded with competition (bright idea!).

Now, after you've read all of this, will you still lie in bed all night dreaming of owning your own store?

THE RIGHT LOCATION

ClassicKicks: Location is important, but it doesn't have to be in a mainstream area. We just happened to end up in a building that used to be owned by Def Jam. We still get LL Cool J's fanmail!

Goliath: People thought Spanish Harlem wasn't a good location. But if it's not already one, make it a destination. Now, we get people from all over the place, New Jersey, Upstate, Downtown and out of state.

Motive807: If you have a store that offers product not seen anywhere else, people will travel. There is a growing sneaker culture in Texas and the customers just need an outlet to purchase the harder-to-find items rather than relying solely on the internet.

Premium Goods: The little guys have to cater to a different customer. Look at Supreme. Ten or eleven years ago Lafayette St was nothing. Now it's a hot place to be. You gotta be able to pay the rent too.

DQM: People will travel but its good to be where others are because you want randoms in addition to your regulars. Anywhere with lots of people is a good location.

Alife Rivington: People will go to any lengths to get kicks. The ALIFE RIVINGTON CLUB is a perfect example. At the time we opened on the Lower East Side, there wasn't shit. It was a residential area, we had no sign and you had to be buzzed in. People still found it and made it a point to tell others.

FINANCE

DQM: At least 50k. The more the better though. Just make your budget work.

Motive807: For startup money, I would suggest at least 125-150k. You have to figure the cost of fixing up the place to your liking, at least one year's rent, purchasing inventory, office equipment and so on. All that stuff adds up fast. Loans are fine, just make sure you shop around for a reasonable rate.

Goliath: It all depends on size, products, utilities, software, renovation etc. It is very costly to carry exclusive sneakers and there is a formula based on space that you have to follow once you figure it out. I would say 200k minimum because you have to live.

ClassicKicks: It totally depends on location - Kentucky is cheaper than NYC. It's good to have extra just in case things go wrong. If you don't have a background in buying, you should at least know the sneakers market and the culture.

Alife Rivington: You don't need much to build a shop, but inventory gets costly because you need size runs of styles. At this point in the game, I think it's more about the connections that you have with the brands. There are so many sneaker boutiques popping up and only so much Limited Edition product.

GAME?

TONY ARCABASCIO

A LOOK AND A NAME

Premium Goods: The inspiration came from a furniture store called Moss, which is uber-expensive, modern, clean and simple. The layout does not foreshadow the product... anything would fit in here.

DQM: In some stores, people feel afraid to touch things, so we made this a very Average Joe place to come in and hangout. The park bench and the hardwood floors make it that much easier to feel more comfortable and familiar. When a customer sees the sneakers instead of meat, they smile, wonder to themselves, and then look up to see some cool merchandise.

Motive807: Having nice clean lines and an inviting feel was important to me.

Alife Rivington: Alife is 'the good life' so we knew the place had to look special. It took eight months and cherry wood from about five different sources throughout NY State to build a space that paid homage to the culture. For Alife, it is more about creating an experience. Who wants to hang out with ugly?

ClassicKicks: Our main focus is the sneakers. All of the clothes that we included were only there to complement the shoes. 95% of our returning customers bring more customers, know the owners and the staff, and understand what we are trying to do.

Goliath: The store used to be a bar and Goliath is still a very social place. We encourage our customers to hang out and talk. You don't have to rock the same clothes or have the same Jordans, we try and educate them...

ACCOUNTS & COLLABORATIONS

Motive807: I don't have a Nike account yet, but should have soon. Every other company I carry was very receptive to my idea of opening a boutique in TX, because I am the only one here interested in these lines. The only collaboration so far has been the art show that Aerosol Warfare put on involving Converse. Thanks again to Christian and Gonzo for that opportunity.

DQM: Working at Zoo York made it a lot easier for me to get a Nike account simply because I already knew a few Nike people.

Classic Kicks: When we first opened we didn't have Nike but we received a 'Hot Spot' award from a magazine. Don't get discouraged if you find it hard. There are other options and if you execute them properly, you will be recognized. Finalizing collaborations is a very long process. We are trying to get some products ready for the holidays. It is so hard to decide on what to do... I mean, we could easily slap two colors on a shoe but we want it to be absolutely perfect.

Alife Rivington: We opened up the first shop in October 1999. We filled it with stuff we liked and thought was cool, hoping others would think the same. Our office was in a loft overlooking the store, which became a meeting spot for a lot of artists and designers. Through these meetings, collaborations would surface, and the store gained new products.

One of the collaborations in the first year was a few pairs of sneakers customized by some friends of ours. Painting on sneakers and clothing was something we did back in the breakdance era, and we thought it'd be cool to rock again. The response was great.

Soon after, we befriended a cat that worked at Nike. He'd come by the shop a lot, and at the time there wasn't much going on in the Lower East Side. One day we all sat down, burned one, and he gave us the low down on Nike. We ended up being a platform for Nike to introduce newer, more innovative designs and our Nike account was on its way.

No promotion or advertising was done, yet lines of customers would form at sunrise each and every time we had a new colorway or style. At that time, we knew that the customer we were already attracting was this sneaker freak. Between the customs and the Air Woven craze, we knew it was time for an Alife spin on the whole shit. Hence, the Alife Rivington Club which we opened in September of 2001.

FAHAD MOTIVE807

CREATING A BRAND

ClassicKicks: We think that it is better for us to carry classic brands and styles rather than create our own line.

Goliath: I think it is best to let the store build the brand. I always wanted to do tees that corresponded to recent sneaker releases to aid in accessory sales. It's just like selling a camera. You buy a camera, you have to buy film too. You buy sneakers, you have jeans, jackets and shirts to go along with them.

Motive807: I think it would be easier to have your store and then do a label to reflect the store. DQM is a prime example of that, they opened a store and had their clothing line directly reflect the concept of the store.

Alife Rivington: By having a store first you are able to learn from the mistakes other brands make. But, by having a brand first (in other stores), you are able to learn from mistakes other stores make. As far as what's easier, starting your own small brand is probably cheaper because anyone can start a t-shirt line and build from there.

ADVERTISING

Alife Rivington: We haven't done any promotions or advertising in the past, and it worked out all right for us. It's not important to us. Everyone has their own style though. We're big on word of mouth. But who knows, maybe our strategy will change in the future.

ClassicKicks: We usually do more write-ups in magazines rather than ads. Some mags include exclusive sneakers and they'll say to get them at ClassicKicks.

Goliath: Our only advertisement for Goliath is word of mouth.

DQM: Word of mouth is our only promotion really. It moves the fastest. But press never hurts.

Motive807: Advertising is definitely important because you need people to know that you exist. You can have the nicest product in your city, but if people don't know where you are you're not going to survive very long.

Premium Goods: A lot of people collect the flyers (postcard-sized with rows of sneakers in different colorways covering up the whole backside and the store info on the other side) that I make. But I started to hear about a lot of crazy things that people have been doing such as bootlegging them and using the image to make t-shirts.

PERKS AND PAINS

Goliath: One of the main problems for me was getting the first month's traffic up. We had a silent opening, so there wasn't any press or publicity. It's hard for one person to do it all. There is so much running around to do every day. On the other hand, I love to go to parties and see people with clothes they bought from my store.

Premium Goods: There weren't too many problems while opening up the boutique. We just found the space and got it poppin'. The hardest part is knowing what to buy. Being able to move general releases can be tricky. Some of your stuff might also be in Foot Locker on sale for two for one. The best part is that I am doing what I want to do. I work the hours I want, I open when I want, I close when I want and I am my own manager.

DQM: Other than the random people who kept taking shits on our stairwell, we really did not have too many problems. Being in the store every day is the hardest. Even on your day off you gotta work. It is not as easy as it seems, but being your own boss is great. At the end of the day, you know that you have worked hard. In the past, others reaped the benefits of our hard work, now we do.

Motive807: The hardest thing I ran into was getting a location. There were days I would get so pissed off because Texans did not understand my concept and wouldn't sign me up for a lease. But things worked out and fortunately I am now open.

ADVICE!

WORDS OF ADVICE

Alife Rivington: No matter what you are trying to sell, always know your game. Credibility is all you have. If you do not have that you don't have shit, which means you are not selling anything to anybody.

Premium Goods: If there is something you want to do, then just do it. Open a store, or make t-shirts, whatever, just do it. Lots of people talk and never act. It's better to do and fail than to not have tried.

Motive807: The thing I have noticed is that everything is starting to look the same. I admire companies who do something original and break away from the norms. Hype is starting to kill the sneaker culture because it has driven prices out of the roof. There is going to be a point where consumers stop buying because everything costs so damn much. Companies also need to start looking at the quality of product that they are putting into the market.

My advice to anyone looking at opening a store is to be patient. When dealing with big companies, you have to understand they work on their schedules, not yours. That can be very frustrating at times, but it's something to get used to. Also, your customer needs to be taken care of as much as possible because without them you will not have a store.

Goliath: Get experience in retail and start out selling. Learn about mark-ups and everything else that goes along with the business side of things because, behind all of the sneakers, there are lots of numbers.

DQM: Be careful what you wish for, because you just might get it.

ClassicKicks: Good luck to the newbies. Just continue to do what you love. We are not masters, but we get wiser as we get older. Yeah, we are busting our ass, but we are doing it for love. Sometimes you want to say 'fuck it' and go to the Bahamas, but you can't. You have to stick with it, have a plan, do your homework and remember that it's easier to go out of business than to stay in business.

THERE YOU HAVE IT

Some very informative guidelines to help you get started. Now all you need to do is save this issue of Sneaker Freaker, make note of this advice given to you by these very smart sneakerfreakentrepreneurs, write up your business plan, get your cash and hit the gas!

If you need any extra information, go around to your favorite boutiques and get the advice that you need up close and personal. Just be sure that you know what you are getting yourself into and remember Dave at DQM's final advice - be careful what you wish for because you just might get it!

THE PEOPLE

Alife Rivington Club :: 158 Rivington St, Lower East Side, New York :: (212) 375 8128
Alife has three partners: Tony Arcabascio, Arnaud Delecolle, and Rob Cristofaro.

ClassicKicks :: 298 Elizabeth St, New York (212) 979 9514
Nick and Jen started their boutique after lots of frustration about not finding the classic kicks that they were looking for!

DQM :: 7 East 3rd Street, New York 10003 (212) 505 7551 :: davesqualitymeat.com
A butcher/meat-themed shop that is owned by Chris and Dave who met working for Zoo York.

Goliath RF :: 175 E 105th St, New York 10029 (212) 360 7683
Started by a sneaker freak named Rosemary who one day acknowledged her passion for and addiction to sneakers and therefore decided to make money doing what she does best.

Motive807 :: 710 Brazos, Austin, TX 78701 (512) 275 7385 :: motive807.com
Owned by Fahad who realized his love for sneakers after seeing the black and red Jordan VI for the first time.

Premium Goods :: 347 Fifth Avenue, Brooklyn New York 11215 :: (718) 369 7477
Clarence Nathan is a Brooklyn native who used to work at Union in NYC and now owns Premium Goods in Brooklyn.

STORY AND INTERVIEWS - DOM SMITH

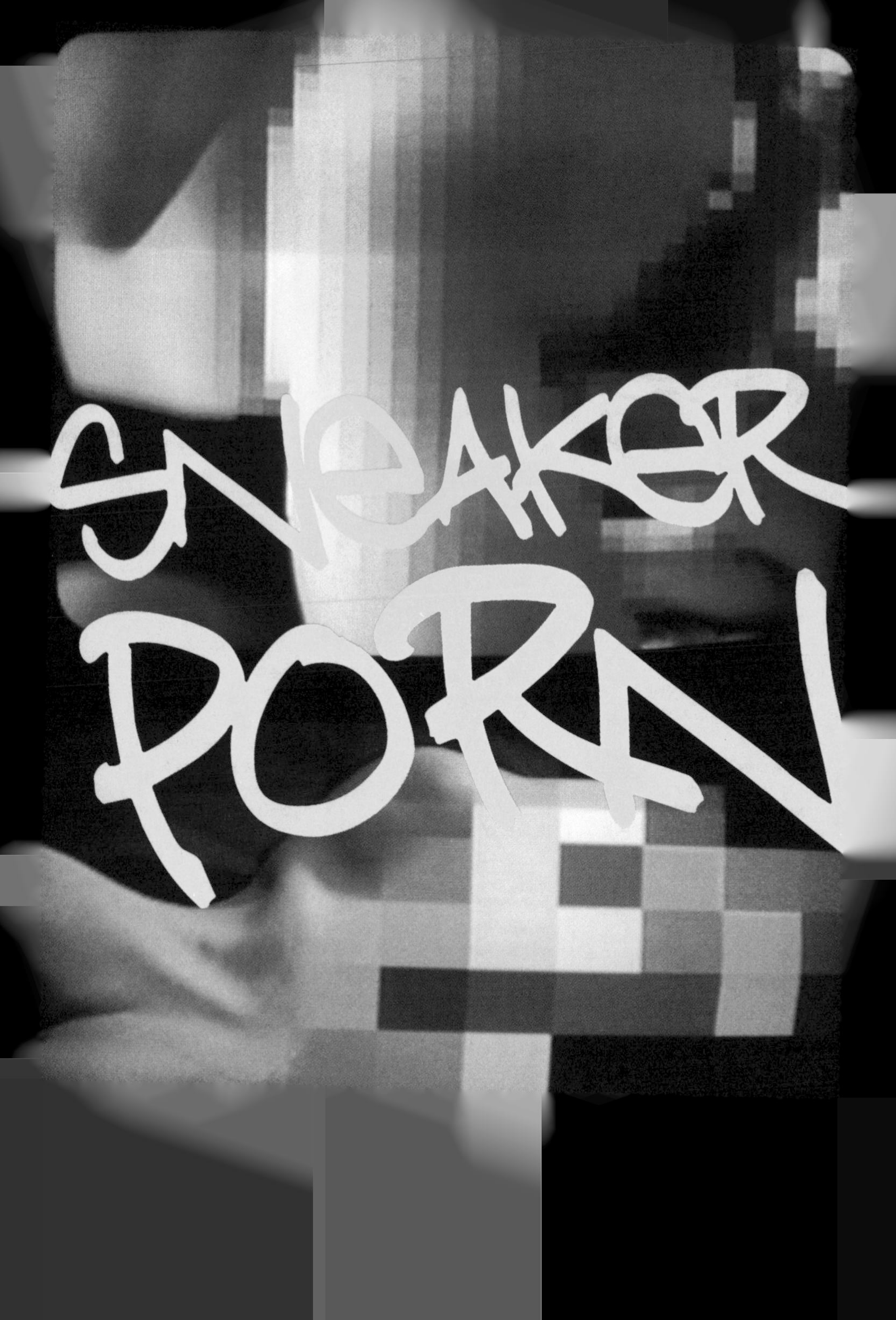
SNEAKER
PORN

Some people are sexually aroused by the strangest things. Whips, cigars, hairy backs, nurses' uniforms, vegemite - if you can name it, you can bet your bottom there's a deviate somewhere who is into getting off on it. It could be your neighbour or your butcher's brother's long lost nephew or even, heaven forbid, your sister's boyfriend. It's a simple fact of life - perverts are everywhere .

Any sexy perversion related to the feet or shoes is known as Podophilia. I have a friend who lets his Great Dane lick between his toes til the cows come home, I suppose he qualifies as a Podophiliac. For others, it's the sight of bright red painted toenails, some get hot under the collar for the big toe, while the smell of fruity gym socks is enough to give some nutcakes the horn. Probably the biggest foot fetish of all is the simple fact that men are bedazzled by women in high heels. It's something about the way it raises the heel and calf and makes the ladeez bum rounder and the bust protrude.

The foot fetish is hardly new - Asian countries have had a love affair with the foot for centuries. The practice of binding lasted nearly 1000 years and left women with tiny feet, sometimes as small as 5 inches long. Encased in tiny silky booties, the feet would stay softer than a baby's bum and chinese dudes were right into it.

There are many reasons why the foot is said to be arousing. Psychologists believe a primary factor is that feet are often the first part of their mother that toddlers touch - if kids want attention they will grab you on the foot, it's the easiest thing to reach. Likewise, parents often play with their children by letting them ride their feet. Quite why that would make you want to do the hokey pokey with a Dunlop Volley 20 years later is another story altogether.

Like any obsession there are layers upon layers of complexity and intrigue. For the purposes of this highly educational article I have roughly divided Sneaker porn into two camps.

On the left foot is the one-armed bandit. Which is to say, they use the sneaker in a variety of ways to bat off. Spanking the sausage with a shelltoe may seem pretty weird to most normal folks but I assure you these fiends are out there and most of them love the internet. A simple google search will lead you to more sneakerporn sites than you can poke a stick at. If you dare...

My investigations have confirmed that the rubber sole is the source of all the Action 'A' Traction. You'll need some grip but more important is a flattish surface so the humble 'Ked' appears to be the sneakerwankers shoe of choice (The Ked is a really boring looking sort of budget boat shoe that your Mum might wear). Suede, for obvious reasons, gets the big thumbs down.

The various techniques even have descriptive names, such as 'Walking the Dog', 'Lazy Girl', 'Total Control' and the 'Flipside Ollie'. I think I'll leave it to your imagination to work out the who, what, where, when and why...

On the other foot, there are those amongst us who enjoy the simple pleasure of looking at pictures of chicks and dudes wearing sneakers, usually, but not always, in the nude. Fair enough I suppose, we live in a free country...

Personally, I think the new shoe smell of virgin vinyl and rubber is definitely a bit sexy, but it's never made me want to whack off with a KT26. I need a bit more romance than that, although, come to think of it, the thought of walking into some middle of nowhere sports store and finding 20 boxed pairs of size 11 Air Force Ones is enough to bring on a mild chubby.

Whatever it takes to float your boat I suppose...

WOODY

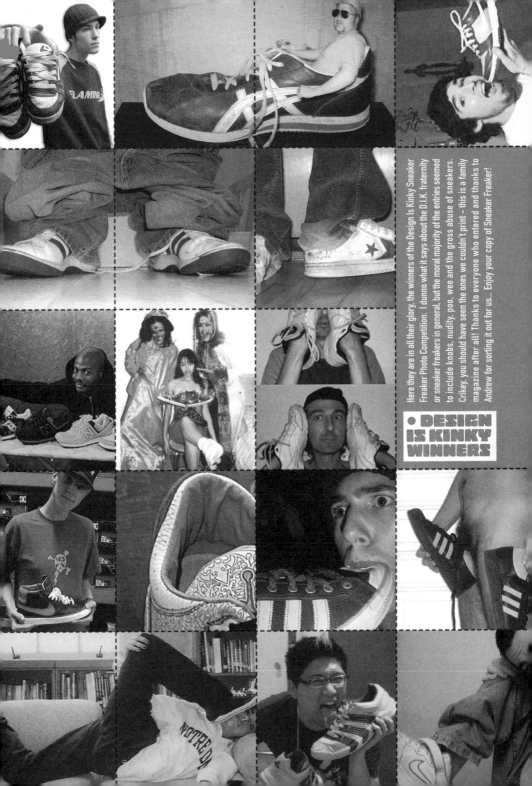

Here they are in all their glory, the winners of the Design Is Kinky Sneaker Freaker Photo Competition. I dunno what it says about the D.I.K. fraternity or sneaker freakers in general, but the moral majority of the entries seemed to include knobs, nudity, poo, wee and the gross abuse of sneakers. Crikey, you should have seen the ones we couldn't print – this is a family magazine after all! Thanks to everyone who entered and thanks to Andrew for sorting it out for us... Enjoy your copy of Sneaker Freaker!

● DESIGN
IS KINKY
WINNERS

TEEN AGE KICKS

At Sneaker Freaker, we pride ourselves on supplying you with unusual and interesting content. We try to get off the beaten track as much as possible but we make sure it always comes back to sneakers in the end. Speaking of which, a while back we were emailed by Rob Heppler who informed us he was writing a story that turned out to be this one... Not wanting to be the victim of some elaborate hoax, we looked into it as much as possible, but we have no way of truly knowing if this story is true. Rob convinced us he was legit so we decided to run it, I hope you find it interesting - we sure did...

June of 1998, I was 18 years old sitting in a park in Everett, Massachusetts, around 9pm waiting for my girlfriend to sneak out of her house. I had just bought a pair of adidas Ozweegos, white with yellow and navy, and was examining them in the moonlight. I believe 1998 was when reflectors on running shoes were the dope hotness. I was amazed at the total perfection this shoe had and I firmly remember thinking, 'Where will these shoes take me?'

September 17th 1998, they took me to a party in Mission Hill, Roxbury. Roxbury was in the news in the late '80s when kids were getting killed for their Jordans, which was the norm in urban ghettos around the country. This party was for my cousin graduating from Northeastern University, one of the greatest parties of all time. I had been drinking the entire week preceding and this particular night was full of pills and more heavy drinking. I don't want to really go into too much detail because it's too gruesome but I did something that I will regret for the rest of my life. In self-defence I stabbed someone and left them to die. Fortunately for me, they lived.

Well those adidas Ozweegos sure did take me places that night. They ended up in a bag with all the evidence at the bottom of a river. **I ended up in jail...**

THESE ARE THE NEW BALANCE RUNNERS YOU ARE ALLOWED TO BUY IN PRISON. THE STORE ONLY SELLS ONE STYLE OF SNEAKER, THEY COST $48.00US AND TAKE SIX MONTHS TO GET TO YOU. THE 'USA' LOGO I FOUND INTERESTING, I DON'T KNOW IF NEW BALANCE DID THAT FOR ALL THEIR SHOES THAT YEAR, MAYBE IT WAS A 9/11 SPECIAL. I DOUBT THEY WOULD MAKE A CUSTOM 'JAIL' VERSION! THESE HAVE SOME MILES ON THEM. YOU COULD ALSO SAY THESE SNEAKS HAVE TOUCHED ON GROUND THAT A LOT OF PEOPLE WILL NEVER GET TO STAND ON...

September 23rd, 1998 - my first day in county jail. I could write novels on the psychological impact jail has on any human who is forced to experience it. But this is about sneakers. I'm now wearing some beat up adidas Falcons, and every time the Spanish kid in the cell next to me wants to go play handball he asks to use my sneakers. Sure, if it keeps me alive another week!

But every time he gives them back they were a little more torn up. Lesson 1. Don't let anyone 'borrow' your kicks.

Overall, sneakers are hard to get in prison, usually a major brand would have a contract with the state forcing inmates to buy the one style and brand.

There are so many levels to the sneaker culture in prison. Gangs would have their brand. Black dudes primarily wore Air Force Ones, while whites choose running sneaks, NB, Asics. Having a pair of Jordans was like owning a Ferarri. So how come the kid in cell 301 has two pairs of Jordans?

You get to keep the kicks you arrive with, which sometimes tells a story in itself. Some people come right from court and quickly realize their mistake of choosing the patent loafer. I mean, you could almost see how long people had been in by judging what they were wearing. Airmax 95s are popular among criminals or maybe that was just a bad year!

This one kid Ryan had a brand new pair of the Nike 'Penny' Hardaway joints, remember they had the 1 cent logo on them? He was in jail cuz he tried to burn down a strip club that kicked him out. He was wearing his 'Pennies' when the cops grabbed him so they still stank of gas and smoke.

After some time, that was the way we could tell people apart. 'You know that new kid?' 'Who?' 'The one wiff da bran new up temps' 'Oh yeah, I seen that dude'.

The other way you get kicks is when someone leaves, they would hit you off with some sneaks, cause they were going home. This was the ultimate sign of honor and friendship.

Please understand. You have no car, no house and no girlfriend to help you standout or describe what kind of person you are. Prison takes away your individuality.

The next 'keep it on the down low' way to get kicks through the walls is have a guard bring them in. Why would a guard risk his $50,000+ a year job for some dirty inmates?

Because inmates are willing to pay astronomical prices for regular kicks you can still get cheap in the stores. A regular pair of Air Max go from $100 to $124, but behind the wall those are worth $500 and up in ANY condition. Guards don't notice the sneakers as much as they would a shank, crackpipe, or tattoo gun. Also you're not going to end up in the hole because you somehow obtained new joints, so it was worth the risk.

Plus it commands respect from the other inmates. We would read about new sneakers, in 'the Source' hip-hop magazine, or 'Maxim'... but when you enter the chow hall and you see someone wearing the new Nike Shox, you'd be like 'Damn he's makin' moves!' Or 'he's snitchin' - which was also another way to get kicks, but not respectable.

Now this brings us to the last way to obtain fresh joints - by force. The most common move would be waiting for your victim to go to the shower - the sneakers are already off and for some reason people don't put up as much of a fight when they are naked.

One of my graffiti buddies from Medford, Eric, he used to write and when he came to Concord state prison with brand new adidas he was only 18 like me, and about 5 feet tall. I was scared for his sneaks. Size was on his side for once as his

TEEN AGE KICKS

foot was like size 6. Who's gonna waste their time beating someone down for shoes that don't fit!

Most people I hung with had their daily beaters and their 'visit' kicks. You know when mom or wifey comes once a week to see you, update you on family affairs, or what's poppin' in the hood... you need to be in the freshest pair you own. These were usually kept in a plastic bag in a locked footlocker.

So now I'm being sentenced, I'm going to go to state prison for 4-6 years with 3 years probation after I get out. Great. I had lost my last pair of A-dogs in a card game, so I've been wearing flip-flops for the past three months.

You come to admire the Nike Air Bubble after three months of wearing flip-flops and having your feet become deformed.

Some new loser was on the tier under me, he had a pair of DC shoes. These were the first DCs I had seen and I had to have them. He told me he'd sell them for $20 in food, they were beat and he was hungry.

State prison has some individuals doing 'Life' which means you are never getting out. We all know sneakers from the '80s are rare, what's even more rare is someone that still wears those original Cortez, or the Bo Jackson cross trainers. And they don't wear them for any reason except that's all they have! You could almost tell what year certain people were arrested by the sneakers they had. Of course after 15 years, kicks come and go, but a lot of solid inmates kept the shoes that touched the ground when they were free.

How does a pair of Spacejam Jordans make over 10 years and are worn at least seasonally?! I knew dudes that on a sunny Saturday

morning, they would fill their trashcan with soapy water find a spot by a window and scrub their sneakers with a toothbrush, as if they were washing their car. Insoles, laces, everything is meticulously cleaned and left to dry by a fan.

Although most of you will never see the inside of prison walls, if they had tours, or a window you could look in like an aquarium, you might catch a glimpse of a huge sneaker time capsule. It's an untouched subculture, full of 'freakers' who have a lot more to worry about than sneakers, but nonetheless are still extremely focused on their feet.

I was finally released on parole August 15, 2002. That day was a unique experience. The next day I went to Foot Locker and this new retro-throwback style is all they sell, Air Force, Dunks, Reebok Classic.

I asked the kid that worked there what was everyone buying, he pointed out white AF1s with a yellow swoosh. I was like 'What the fuck!'

I just came from state prison where that's all anybody could wear cause that's what everyone was still wearing in the '80s and '90s. Now that's what people want to wear?

I was hoping on some new sneaker technology, or patterns that will make people remember the early '00s as great sneaker years. Not re-make great sneakers and bring them back like they were just invented.

So before you head out to the Bar, Pub, Club, anywhere you could get really fucked up - tie your shoes tight - you might be wearing them for a lot longer than you think!

ROB HEPPLER

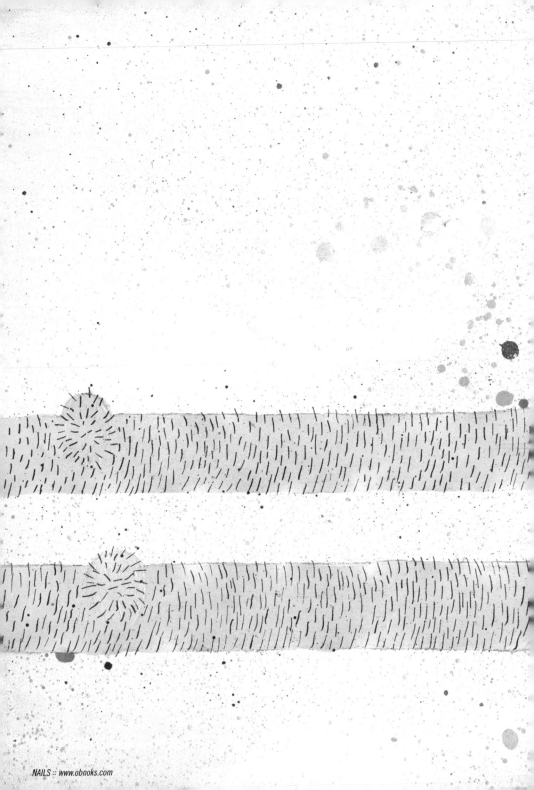

PHUNKSTUDIO

IVAN TANG :: kingtangy@gmail.com

In issue 2 we started a series on fakes. At that time the fake scene was already well entrenched but still fairly primitive, especially in terms of quality control and attention to detail. Well it's not now! These shoes are getting very, very sophisticated and very, very hard to pick. When you can find fake Shox that are seemingly flawless, you know that the bar has been well and truly lifted.

So what exactly is wrong with fake sneakers - they look the same, right? First off, they are shitty shoes. They fall apart and they have no performance at all. They hurt your feet. They aren't the right size. So what may look like a bargain is invariably not. And they just don't last, because they weren't made to.

The other reason is that they are sold under fraudulent pretences online. There are so many it is pointless to list them all, and it took only minutes to find over 30 sites, from where we sourced many of the pictures in this report. Most times they are called 'variants' in their Terms and Conditions but that's a lie. There is no such thing.

Since counterfeit crime would appear to be only committed against mega-corporations, many people feel it is a victimless crime. I just feel sorry for the newbie kid who saves his bucks only to be bitterly disappointed when his order never arrives, or the shoes fall apart on first wear! That argument also discounts the poor souls who have to make the stuff in oppressive conditions and the fact that criminals earn all the profits. You'll know more about this after you read the interview on the next page.

Why does it happen? Simple economics. If people are still gullible, stupid or at best, ill informed, fake factories will keep churning them out. And with prices of some Dunk SBs still hovering around the $3-500us mark, there is a massive incentive to stay in business.

In light of all this, we thought it was time to point out faults in some of the most faked models. This time we have chosen the adidas/Bape collabs, the NB MT580, HTM AF1, Jordan III, Dunks and the VC Shox.

Aside from overall quality control, the details that really stand out include incorrect logos, dodgy tags, weird barcodes, boxes that don't match the model and crazy colourways that have never been seen before such as pink/black Jordans IVs and purple/yellow Jordan IIIs. (LMAO). Plus, when you know every nook and cranny of your favourite sneaker (just like your girlfriend), you'll be left with a feeling that something just ain't right... However, this is only helpful when you have the shoes, and by this time it is usually too late.

There are a few things you can do to protect yourself. The first is to only buy your shoes from reputable sources. A dude selling out of his boot at a flea market is suss. If you're hunting on eBay, make damn sure you thoroughly examine the feedback. Be patient, most styles will come up again. Plus, the longer you hang around the more you'll learn and the less likely you will be ripped off.

I also highly recommend research on respected forums to see what other people are saying. They list regular offenders and info on how to spot fakes. As far as fake online retailers go, there are a few ways to weed them out. The general look of their site is often amateurish, but not always. Sometimes they use photos pinched from other sites. However, strictly going by the photos is a pointless exercise. Some sites use pictures of real shoes and then send you the duds. Many won't have credit card facilities hooked up so they'll often ask you to pay with a money order. Don't. You'll never see your money again. And they probably won't have a phone number listed so you can't call them to discuss your order.

And finally, just use your common sense. If you think it is too good to be true, it probably is. If you see a total bargain, think about it before the blood rushes to your cranium. Don't be misled by greed and lust. These vampires make their money preying on the human emotions of sneaker freakers. Hang on to your hard earned cash and never give a conga line of suckholes an even break.

Suitcases full of fake Jordans seized by Nike and Australian Customs

FAKE SNEAKERS PART 1

RICHARD STANWIX

We'd been trying to land this interview since the beginning and it took until Issue 5 to finally get our man - Richard Stanwix, Head of Brand Security for Nike. Suffice to say, he is a very busy man. Here he gives us an insight into how pervasive the fake industry is and how complicated it is to catch these mongrel fake selling bastards!

What do you call what do?
Well I'm Nike security manager for the pacific region. Primarily my role is brand protection and anti-counterfeiting. Shipping, transport and event security, retail loss prevention and a holistic approach to generally managing risk in business, whatever the cause might be. Counterfeiting for footwear or apparel is probably about half of my role. I could easily spend all my time catching these crooks but we have limited resources...

How big a problem is the fake industry?
There are a whole bunch of reasons why it is wrong. One of which is that the huge trade in fake Nike and other brands' product drives the whole blackmarket industry. They evade taxes and they work outside of proper work conditions. The factories which produce counterfeits are often the ones for which we get the blame. The media goes in and there's a bunch of juveniles stitching a swoosh on shoes and historically you'll find that most of those are counterfeit factories. So we have a corporate responsibility to solve this problem. We think the whole counterfeit trade in Australia alone is about one billion dollars.

Just in Australia?
Yes. Of which Nike is probably 40-50 million dollars a year. It's certainly a big problem for us, but it's not just about revenue. Where it is important is if you do buy a counterfeit item thinking it is the real deal and it falls apart, it's a brand disconnect that is a real killer. Most of the counterfeit sellers have a pretty good spin on why they are selling. 'Oh we got some excess stock from Japan or a chain of sports store closed down in Korea and that's why it's forty bucks.' So, it still doesn't mean you're expecting anything less than the full performance of a Nike shoe. This is demonstrated because we get calls to our customer service centre and people want refunds. That happens almost weekly where people want refunds for fake shoes.

People are suckers aren't they? There's all sorts of scams like buying sapphires in Bangkok or carpets in India, why do people never learn that if it looks too good to be true it probably is?
You'd think that history would educate people but still it goes on. Now whether the counterfeiters are getting more sophisticated in the stories they spin I don't know. Look at eBay, they build entire stories around the origin of their shoes. They say they've got contacts at factories or it's excess inventory Nike has cleared for some reason.

Have you caught people selling fake shoes in Australian shops?
Yes, there's retail shops but they are in the lower end. Certainly not chains you'd expect to sell legitimate goods. One issue that is always a concern is, and this doesn't apply to your readers because they are a bit wiser, is the blatant rip off of an entire design of a shoe. They don't apply the trademarks and they leave the swoosh off, but it's an identical copy of the Presto for example.

Yes, I saw that one! Do you take action over that?
Well we don't register designs in Australia, but we always enforce our rights according to the brand violation. You need to sell a pile of shoes in a single style to warrant registering the design. The process is long and involved and the legal expenses are huge and in a fast-paced footwear environment, sometimes the shoe has been and gone before the registration is complete. So you make a qualified assessment of risk. If some bozo wants to buy it without the brand and convince themselves that it is a genuine Nike then go ahead, knock yourself out!

I get emails from lots of kids who've just found out about sneakers and they are seduced by the price and availability of these fakes. Out comes mum's credit card and the shoes never arrive or they are fakes... How are those websites able to stay in business?
Conceptually, they are not. It's an offence if you have counterfeit shoes in your possession; if you offer them for sale; if you import or distribute them; these are all separate crimes under the trademarks act. The loophole is that they stay under the radar just long enough. We stumble upon them, we deal with the offender, and it could mean false names and addresses, we shut down the site and then 24 hours later they are up under a different name with the same product! You'd need an army of people surfing the net to find and shut down the offenders. So the fundamental message is that it's all about educating the consumer. Like you said before, if it looks too good to be true you can bet your bottom dollar it is.

We need to educate kids at the early stages in their interest in the sneaker freaker world that starting your collection and buying the hard to get shoes, if it was as easy as logging on and running a search, well how come 50,000 people in the world didn't notice this shoe before? You don't have to be a rocket scientist to work that out.

These sites can be based anywhere. They ship from Korea, receive US dollars, their server is in Mexico... how do you prosecute them?
You can, but you have to fall within the legal framework of whichever country ultimately ends up being their base. Enforcing intellectual property rights in Asia is incredibly difficult. For one, there's so many infringers. Second, their fundamental belief in intellectual property is different to ours and thirdly, in a lot of these countries, this is huge business for them. If we shut down the whole counterfeit trade tomorrow, motor vehicle parts, apparel, drugs etc... we would take a massive chunk out of their revenue and they know that. On face value they try and get WTO registration by pretending they're keen to enforce copyrights, the reality is different.

Conversely, we did one a while back where the site was based in China but the guy was in country Victoria (Australia). His son had moved to China. Imagine a little 30 acre hobby farm, he employs a few locals, has his lounge room set up with a bank of computers, rings his son at the end of each day and the son goes down the market, buys the shoes/apparel and ships it back to Australia and they mail them out locally. We tracked it and sure enough they had a lucrative trade going on. So you get lucky sometimes, and up we went with the police and arrested them.

Were they jailed?
No. Intellectual copyright is seen as a victimless crime. For that reason it is the fastest growing crime of this century. There's very good evidence of South American drug cartels getting into this business because downtown Ma and Pa wants them hung, drawn and quartered for selling cocaine to kids but sell them a fake pair of Jordans and nobody cares and they have twigged to that.

I think for Australians it has become synonymous with getting a trophy on holidays. Go to Bali, come back with a tan and DVDs. Go to Hong Kong and come back with fake luggage and handbags. Go to Bangkok and get a Rolex...
Yeah, and the market has got much more sophisticated in the past few years. I saw some counterfeit Shox the other day and a lot of money and work has been put into creating the tooling of that shoe. That is no fly-by-night organisation, they have very serious dollars, setting up factories to make Shox.

It's easy to make a Nike tee shirt but how the hell do you make a fake pair of Shox? How do you think it happens?

There is obviously a whole bunch of technology required to make shoes. Now, anything that you can build you can reverse engineer, and making a mould is easy. A sole needs a number of different moulds stitched and glued together. They unstitch the upper of the shoe and mimic the individual components. I mean they can make anything, I've seen counterfeit cars (laughs).

Really?

Yeah, they just buy the car and strip it apart and they reverse engineer it. In fact I saw a customs report where they had a Mercedes front of the car but the back end design was a BMW! They can make it look the same but in the case of shoes the breathable material isn't the same, the leather isn't as good, the Air Unit doesn't work, the polyurethane doesn't cushion the way it is supposed to... These Shox came back to our service centre, the soles were snapping. They are not interested in performance, they just want their dough today.

So, as rumoured, are some fakes made by legitimate Nike manufacturers?

There are some, and we'd be foolish to think that there wasn't some backdoor action at these factories because of the huge amount of money available. The way to close these loopholes is to lock in very tight contracts, and that includes B Grades. In some cases the contracts are worth tens of millions of dollars so the risk of factory owners is so great that they wouldn't run the gauntlet.

It's not always possible to stop the night shift from running a small scam but we find them out. I can look at a pair of shoes and know which factory it was made in and what time it dropped into market. It might be that a particular factory in China was the only place that had a contract for a particular colourway, so if I started to see a whole bunch of them in the market, it's a no-brainer. And the factory knows that. That's through a combination of the letters and numbers on the bar code system. For example, last week I found some counterfeit Tuned Air. The bar code told me it was a Footlocker exclusive but the counterfeiters said, 'Oh we got these from a sportswarehouse in Korea'. But we all know that Tuned Air is a Footlocker exclusive.

So, they don't know everything. Style codes, colour codes, factory codes etc. They do a perfect copy of a label and invest money in it by ordering 10,000 labels. Twelve months later they are on their 17th style and they are still using a label that says it is a blue Air Max but they are doing a red Presto. That's the greatest tool for us to undo them at the end of the day.

Is that why the boxes are never right? They go to all the trouble of faking a shoe but couldn't be bothered faking the right box! Is that because they don't care if people know it is fake?

No, I think that they miss the detail. Nike is 30 years old and I am constantly staggered to see some of the stupid things that counterfeiters do that are no-brainers for people who know the brand. The swoosh is wrong, the box is wrong, the colours aren't right, there are simple spelling mistakes on labels. It's almost like there's such a sense of urgency to get after the revenue that they miss the small stuff that your readers notice.

But you have to get them in your hands to find it out. The deception only has to live long enough for your credit card to go through. I've seen tracksuits with three stripes and Nike logos. Jackets that are adidas on one side and reversible with Nike logos on the inside. They put the swoosh on sandals and write 'Nice' as if we can't tell it is a Nike. We had an offender who was selling DKNY and he said it wasn't Donna Karen New York, it was Don King New York (laughs) so they weren't infringing trademarks.

Plus they can always put pictures on their site of real shoes anyway...

Exactly. That's right. It's a lot easier in apparel because they can go to one of the many Nike websites, copy the photographs, print out the designs and embroider 10,000 blanks.

With some SB Dunks going for $3-500us, it's just too easy isn't it?

It is, and I think the danger lies ahead of us, not behind us. One of these days the counterfeiters will realise that if they charge the going rate, rather than what they usually do which is charge say $65, they will make more money. Now, when they truly get their criminal minds underway, that's when the consumers will be even more likely to buy them in my view. I don't say this to scuttle the genuine sellers of goods at high-end prices but counterfeiters are foolish to offer stuff so cheaply.

Ok, we better keep that one quiet. One thing that pops up regularly is that the sizing is always way off, why is that?

Yeah, in fact they are nearly always one size too small. This Tuned Air that I got a few weeks ago was all wrong. I'm not sure why. Perhaps they don't care what label they put on shoes. A size 9 can be anything from a size 7 to an 11 so minimising sizes would maximise $$$. Again, I think it's because they know that when you get it, you will discover it's counterfeit, so they therefore put more energy into disappearing when you want your money back.

Do you see a time when we have some sort of electronic means of validating product?

Yeah, there's a lot of these things around like holograms and DNA thread. What we need is some tech that the consumer can interpret. DNA impregnated ink in screen printing and tongue labels is great but there's nothing that can't be copied. The only way consumers can be certain is to buy from authorised retailers. I know it is a lame thing to say but it's true. Nike doesn't sell on eBay, or in dodgy retail stores, we have a very particular supply chain and if any Nike retailer thought they could go down the path of trying to pepper and salt some fakes into their real product to make some dollars the consequences are enormous.

I hate the language. Calling them variants or factory samples as if it that makes it OK!

Yes. I agree. I feel sorry for them when they buy, but sending them back to us is just gonna get a letter back saying you've spent $114 on a pair of fakes. You didn't buy them from a legitimate Nike retailer. Sorry about that. All you kids need to understand, if we have excess inventory we have very strict rules on where it can go. We don't sell B Grade stuff unless it clearly says so. We don't clear any product through any company which doesn't have a direct relationship with Nike.

What do you do with the fake shoes?

Sometimes we have container loads of them. But depending on whether we can get them released, well, we are actually the largest gift-in-kind donator to World Vision in Australia. We will provide the product seized and send it to countries where we don't have real business. Yes, they are fake but if you don't have any shoes they must be fantastic. We've got some great stories about places where the shoes have ended up in remote and harsh locations where otherwise they had no shoes at all.

So there might be a whole tribe of African dudes wearing fake Unkle Dunks out there?

Yeah I guess so!

Thanks Richard, may the force be with you! Any other thoughts?

I always welcome your readers emailing us with info and we always follow these things up, to the extent the size of the problem justifies it. We enforce counterfeiting in the same way that drug enforcement occurs. The guy at a flea market selling shoes will lead me to his wholesaler, who will lead me to the importer, distributor and the manufacturer, they're the people we want to take out. It's good fun to go after those guys who commit deceptions, especially against young kids. These bozos are profiting from the naivete of consumers. Anybody who wants to set me and my team onto a bunch of fakers is most welcome. The best email address to use is security.aus@nike.com

Be alert and not alarmed!

Yeah!

Turn the page for some samples of some more fakes we have spotted!

The Nike logo should be even horizontally, here you can see that the angle of the dangle is all wrong!

Notice anything weird about this inner sole? The Tuned Air Logo has been reversed!

Bizarre Jordans

Fake Unkle Dunks

JUMPMAN?

JORDAN II (RETRO)

Prior to their re-release this year, the JIIs were one of the least popular Jordans back in the day. As a result, the 1994 retro model is now fairly rare and worth a mint, perhaps as much as $4-500. I have no idea what a deadstock OG pair is worth, maybe twice that. Anyway, they're currently being advertised on the counterfeit sites for around $55-150USD. You can bet your bottom that they are fakes. Why would anyone with the nous to open an eBay account simply give super rare stuff like this away?

They wouldn't. They are 100% phoney.

Also, when shoes are this rare, how do you think it is possible to have a full size range available at all times?

They wouldn't. They are 100% phoney.

As far as online sellers go, Jordan Brand is probably Numero Uno for fake sneakers. Every model in every colour is available, to varying degrees of quality and price. Nike is not far behind, with Dunks, Air Max and Air Force widely faked, as are Le Brons and Huaraches.

We did find some fake Reebok G Units which were pretty bad. Bapestas are now everywhere. Some New Balance can also be found, though not online so far as we know. As far as adidas product goes, the Bape collabs are badly faked and the new 35th anniversary Superstars are sure to be a target as well. On the next pages you'll find guides on how to spot the flaws in some of these models.

HERE ARE SOME TERMS YOU MIGHT COME ACROSS ON WEBSITES THAT SELL FAKES...

FAKES What do I mean by that? I mean they're not real. They weren't made by the brand. They are copies, made by a bootlegger to low standards using inferior materials. Fakes can be relatively unsophisticated and easy to spot or they can be damn near perfect. In many cases you would need to have a fake and a real shoe to be able to tell them apart. Sometimes they smell different, look different, feel different. In most cases however, they deteriorate quickly.

VARIANTS These are fakes. Pure and simple. Loads of sites use this term but it is deliberately misleading. Variants are fakes, straight up. Look at the Policy section on their site, it might be hidden somewhere but will usually say "these shoes are factory variants" as if that means they are some bona fide product. They aren't.

SAMPLES Everyone surely knows about samples but briefly, for the uninitiated, 'samples' usually come in Size 9 with no box and are used to roadtest different looks for a shoe. You can come across some unusual samples, some of which are valuable for sure.

LOOKALIKES These can be found in cheap stores, are made by anonymous brands and are very cheap replicas. Personally I find them more odious than fakes in some ways, but I guess they don't pretend to be anything they are not. The Shelltoes and the Nike Presto have been badly 'lookaliked' locally. These shoes must infringe copyright so I don't know how they get away with it but they do.

CUSTOMS If you see a shoe in a non-original colourway, it is either a sample, a fake or a 'custom.' Customs are shoes that have been hand-detailed in some way. Some sites call their shoes 'customs' but they are fakes. Pretty much anything that has been structurally altered is fake, such as all the Gucci, Louis Vuitton and Burberry AF1s.

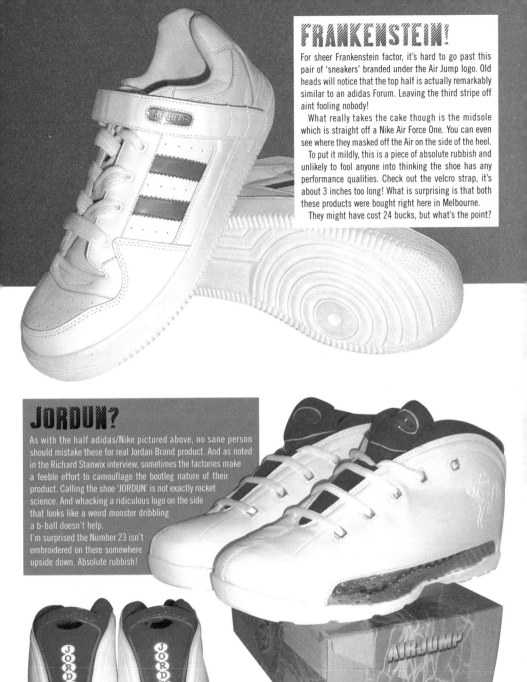

FRANKENSTEIN!

For sheer Frankenstein factor, it's hard to go past this pair of 'sneakers' branded under the Air Jump logo. Old heads will notice that the top half is actually remarkably similar to an adidas Forum. Leaving the third stripe off aint fooling nobody!

What really takes the cake though is the midsole which is straight off a Nike Air Force One. You can even see where they masked off the Air on the side of the heel.

To put it mildly, this is a piece of absolute rubbish and unlikely to fool anyone into thinking the shoe has any performance qualities. Check out the velcro strap, it's about 3 inches too long! What is surprising is that both these products were bought right here in Melbourne.

They might have cost 24 bucks, but what's the point?

JORDUN?

As with the half adidas/Nike pictured above, no sane person should mistake these for real Jordan Brand product. And as noted in the Richard Stanwix interview, sometimes the factories make a feeble effort to camouflage the bootleg nature of their product. Calling the shoe 'JORDUN' is not exactly rocket science. And whacking a ridiculous logo on the side that looks like a weird monster dribbling a b-ball doesn't help.
I'm surprised the Number 23 isn't embroidered on there somewhere upside down. Absolute rubbish!

Hmmmh, JORDUN. Now how do I know that name?

FAKE SNEAKERS PART 2

By Iori
Photos from eBay, HKK and X-Why@Kix-Files.

Back in Issue 3 of Sneaker Freaker, I supplied a detailed description to help you all spot the fake Dunk SB shoes. But it seems nowadays that the fake factories are turning out other fakes besides the Dunks, so Doctor Iori has bestowed upon himself to do some fake shoe research again. This time we will concentrate on adidas, New Balance and Bapesta as well.

ADIDAS: SUPER APE STAR AND SUPER APE SKATE

Luckily for us, the quality of the fake Super Ape Star and Skates is not that high. There are a few areas where the manufacturers cannot, or are too lazy to, replicate. You can determine if they are fake or not at the first glance.

The first point to look at is the tag that is attached to the shoe. On a real pair of Super Ape Star/Skate, the tag is attached by a black metal chain. On the fake pair, they use a plastic string to attach it on the shoe, which is the same as the ones which Nike use to tie the spare laces on the SB shoes.

Secondly, when you break out a pair of fresh Super Ape Star or Skate from the box, the shoes should be laced up using a pair of ordinary white laces and the 3 optional cammo laces are put aside. But with the fakes, they will use one of the 3 cammo laces and the white laces are nowhere to be seen.

Thirdly, Super Ape Star/Skates are made in US half sizes: an example would be US8.5 and it will be UK8. Some fakes I have seen have US9/UK8.5.

And lastly, adidas never released a grey colourway for the Super Ape Star: I've seen one on eBay and it was funny as hell.

REAL!

REAL!

FAKE!

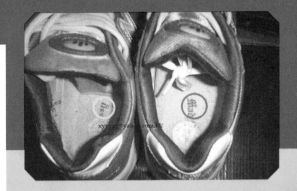

NEW BALANCE MT580: X MITA X STUSSY X REALMAD HECTIC

Until recently, most only knew New Balance for its outdoor and recreational shoes. The Offspring edition and Crooked Tongues combo gave us the insight that New Balance could be trendy as well. But turn the clock back to two years ago and you'll discover New Balance Japan were already retroing their classic mountain trail shoe, MT585, first with famous sneaker store Mita and then with renowned Ura-Harajuku streetwear brand realmad HECTIC. When they teamed up with Stussy they renamed the model 'MT580' and it has been the pinnacle for New Balance in the mindset of trendy Tokyo teenagers. Fake producers then saw a good chance to rip them off...

Spotting fake MT580s isn't that easy, but there are a few key points to check: the rollbar, insoles, the plastic ankle protector and the box.

Basically the NB rollbar is a similar shock-absorbing technology to Reebok's Graphlite system. If you look under the shoe, you will see there is a little window that shows the plates of the rollbar. It should be blue with black dots on it. If the MT580 is real, the black dots should be spaced apart evenly. If it's on a pair of fakes, the black dots are dotted randomly on the rollbar.

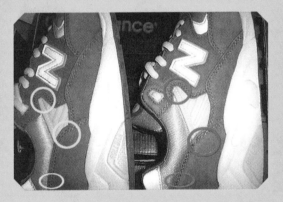

Secondly, if you look on the side of the outsole, you'll see a plate on the side that says 'rollbar'. If it's a real pair, the letter 'R' will have a tail that stretches to the bottom of the plate and the checkered squares will merge with the tail. But if it's fake, the checkered squares won't meet with the letters on the top.

On the insoles, there should be the words 'Mad Stussy' on it. If the shoes are real, the word 'MAD' will be on top on the right-hand shoe.

The ankle plate is the trickiest part. If it's a fake pair, the stitching will be straight and have sharp corners. If it's real, the stitching should be curved nicely, and the plate will be much larger compared to a fake pair.

And lastly, check the box label: on a pair of real MT580, there should be no space between the words 'MT' and '580'. The sticker on the lower corner of the box should be stuck in the middle, but not on the top left-hand side like the fake boxes do. Also the box should be 300mm long. The fake boxes seem to be at least 350mm in length.

And lastly, here's an update on the fake Dunks currently available on the market:

- HEMP SERIES
- CITY SERIES (LONDON, PARIS, TOKYO)
- CALIFORNIA DUNK
- JEDI
- HOMER
- LUCKY DUNK HI SB

FAKE SNEAKERS PART 3

FAKE!

NIKE: VCII

I got a brand new pair of VC IIs from eBay thinking the seller was legit cuz he dropped photos of the actual kicks. I was psyched because I had been looking for these for a long time, so I felt like it was Christmas when I finally got them in!

The warning bells still hadn't rung, even after trying them on and realising they didn't quite fit me. After some inspection I came to the conclusion that these are fakes or variants - whatever you may want to call them.

Here's a few things I noticed. The size states it's a 9.5 but it feels more like a size 9. The Shox logo on the heel is mirrored. The stripe lining is a maroon colour instead of the bright red.

And they didn't come in the original box. They sent me a busted-ass box that belonged to another shoe.

Another shocking thing was that I wore them for a day and my socks went bright red! And we all know OG Nikes don't give off any colour to your socks.

The crazy part is the kicks are so well-made you hardly notice any flaws. But when you start wearing them you will know the difference. These things feel like a brick!

Quincy Renon

NIKE: HTM AIR FORCE 1

One of the hottest releases of 2004 has already spawned some fakes! According to rumour, they were released into the market as B Grades but they didn't deceive the expert eye and were instantly recognized as fakes. They were reportedly produced by the same factory that did the real HTM AF1, using identical croc skin which was ordered in huge amounts.

The fake HTMs aren't hard to identify. Firstly, they didn't come with a special HTM box — they come with the normal orange Nike boxes which were given out when the shoes were sold in the US and EU. For some reason, Singapore and Australia received the special boxes.

Secondly, the build of the shoe is pretty shabby. It has a lower cut and a fatter toecap area. The tongue of the shoe was made out of patent materials on the real version, but on the fake ones they are made out of the same crocskin. Also the word 'AIR' is white in colour, not black which is what it is on the real version. The fake version has no individual numbers as well.

Iori

REAL!

Image :: Billie Stone

ADIDAS FAKES

While imitation is the greatest form of flattery, counterfeits hurt the sneaker purchaser and the manufacturers of this illegal product are criminals. Fakes are easy to spot. They are usually cheap, don't look quite right and are sold at markets and through non-reputable stores. Lately criminals have moved the market stalls to the internet.

The main reason that counterfeit and 'knock offs' are a problem is that the buyer inevitably gets very poor quality. All adidas product goes through strict quality checks to ensure that the consumer gets great quality.

In order to protect the public, adidas has investigators out checking the market. Each year adidas performs hundreds of raids and we prosecute all offenders. Most fake shoes are made overseas and so adidas works with Customs as well to ensure

illegal product never gets into the market place.

Each adidas product has subtle features to allow Customs to identify illegal product. Many of these features are not widely known so that the counterfeiters cannot replicate the product. Some of these features purchasers can spot for themselves. Eg: all shoes come in an adidas shoe box. They all have proper branding with our name spelt correctly (only 2 d's) and adidas is always spelt with a lower case 'a'. adidas trademarks always have the registered symbol as part of the logo.

If you suspect that shoes being offered for sale may be dodgy then don't buy them. Lastly, if you are overseas or purchasing on the net use common sense, ask questions & remember 'Buyer Beware'.

Paul Sweet :: adidas australia

FAKE SNEAKERS PART 4

NIKE: JORDAN III RETRO

I've been collecting Jordan since 1990. I was in high school and that's when I could afford my first pair. They were Jordan V white/fire red sz 10.

I won these Nike Air Jordan III retro off eBay about a year ago. They were a US size 11, but auction stated that this model of shoe 'ran a little small' so it would fit like a 10 to 10.5. After waiting up until 4am, I won the auction for $175. Shipping was $35. So the grand total was $210us.

The seller had a feedback of 1000+, was 97% positive and was one of those 'verified trusted square traders'. I paid for the shoes by money order, had my shoes within 2 weeks and I was very happy. Months later I bought another 10 to 12 pairs of Jordans for myself and friends. Some of these were models that hadn't been retro'ed yet Eg. XVI, XVII, but there were others that had been.

Then I noticed that some sellers had multiple pairs and sizes of the III, IV & V up. They were selling for around $100us. Some sellers were giving away info on fakes for free. This is when I suspected that I had fakes and that I paid a whopping amount for them. I emailed pics to this seller and he sent them back, pointing out what makes them fake. I haven't purchased Jordans from eBay since although I have made purchases from Eastbay, but they're legit

I recently bought a real pair of Nike Air Jordan III white/cement/fire red size 10.5 for $300us shipped. I made sure the production dates and numbers matched up to the info I had. I had the person send me detailed pics of the shoes from every angle. When I received the shoes I compared them to my fakes. The fakes are almost the same, but not good enough to get past a smart Jordan collector.

I hope this helps everyone out there collecting Jordans. I've been ripped off a few times, but I didn't know that there were fakes out there. The more tips on spotting fakes the better. Hopefully one day we can rid eBay of fakes for good!

Cheers - JC

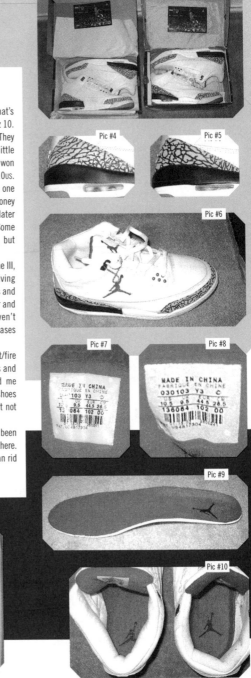

Pic #3
Pic #4
Pic #5
Pic #6
Pic #7
Pic #8
Pic #9
Pic #10
Pic #1
Pic #2

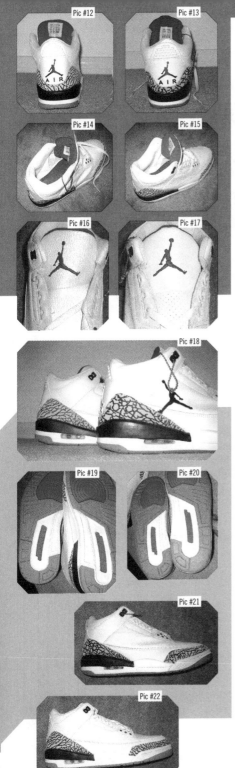

Pic 1. These are the fakes. Notice the tissue paper is real thin and crappy and the material inside the shoe is slightly discoloured. It has a light blue tinge to it. Also there is the metal Jumpman keychain attached to the shoe. Authentic IIIs do not come with this keychain

Pic 2. These are the authentic IIIs. From first glance everything is good. You can see the quality of the materials and the tissue paper looks right.

Pic 3. Side by side. The authentic IIIs are on the left. Here you can see the difference between the two. The cement on the fakes is slightly darker. The fake box is of poor quality construction and it is a lot smaller. The seller used brown tape to wrap the box with the shipping slip. I was pissed about the box being covered with tape because it ripped the label off if I tried to take it off

Pics 4 & 5. Pic 4 is the authentic III. The stitching on the cement is grey as opposed to white on the fakes in pic 5. The elephant print on the fakes is much bolder than the authentic. The visible air is clear on the authentic as opposed to the fakes. The visible air on the fakes is a lot smaller and the black finish around the heel is not as nice as the authentic.

Pic 6. Fake!

Pics 7 & 8 Authentic tag in pic 7 and the fake in pic 8. My camera aint so good but it's the fake tag that is actually that blurry! The letters are larger and squashed down. The production date on the authentic is 01-13-03 and the fake is the same.

Pic 9. This is the innersole of the fakes. It is red on top and red on the bottom. Its is very flimsy. The innersoles I buy from Rebel Sport are ten times better. The authentic innersole is red on top and black on the bottom. I couldn't even take it out because it was stuck from all that glue they put in there.

Pic 10. This is the overhead shot of the IIIs side by side. Authentic on the left, fake on the right. You can notice the heel fit on the fake is very wide and boxy. The tongue of the fake is arched as opposed to the square tongue on the authentic. You can also notice the poor quality of the materials of the fakes

Pic 11. Another shot of the tongues. Authentic on the left, fake on the right. You can notice the red on the fake is much darker and almost 'velvety'.

Pics 12. & 13 Pic 12 is the authentic, pic 13 is the fake. Once again we see how wide the heel is on the fake. The cement on the rear of the sole is darker and has very poor construction.

Pic 14. Fake

Pic 15 Authentic

Pic 16. Authentic tongue. The finish of the embroidery of the Jumpman is far superior to the fake in pic 17. The tongue is not perforated on the authentic.

Pic 17. Fake. Perforated tongue. Poor quality of embroidery

Pic 18. Authentic in the background, fake in front. Once again we can see the difference in the visible air unit.

Pic 19 & 20. Comparison of soles. Fake on top, authentic on the bottom. The cement is much darker on the fake and there is detail to the sole. The authentic shows much more detail to the tread on the sole. When I tried the fakes on, they felt blown out. The soles on the fake are not flat.

Pic 21 Fake

Pic 22 Authentic

MVP?

Sometimes all this fake stuff *can* be a laugh and I've not seen anything much funnier than this pair of weird-ass Jordan IVs, I mean MVP sneaks. They were bought in Sydney for fifty bucks and by all reports have actually performed quite well and survived a few months wear and tear.

Now just check out the details. The silver box and the label are eerily reminiscent of a well known sneaker brand and the Jumpman has been changed to what looks like someone parachuting with a bowling ball! But mostly it's the thick leather used in this MVP that creates the optical illusion. The way the leather wraps around totally changes the dynamic of the classic Jordan IV shape, so much so that it almost looks like a different shoe. Weird huh?

Thanks to Garry Trinh for the photos....

The latest trend in the sneaker game is not sourcing rare kicks but trying to spot the fakes! Try taking a stroll in any auction site and see for yourself – the growth of the fake industry is alarming. There is an easy way to avoid buying fakes and that is to stop buying shoes altogether. That's obviously impractical, so you'll have to have 'the knowledge' to avoid being ripped off.

Because there's so many fakes around, we will concentrate only on the Dunks listed here. There are several consistent major flaws in the fake Dunks. Most are noticeable at a glance, but some need an experienced eye, even at close examination. Here's a pretty good list of things to look for. It won't guarantee you are buying a legitimate Dunk, but it is better than a poke in the eye with a stick!

CURRENT LISTING OF KNOWN FAKE DUNKS...

CHOCOLATE SB (Anthracite/Black)

ZOO YORK SB (Paul Brown/Black)

DANNY SUPA SB (Safety Orange/Hyper Blue/White)

RICHARD MULDER SB (White/Orion Blue/White)

REESE FORBES SB (Wheat/Twig/Dune)

DENIM SB (Denim/Denim/Denim)

HEINEKEN SB (Classic Green/Black/White/Red)

SUPREME SB (Black/Cement and White/Cement)

REVERSE SUPA (Orange/Hyper Blue/White. EU exc)

ALPHANUMERIC (Lightning grey/yellow)

RAINBOW/VIOTECH (Viotech/Lemonade-Crimson. co.jp)

DUNK HI PREMIUM (Curry)

HAZE DUNK LOW/HI PREMIUM (Black/White/Grey)

SPLATTER (Silver Ice/Team Red-Lt Graph)

UNDEFEATED HI (White/Yellow gum soles)

METHAMPHIBIAN X UNDEFEATED (all colours)

GOLD DUNKS (Gold Olympic Issue)

CONNERY (Tweed Issue)

+ HUF, RAYGUN, HOMER, DUNKLE & HUNTER...

▶▶ *1. THE SOLE* Generally, the fakes have a few flaws on the sole. Firstly the Nike logo in the middle of the sole. There should be a little ® above the swoosh. For fakes, this won't be there. The real pair should curve up towards your toes, but fakes curve up from the middle of the shoe, both forward and back. If you put them on a flat surface, it will rock like a boat!

▶▶ *2. THE HEEL* Easily spotted again. The words on the real Dunks should be stitched in line with each other and be equal in size. Fake Dunks have crooked stitching, the letters don't line up and the N-I-K-E letters are a lot bolder. Now look down a bit more and you should see 3 evenly separated stitching lines right? On fakes they are packed together and are uneven.

▶▶ *3. THE TONGUE* Fakes have less padding inside and the arch inside the tongue will be curvier than the real SBs which have a more rigid, fatter and straighter tongue. This won't be easily spotted so wear a pair of SBs when you go shopping to compare them.

▶▶ *4. THE TOE* Fake Dunks have a bigger compartment for the toes. Also, the cutting on the leather/suede for the toe cap area should be cut by machine so it should be clean, neat and without any material sticking out. The leather/suede for fake shoes is often cut by hand – edges will be uneven and messier than the real ones.

MADE IN AUSTRALIA
13
NOV 77MI

WORDS — lORl

MADE IN AUSTRALIA
64M

A309999

For further information go to the www.sneakerfreaker.com website for detailed updates of the fake kicks scene.

▶▶ **5. SB LACES** When you buy a new pair of SBs, there should be another set of different coloured laces and they should be tied with a CLEAR plastic band on the right hand side of the RIGHT shoe. Fakes Dunk laces are usually tied on the LEFT side of the left shoe with a white plastic band.

▶▶ **6. ZOOM AIR INSOLE** You'll only be able to tell if it's fake by feeling the Zoom Air insole. The fake insole feels like it's made out of foam. It's not stiff and won't retract into place. For real SBs, the Zoom Air insole should be hard, stiff and bounce back into its original shape when bent. Also the 'Zoom Air' logo is printed more clearly on a real pair - fake SBs have a muffed up look because there's little space between the paint and the colour of the insole, therefore the word 'Zoom' is a bit smaller than usual.

▶▶ **7. THE TAG** The words in the tag of a real pair of SBs should be bold and clear. For fake Dunks, they will be lighter in colour and thinner.

▶▶ **8. THE SHOEBOX** Check the sticker on older orange boxes. There should be a white border that spaces out little boxes for the size, colour code and name. For fakes, they will be thicker than usual. The sticker is stuck onto the box on a slanted angle. For the new silver SB boxes, check the font for the shoe size — the font for the number is different than the real silver box which is smaller and thinner, and the sticker is stuck on the lower left hand corner. Real silver SB boxes have the sticker stuck in the middle.

▶▶ **9. CHOCOLATE/HEINEKENS** Fake Heinekens have the red star stitched lower than the real ones and it's slightly bigger. On the Chocolate, the little blue and red stitching on the bottom of the cross will be different — fakes have the red on the outside and the blue on the inside. Real Chocolates are exactly the opposite. The black markings in the yellow cross will be mirrored as well.

▶▶ **10. DENIMS** Real Denim Dunks should have a messy look but the fake shoes are totally clean, corners cut neatly. Also the blue denim colour is darker the real Denim Dunk.

▶▶ **11. SPLATTERS** On the real Splatter Dunk, the white paint should be splatted on the shoe evenly. On the fakes, the white paint is splatted in big blobs and unevenly on the shoe.

▶▶ **12. SUPREMES** The cracks on the real version are dark in colour and embossed into the leather. The fakes appear to be lighter in colour, are embossed less and the cracks are uneven. The Supremes are by far the most common and the best quality fakes ever produced and can even fool the most experienced sneaker headz in the world. Be extremely wary of buying these...

▶▶ **13. HAZE** These are hard to spot and can fool the best headz as well. The difference is the painting - fakes aren't sprayed that evenly on the edges and the colours are slightly lighter.

▶▶ **14. PREMIUM** The colour of the fake soles are white, but the real ones are light yellow. The leather is cut by hand so they look untidy. Stitching is messier, the leather colour is lighter and the Nike tag on the tongue is stitched on at a tilted angle and it uses white lining instead of gold.

REMEMBER! Before bidding for a shoe always ask questions and request photos of the above mentioned areas taken from different angles. This will determine if they actually have the shoes or are simply using photos pinched off legitimate websites. And remember, keep your guard up, happy sneaker hunting and don't let those mongrel fake selling bastards pinch your hard earned cash!

CHAPTER XI.
SHOE SOLE HÆMORRHAGE.
HOE

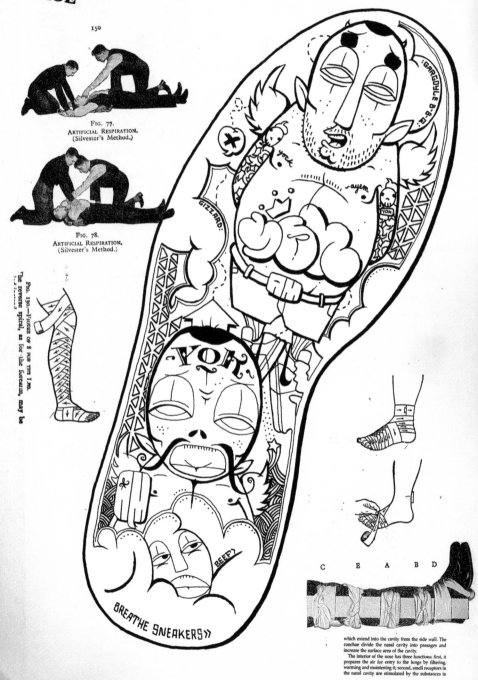

FIG. 77.
ARTIFICIAL RESPIRATION.
(Silvester's Method.)

FIG. 78.
ARTIFICIAL RESPIRATION.
(Silvester's Method.)

FIG. 130.—FIGURE OF 8 FOR THE LEG. The reverse spiral, as for the forearm, may be

which extend into the cavity from the side wall. The conchae divide the nasal cavity into passages and increase the surface area of the cavity.

The interior of the nose has three functions: first, it prepares the air for entry to the lungs by filtering, warming and moistening it; second, smell receptors in the nasal cavity are stimulated by the substances in

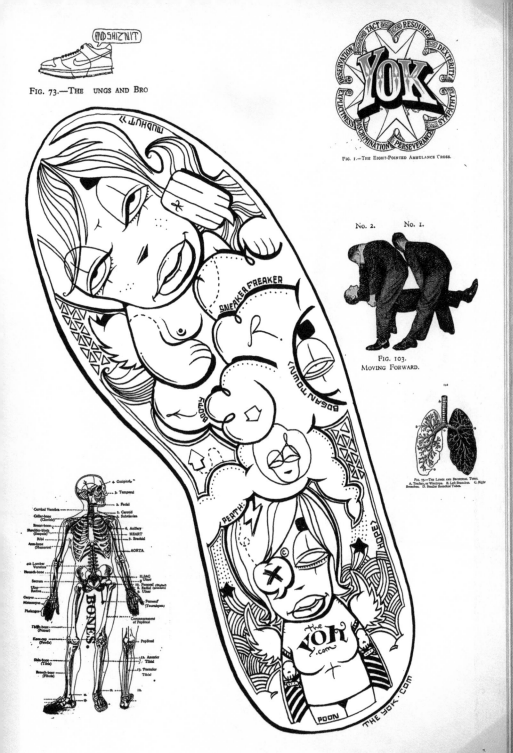

FIG. 73.—THE UNGS AND BRO

FIG. 1.—THE EIGHT-POINTED AMBULANCE CROSS.

No. 2.   No. 1.

FIG. 103.
MOVING FORWARD.

FIG. 73.—THE LUNGS AND BRONCHIAL TUBES.
A. Trachea, or Windpipe. B. Left Bronchus. C. Right Bronchus. D. Smaller Bronchial Tubes.

XI.

TALKIN TURKEY WITH MISTAH JASON BASS

WAY BACK IN ISSUE 2 WE CAUGHT UP WITH SHOE DESIGNER JASON BASS: GURU, URBAN EINSTEIN, CAPTAIN COBBLER AND FRANKENCREATOR OF JB CLASSICS! STARTING IN SAN FRAN IN 2002, JB HAS TAKEN SNEAKER DESIGN AND MANUFACTURE INTO THE LOFTY REALMS OF WEARABLE HIGH-ART. JB'S OWN NATURAL SENSE OF DESIGN ANARCHY AND INDIE COLLECTIVE APPROACH, (AS WELL AS ALWAYS TYPING INTERVIEWS IN ALL CAPS) HAS KEPT US IMMENSELY ENTERTAINED OVER THE YEARS!

Hey JB, how's those world domination plans coming along?
HAHAHHA! IT'S BEEN GOING REALLY GOOD BROTHER! IN TERMS OF THE BRAND, IT'S BEEN AS ORGANIC AS EVER, JUST MELTING AND MOVING THRU OBSTACLES DAY AFTER DAY. WE'VE STUCK TO OUR GAME PLAN SINCE DAY ONE - INDEPENDENT!

How the hell did all this sneaker business start?
BASICALLY, JUST LIKE ANY OTHER TRUE SNEAKER HEAD, I WAS ALWAYS SKETCHING DESIGN CONCEPTS DOWN IN MY BOOK AND SORTA DREAMING THAT I WOULD BE ABLE SOMEDAY TO BRING THIS SHIT TO LIFE! THEN ABOUT A FEW YEARS AGO, IT WAS KIND OF LIKE A MATRIX SORT OF THING, I MET SOME HEAD WHO COULD BRING MY SHIT TO LIFE.

Sounds like you're underwater, where the hell are you now?
JUST SITTIN HERE IN SAN FRANCISCO AT THE JB LAB AFTER RETURNING FROM THE LAS VEGAS SHOE SHOW (WSA). IT WAS COOL! FOOTWEAR NEWS MAGAZINE FEATURED US IN THEIR TRADE MAG WHICH WAS RELEASED TO ALL THE SUITS & EXECUTIVES AT THE SHOW. SOME MAJOR EXPOSURE TO PEOPLE THAT USUALLY STAY WITHIN SECURE BOXES OF CORPORATE BRANDS. SO THAT WAS REALLY FRESH AND FILLED WITH TONS OF POSSIBLITIES FOR OUR FUTURE GROWTH.

It's quite tricky making shoes, are you off to the factories all the time?
YAH, BUT ALL OF MY STUFF IS HAND-MADE, SO IT'S MORE LIKE A LAB, EVERYTHING IS SUPER-MINIMAL. ONLY A FEW STITCH DOCTORS AND MATERIAL HUNTERS. FOR THE MOST PART, I JUST DEVELOP EVERYTHING GRAPHICALLY AND THEN STEP TO THE LAB AND BRING IT TO LIFE. SOMETIMES I GO WITH ONE IDEA BUT BY THE TIME THE PROTOTYPE IS FINISHED IT IS TOTALLY DIFFERENT. THE LAB IS A FRESH SPOT!

Can you explain the design process involved with shoes?
WELL, SHIT! MY INFLUENCES ARE DEEPLY ROOTED IN DESIGN ELEMENTS OF PACKAGING AND ILLUSTRATION AND VIDEO AND WHEN WE GET TOGETHER WE JUST SORTA TOSS MAD IDEAS AROUND WHILE DRINKING RUM AND 7-UP UNTIL SOMETHING WORKS... OK, LET ME EXPLAIN, WE JUST TRY TO DEVELOP CONCEPTS THAT BREATHE BY THEMSELVES. WE DON'T HAVE A MARKETING TEAM TO PUMP OUR SHIT, IT NEEDS TO BE ABLE TO PUMP ITSELF, WHICH IS TRUE OF ANY REAL CONCEPT.

I like the printed stuff, is that where it's at?
YAH! OUR PLAN IS TO HAVE GRAPHIC FUN, SO YOU CAN EXPECT MORE PRINTS TO COME REAL SOON!

ABOUT HIS DESIGNER SNEAKS

The retro buzz is still so strong, it makes you wonder why the big guys keep developing new projects... what is the future of sneaker design?

WOW! THE FUTURE OF SNEAKER DESIGN!! YOU BETTER CALL NIKE AND THE REST OF THE GIANTS, THEY THE ONES PUMPING MAD UNITS ALL OVER THE WORLD. I'M PRETTY MUCH A DESIGN CONCEPT. ONE OF MY IDEAS I FEEL THAT I WANT TO EXPLORE IS GOOD GRAPHIC PRINTS THAT CAN BREATHE ON THEIR OWN. I FEEL THAT GRAPHICS ADD FRESH COMPOSITIONS TO TRAINERS, AND HEADS WHO ARE INTO MATCHING THEIR FITS OR WHO HAVE A GOOD SENSE OF DESIGN WOULD BE DOWN TO ROCK MY COLLECTION. AS WELL AS DEVELOPING DIFFERENT PACKAGING AND BOOK DESIGNS.

What was the Motug show all about?

THIS WAS AN AMAZING PROJECT, PUT TOGETHER BY LASE NYC. MOTUG STANDS FOR 'MONSTERS OF THE UNDERGROUND' AND I WAS TRULY BLESSED AND EMBRACED BY ALL THE LEGENDS INVOLVED WITH THE PROJECT. THEY ARE: TOOFLY, EWOK, FUTURA, GHOST, DIZMOLOGY, CES, SHEPARD FAIREY, TKID 170, DOZE GREEN & NYC LASE... THIS WAS A STATEMENT TO ALL GIANT BRANDS, DISPLAYING THE POWER OF THE UNDERGROUND MOVEMENT. THERE WERE ONLY 24 PAIRS PRODUCED. EACH ARTIST GOT ONE PAIR, THE GALLERY RELEASED 7 PAIRS TO THE PUBLIC ON THE OPENING NIGHT, AND LASE AND I EACH KEPT 3 PAIRS. THEY SOLD FOR $1500 US A PAIR AND UP!

Any new shit we should know about?

SURE. WE GOT THE FIRST EVER FOOTWEAR COMPANY TO FOOTWEAR COMPANY COLAB BETWEEN DC SHOES AND JB. PLUS JB CLASSICS ARE DROPPING SOON. WE ALSO GOT A PROJECT WITH THE CARTOON NETWORK IN THE PIPELINES AS WELL AS KID ROBOT TOY BOUTIQUES. SHIT, I THINK THAT'S ENOUGH TO LEAK AT THE MOMENT. BUT ON THE REAL, EVERYDAY WE HAVE SOME EXCITING NEWS THAT LEADS US INTO THE NEXT DAY. WE ALSO ARE GETTING TO READY TO DROP 10 USA EXCLUSIVES, LIMITED TO 200 PAIRS PER STYLE SO THAT WIILL BE FUN. WE ALSO HAVE THE BULLY TOY DROPPING IN LONDON AND THE US PRODUCED BY JB CLASSICS AND SUPERDELUXE/GLORIAS! PLUS SOME REAL ILL SHIT WE ARE DOING WITH PETE FROM SNEAKER PIMPS.

Well that's not much - what else have you got planned?

JUST KEEP COMING CORRECT, ALTHOUGH, I'M DEFIANTLY PULLING MY HAT DOWN AND BUYING SOME PITBULLS CUZ NO-ONE WANTS TO SEE AN UNDERDOG WIN..

Turn the page for a huge selection of JB's work...

"TO LIVE AND WORK CLOSELY TO JB IS MUCH LIKE BEING IN THE EYE OF A TORNADO. THIS WHIRLWIND OF MATERIALS AND THOUGHTS WHIPS AROUND YOU, BUT IN THE MIDDLE IT IS CALM. FROM THE OUTSIDE LOOKING IN, YOU SEE A CRAZED MASS OF SNEAKERS, CIGARETTES, EMAILS, STARBUCKS CONTAINERS, SKETCHPADS AND SMOKE, FLOWING TOGETHER IN A SORT OF ODD HARMONY. THIS IS MY TAKE ON LIFE WITH THE CAPTAIN COBBLER" :: MDOT

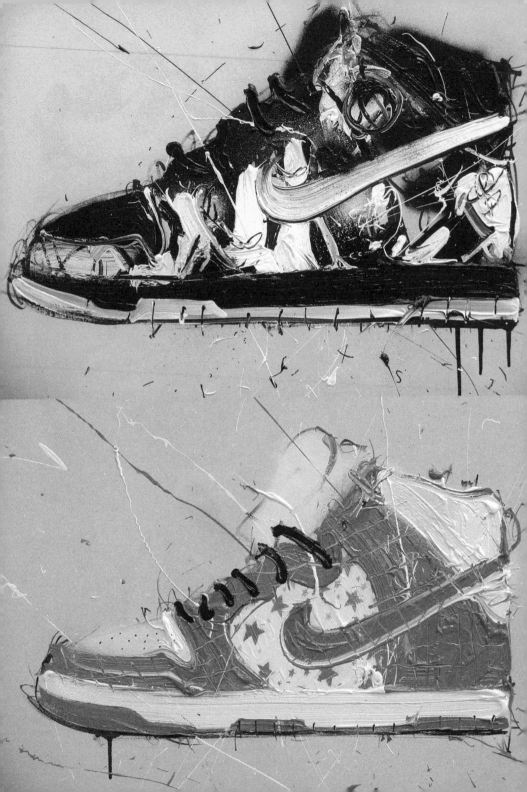

As an avid collector and artist, painting sneakers was an obvious choice. I've been into the design and colours of sneakers since I was a kid. Saving up for my adidas Colombias and then finally getting them was the start of my obsession at age 14.

I actually started painting sneakers in 2002 when I was looking for a new subject. With my work, I am immortalising the kicks that we all know and love, presenting them in my own style of painting, which has always been explosive and expressive.

I see the form, shape, styling and texture of sneakers coming together to complete objects of extraordinary beauty. Much the same as a Ferrari engine or the curves on a Spitfire plane. I think the Jordan V is up there with the greatest designs of the 20th century.

To start a painting, I produce a very quick line drawing which forms the skeleton and structure of the shoe. Then I use spray paint to create form. The actual act of painting is dynamic and spontaneous.

As I look at the early works, I feel the actual expression of the paint is much more dominant than the description and character of the shoe itself. But as time has progressed, textures, details, lines and pattern have all evolved to give a much closer representation, balanced with my style. Icons such as the Rayguns, Staple Pigeons or Kid Robot have all formed backgrounds, giving the character and branding an importance equal to the sneaker itself.

Will I ever stop painting them? The answer to that is no. I started painting them for the joy they bring me, and others. As long as companies keep pushing, developing and designing things that I find visually stimulating, then sneakers will always be a part of my subject matter as an artist.

dave white

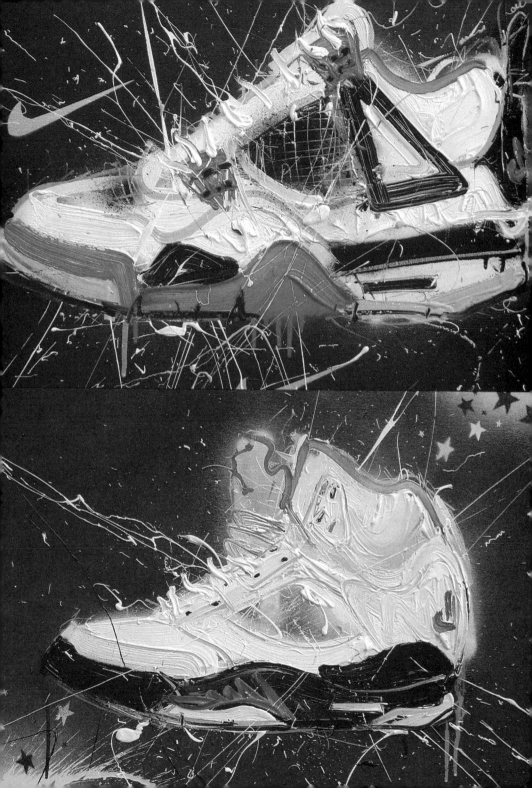

LONDON

LOCK, DEADSTOCK AND TWO SMOKING AIR MAX!

Welcome to sunny London! A place of dreamers, schemers, wieners, double-teamers, cheeky chavs, Reebok hustlers, fashion wankers, Nathan Barleys, council estates, nail bomb experts and more quality sneaker stores than anywhere in the world. That's right - I'm telling you - London is now numero uno for hunting kicks! You may go a bit chicken oriental as every High St seems to have the same stores all in a row. Luckily, they are all pretty good, but there's also a brace of great indie stores worth checking out. And that's what we did! Luvvly jubbly...

EAST AND SOUTH

Let's start in the East and stay there! Our favourite store in London is the gorgeous **Gloria's**, (as in Gloria Gaynor, rhymes with trainer) the location of our incredible Snkr Frkr 6 launch! Andy, Pete and Matt went so far out of their way to help us we are beholden for all eternity - we're not worthy! So we might be biased, but they have a great-looking store in a great location and they stock a sincere range of killer kicks, including **FEIT** and **JB Classics** plus all your usual suspects. I might point out, Gloria's don't have major brand accounts, instead they are determined to do things their own way by importing the best of the best from wherever it takes. And that commitment requires a lot more creative and commercial effort than you'd think. Cheers Gloria!

In fact, the whole Truman area is a bonanza for shoppers. There's a whole cluster of stores down here selling art books, vintage clothes and other cool stuff. Plus it's nice and quiet, there's a great pub at one end of the street and a great café at the other. If you have time for a Bengali curry or a legendary corned beef bagel from the shop on Brick Lane you'll be well stuffed as well. From here it is just a short walk to visit our friends at **Best Shop** as well. You might even run into Nathan Barley if you're lucky - say hello for us!

A quick five minute walk away is **Meteor Sports** in Bethnal Green Road. For a dose of legit East End London, check this out - lock, deadstock and two smoking Air Max! A proper old school sports store but with a modern twist, Meteor specialise in Nike, Air Max, Air Force, anything slightly on the Chav style of things. They couldn't give two figs for modern fashion wankers, but they are dead serious about their sneakers. All the same, I have to say their selection this time around was a little disappointing. Two years ago when I was here last, the shop was going off! I guess things change and you can always have a flat spot. Anyway, there's also some wild bling jewellery stores down here on the same street, which seem so out of place it is just surreal.

Sports & Things is on the south side of London, deep into downtown ritzy Streatham. Best be keeping your wits about you in this neck of the woods! Readers of Issue 6 will remember Craig Leckie's amazing review of this store. To briefly recap, it is a massive sports store that seems to have existed in some sort of time warp for the past 15 years. They have a lot of great stuff, a shitload of weird relics, incomplete sizes, jaded and sun-damaged stock, old tracksuits, Hi-Tecs, Jordans, adidas, Brooks... there's just mountains of stuff everywhere you look! There's also an enormous archive of deadstock goodies hiding downstairs away from prying eyes, so go in and ask them what's cooking, you may get the surprise of your life. Especially when you ask for the price! A truly unique London experience.

EAST LONDON

Best Store	No.5 Back Hill :: 0207 833 5844
Gloria's	Truman Brewery, Brick Lane
Magma	117-119 Clerkenwell Road
Meteor Sports	408-410 Bethnal Green Rd :: 0207 739 0707
OFR Books	Truman Brewery, Brick Lane

SOUTH LONDON

Sports & Things	Streatham High St

SOHO AREA

In case you're wondering, Soho is a compact central area of London bound by Oxford St, Shaftesbury Avenue and Regent St. It is home to a labyrinth of tiny streets packed with ad agencies, media companies, down-and-out bums, sandwich bars, horny secretaries, sex shops, gay bars, a nice park, several quality record shops and fantastic pubs. There's also a stack of quality sneaker stores to check out - so let's start in the dead centre!

Carnaby St has undergone something of a change over the past few years. Its reputation as the swinging centre of London has long gone. Unfortunately, in the past two years it has become indistinguishable from any London High Street destination. As far as sneaker hunting goes however, it's the cat's knackers!

First stop is **Size?**. Put simply, they are the most complete sneaker store in the world. I know it is high praise but I can't think of a single store that comes close to matching the impressive breadth of their product mix. They have more kicks, more brands, more styles, more colours, more choice, more, more, more, more of everything! Size? is a sneaker freaker's wetdream. They have so many shoes you won't know where to start, plus they have their own special make-ups like the Night Jogger, Trimm-Trab and NB577s - all well-chosen and progressively remixed. For a chain store they are doing it right and their focus is definitely the chosen path of the righteous sneaker fiend.

Next door is the **Converse** store. It featured an installation of artwork from 2000AD when we were there which made up for some otherwise dull sneakers. You'll also find a Casio store which I always check out, even though I haven't seen a decent G-Shock for nearly a decade. Across the road is a branch of **Office**, another commercial chain with a wide range of sneakers. There's also a **Puma** and a **Vans** store - see what I mean!

But there's more. Just one street back from Carnaby is Newburgh St - home to **Bond International**, a longtime staple of the London streetwear scene. They stock a compact selection of imported kicks plus a well chosen range of tees, toys and mags as well. The best part is the Bond friendly vibe, you won't get any attitude from skinny upstart shop kids on two quid an hour in here...

A few doors down at #6 is the **adidas concept** store, one of the more pretentious excuses for a shop we've come across. Actually that's a bit harsh, but it's not really doing much to float our boat. Not sure what is going on here. At #15 Newburgh is the **Onitsuka** store, a twin sister (in looks) to the Tiger Amsterdam store. They have a stellar line-up of shoes and their silky signature jackets are a class above anything I've seen produced by a footwear brand for some time. If you're into it, check it out.

FOOTPATROL

OXFORD CIRCUS

NIKETOWN

ONITSUKA

SLAMMIN KICKS

From Newburgh St, walk down to **Slammin Kicks** on Beak St. Run by the effervescent Magdi, Slammin deserves the support of all you heads out there. It's a true indie store doing their best to bring choice to the London massive. They've also started their own tee range which is looking sharp as well. Just a few yards up the road is **The Hideout**. That's where you'll find a fairly complete range of Visvim shoes and a bunch of other stuff you can wear.

From here, **Maharishi** is one or two streets away. Well known for their obsession with cammo, Maharishi also stock their own range of clothing as well as toys and a few sneakers. They've done their own make-ups with Nike in the past and the store has an exhibition space where the likes of Futura have been known to show off their doodles. Quite an incredible store...

Footpatrol is our last stop in central Soho and a little harder to find than the others. It's not actually in a street, it's more of a walkway and from the outside, you'd be hard-pressed to know what's going on. Footpatrol have a fine reputation for getting the rarest shits, and with all proddy locked away in the trademark cages, the fitout is still a novelty. If you want some super-duper Nike shizz like Undefeated Jordan IVs you'd be best advised to buddy up with the FP gang, it's the only place you'll find them. All you had to do was enter a raffle and venture into central London the day after the bombings for the drawing of the prize!

No doubt you'll also walk up to Oxford St at some point, most likely because you'll run out of squids and need to hit the bank. You will always run out of money in London! Up here you'll find **Niketown** and **JD Sports**. Y'all know what to expect from Niketown so no elaboration needed from me here. JD Sports have sharpened their product mix into a premium sports store. You'll find all your performance gear and the store is run like a well-oiled machine. JD are also big enough to warrant their own exclusive sneakers and for my money, they have produced some of the best colorways of the Air Force One seen in the past few years.

adidas	6 Newburgh St :: 0207 734 9976
Bond	17 Newburgh St :: 0207 437 0079
Converse	33-34 Carnaby St
Footpatrol	16A St Annes Court :: 0207 734 6625
JD Sports	172 & 268 Oxford St :: 0207 323 3379
Kokon To Zai	57 Greek St :: 0207 434 1316
The Hideout	7 Upper James St :: 0207 437 4929
Maharishi	2-3 Great Pulteney St :: 0871 218 0260
Niketown	Oxford Circus :: 0207 612 0800
Onitsuka	15 Newburgh St :: 0207 734 5157
Size?	31 Carnaby St
Slammin Kicks	37 Beak St :: 0207 439 0180
The Hideout	Upper James St :: 0207 437 4929

COVENT GARDEN

The second major destination for sneaker hunters in London is Covent Garden and the best way to get there from Soho is to walk. I'd deffo avoid going there on a weekend, it's just totally rammed with continental tourists.

As we walk towards Covent Garden, take Earlham St. You'll pass the **adidas Originals** store and the **Stussy** store. I've never really bought anything in either of them but I always take a look just the same - hoping against hope! On the other side of the street is **Magma Books,** London's best book store and a great supporter and stockist of Snkr Frkr.

Eventually you'll hit Neal St which has a crazy chicken run selection of sneaker stores. Starting at one end you'll find **Office, Reebok, Offspring, Footlocker** and then **Size?**

How's that for an intense 100 yards of sneaker retail?

Offspring have some nice collab New Balance under their belt so they're worth a visit. Some years ago I bought the Atmos Safari Air Max there as well, so that's a nice memory I can share.

Just around the corner is **Slam City Skates**. It's been here for ages, has never really changed and if you need a fix it's one of the very few skate stores in London that I know of. I've heard you might find over-priced Nike SBs here but I've never seen them. There's a record store in the basement as well.

On the other side of the Tube station is Floral Street, home of more over-priced clothes stores. You'll also find the second **Maharishi** here as well. It has a slightly different proddy mix to the Soho store but also has an exhibition space outback where they had the best collection of Six Million Dollar Man stuff I have ever seen. Go the Bigfoot!

Past visitors to London might remember another Covent Garden store called **My Trainers**. Alas, my news is that the store has closed down. Someone said they had moved to Brixton but I'm not sure if this is true. My Trainers was a pretty good store last time I looked, so that's a bit of a bummer. I guess sky-high rents and intense competition have claimed another independent store victim.

adidas Originals	9 Earlham St :: 0207 379 4042
Maharishi	19a Floral St :: 0207 836 3860
Magma Books	8 Earlham Street
Offspring	60 Neal St :: 0207 497 2463
Rbk Store	51 Neal St :: 0207 240 8689
Size?	Neal St
Slam City Skates	16 Neal's Yard :: 0207 240 0928
Stussy Store	19 Earlham St :: 0207 836 9418

SLAM CITY SKATES

size?

JD SPORTS
Air Force One

SIZE?
Night Jogger

SIZE?
NB577

OFFSPRING
NB576

After postponing our original SF6 launch due to the London bombings, we rescheduled for the following Tuesday at Gloria's in Brick Lane. I wondered who would come down at late notice but the London summer turned on a perfect night, the Tiger beer was nice on ice and the whole crowd was going gazongas to some ill beatz from Jerry Dammers! I dunno how many heads came along but it was probably 7-800 or more maybe, who cares, it was a killer party and we were all very jolly with ourselves, especially by midnight when we finally left for the after party! Thanks to a lot of hard work, Glorias also looked a treat... cheers to Andy Holmes and the gang. The event was co-presented with the guys at FEIT - huge bignobs to Tull, Vlad and Rodney who were also brilliant. To the ladeez on bar duty who did a phenomenal job, to Justin & the boys from Camden, Dave B, Leckie, Hughie, Nathan Barley, Christo, Belle, Zissou, Insa, Matt Pidgeon, Easley, Bert & his nephew and Pinky (for the room)... **London was burning!** What else can we say?

FRASER COOKE

FOOTPATROL, LONDON

Foot Patrol x Nike EPIC

Did you enjoy the Laser event in New York?

Definitely. I thought the presentation was really interesting to see everything and to meet Mark Smith who did it was very nice. I think the party was pretty good, I don't now how many people actually really knew exactly what they were there for but nevertheless everyone I have spoken to said they had a good time.

I thought it was a great piss-up. How's London these days?

London has actually picked up a bit, there's a bit more energy. There's no scene going on at the moment as far as nightlife, there's always those little trends but nothing really that special.

Club Culture seems a bit flat all around the world these days.

The bottom's fallen out of it. People want lots of different eclectic stuff which is good and over here the thing that always drove club culture was the fact that clubs used to be the only place that you could go out to till 4am. Bars would shut but they've loosened the laws so you could go to a bar that has a DJ and you don't have to pay to get in. Plus music hasn't been that inspiring and a lot of the younger kids have been rebelling against my generation, getting back into rock.

Going back to the sneakers, London is a bit flooded with stuff right now I think, compared to Australia. It's closer to Tokyo or New York where you can walk down the street and find 5 or 6 shops that have a very similar selection and a lot of so-called special stuff is too widely available in a small radius. Everyone is looking for something special but at the same time people want to be different, exactly like everyone else in the world.

With only one shop, how do you stay ahead of the game?

It's difficult, you have to rely on having a strong relationship with the companies. We have a good relationship with Nike and adidas. For example, when HTM was around we were the only place to get that. The Stash AF1 we had as well. We had the Laser series so we do get exclusives. Like the Haze Dunks in a low and the Beams Huarache. That's really the only way because there is only so much product. There's so much quick strike special potential but then they've got 'X' amounts of stores to service and there is really not enough special versions to be able to really get exclusives. I do understand their side of it, they've got people they work with in more mainstream stores and they spend a hell of a lot of money, same as in all parts of the world.

In that case, doesn't everyone end up unhappy - the consumer, the retailer and the company?

I have said this already to the company but I think that the Safari was one I thought could have been better dealt with. It was definitely a shoe that should have been in Footpatrol. I realise we can't have everything but in New York and in Los Angeles they did special events around it with Biz Markie, they referenced directly one of the reasons why that was an iconic shoe and then to put it into a mass shop. It just ended up languishing and people don't really care.

I was glad Australia only got a few pairs because it kept them on people's feet who truly loved them. It's a shoe that requires a sophisticated taste, plus you have to know the whole story...

I agree, it's not the kind of thing where the Average Joe is going to look at it and go 'that looks cool.' It is challenging so you got to want it for the right reasons. I'm just picking that one out, its not like major big deal but little things like that are where you get frustrated. To be fair we are all trying to do our best...

London seems starved of Dunk SBs, I'm surprised they are almost the most exclusive shoe in town.

Basically from what I understand Nike want to keep the SB as a skateboard product so they want to sell them just to skate stores and there is only one really serious one in London, Slam City, plus Ideal in Birmingham. They just took their time to launch them into this market. I heard they were going to start with Germany and maybe they changed it but the only thing that's a bit sad is that everyone sells these shoes at quite a high price and I have spoken to skaters who would love to have them but they're not going to spend that money and skate in them.

They're going for 150 quid aren't they?

Yeah, I think that is going to drop, it wasn't Slam. I think the other store put them out at that money and then Slam were like 'if they're doing it we are going to match it'. It's a shame cause there's actually people grey marketing them for like 75 quid, half the price. Doesn't really make anybody look good apart from the guy who is selling it for 75 quid who shouldn't even have them, so it's a bit screwed up really.

The obsession with retro - not just in sneakers, but in film, music, television and pretty much any realm of pop culture... is it self-destructive when everything's not as good as it used to be?

I think it's okay in its own right as long as there is a balance. It's good to look at classic things but people are scared to step out and do anything on their own. They wanna follow the crowd. So there's a whole generation of kids that are coming through in the past few years that won't have seen much new product at all. When I was a kid, it was always about some new stuff that was coming out and you wanted to have it. The shoes that are retros now were once the newest thing. So how do you create a new classic if people aren't interested? That's what worries me...

Is there any new product that you think will go down as classic?

The last one was probably the Presto. That was a great shoe. there's been a lot of over-techy stuff so it's a bit tricky. The Mayfly shoes, I don't think they'll be a classic but they're interesting, crazy colours. It's a good story.

What about the Shox? They seemed to have finally kicked in America, how about London?

They have been quite big here. It's funny, you have a couple of different types of customers. You have sneaker heads, quite a small group. You have a younger group who are into retro and rare stuff and following a story, particularly the Asian crew who come in from HK and Japan. Then you've got the old football crew who favour adidas, the casuals who are very loyal. Then you've got the averages who see the Reebok travel trainer and love it, in a way they're the most honest because they buy what they like. Then you've got street kids who are into the urban look, they wear Shox, but the AF1 and the Dunk have blown up, due I think to watching rap videos. Obviously we don't have the basketball thing in England but Nike have become quite big on that Council Estate kinda vibe.

Have they offered you a collab shoe?

Yes. We've got a Foot Patrol shoe, you know like the Berlin Vandal, a limited number of pairs. 24 maybe...

Any hint as to what that might be?

It's the Epic. It's more of a sneakerhead kinda shoe. We've tried to tie the design and colours of the shop into the shoe. There's some nice details in there. We are just trying to work out how to distribute them, I was thinking I might actually do a raffle. I know Undefeated did something similar. I would prefer people got it to wear... The only other collaboration I've been involved in is the Stussy one cause I have been involved in the colours for the past 3 shoes.

You strike me as someone who likes to wear their shoes. Does it amaze you that people just ice all this stuff to retain its value?

I understand it but for me it was always about that day when you have a pair of shoes in a different colour or whatever and you walk that little bit taller down the street, you know. I'm 36 now but I spent a lot of time in NY from 1989 and at that point you could get different shoes in different areas so there was always something special. When I came back people would be like WOW! I have a lot of shoes and I wear them. Simple. I never really thought about collecting as such, I mean I've worn out a lotta great stuff that is now worth a fortune.

Actually, it only became a business in 1989 when I was cutting hair, I was into hip-hop and it was always about fresh sneakers and a bloke opposite me asked me to work for him as a buyer and at that time the old school thing hadn't been exploited. There were no reissues, no Clydes, no Superstars, so anyway we went to NY and bought tons of it dirt cheap so that's how it became a business. I was a bit naive I suppose, I was just into it.

Did it spoil your enjoyment of the shoes?

Yeah it did, first time around... I was younger, I was much more inflexible, some of the people buying it pissed me off, I thought 'fuck this', but you get a bit looser as you get older and things have changed now. I enjoy it, I like it, I still do.

That's good to hear. Do you feel protective of the culture?

In a way I do, I suppose. The biggest shame for me is that I really wanted the people who wanted this stuff to be able to just walk into our store and buy it for a good price. I could really jack this stuff and put it on eBay but I will never do that because I was always that kid who dreamed about sneakers. I can make enough money on a regular mark up. And I hate resellers. We have a limit of one person per shoe, but you can't stop it. We thought about doing a membership thing with a database and a card and a preview, maybe that's worth it, I don't know.

There's no going back, it is what it is. We have had some crazy situations in the past, with the HTMs, it was nuts. We literally saw them go up on eBay that afternoon after we had sold them, they even showed our bag on the picture. It's unfortunate, because you start to mistrust everyone. I mean you're trying to sell shoes but then you're trying not to sell them. It's madness.

Amen to that! Thanks for your time Fraser...

SPORTS & THINGS

During the first couple of weeks of October 1999, I was fortunate enough to experience something that may make certain others green with envy. Whilst on holiday in New York I was granted access along with another pal to scour the shelves and stockroom of one of the most prolific record emporiums in the world before it opened for trade, the Sound Library on Avenue A in Manhattan. If you have a passion for collecting vinyl then you'll know this shop, period!

My buddy and I had been hangin' out with another friend who knew one of the owners and he generously offered to give us a tour. He asked us if we'd like to have a snoop round before the shop opened and we headed back to our hometown of London the following day. We naturally jumped at the chance.

The memories of trawling through the racks that day are still clear in my mind as is the fragrance of the last few licks of paint that were being applied around us. The excitement I get when thinking back to the redolent air in that basement as we hot-stepped down the stairs is also there. The vinyl was racked sky high. Bulk quantities of rarities that I still haven't seen to this day were fastidiously propped against walls, and flicking through the overflowing crates of classics that were screaming out to be bought was almost too much to withstand. The experience was a humbling one, and the same emotions came back to me recently when I experienced a find of a similar magnitude.

If you've seen the Doug Pray documentary 'Scratch', you may recall the scenes of DJ Shadow gaining ingression to yet another basement of dreams. One of the most magical pieces of the film focuses on the notoriously camera-shy Shadow surrounded by mountains of vinyl relics. Shadow had been a regular at this store in California, just as I had been a returning customer at a local sports store in Streatham, South London called **Sports & Things**. Just as it was customary for the Sacramento store clerks to [taunt and] inform the world-famous producer of the gems tucked away in their basement, the store owners in London had often teased me and referred to a similar hoard of sneakers: a mass of stock that they had been selling off at irregular intervals over the few years I'd been a customer and further back.

During the summer of 2001, myself and a pal were fortunate enough to be granted access to the stockrooms. Yep, that's plural. At that time, one small storage area had nothing but a desk, a redundant old computer and hundreds and hundreds of pairs of original Stan Smiths. They were strewn all over the floor and piled to the ceiling [this room is now FULL of OG Neon Yellow and Cool Grey Air Max '95, some samples even in leather]. We had a brief, excitable, yet fanatical, look around the other two huge stockrooms. One was full of working stock [shoes and clothing actually for sale] and another basement floor that wasn't particularly easy to access was entirely dedicated to boxes of dead-stock.

Bringing things up-to-date, after a long hiatus of non-attendance, and discovering that the owners ['Boss' and his son, 'Junior Boss', no joke!] are now actively seeking a buyer for the business [a cool £1Million ONO], I decided that this 'Holy Grail' was something that had to be documented and, more importantly, shared with the world.

If one was to peep a collection belonging to some true sneaker pimps, say, Jeremy Howlett, Charlie Perrin, Adam Levinson, or any other notable collector from around the globe, it's a guarantee that you may come across some repetition [Damon Dash owning 60 pairs of the same re-issues he's just blagged does not maketh a collection], but not a stockpile of this size or volume of duplication on this scale.

The first time I stepped back into the basement of Sports & Things was very recently. I felt like I was being ordained into some secret priesthood, it was an intimate experience that, to be honest, set my soul on edge. The main basement floor is an old storage room that still has a biting chill about it. The ceilings are high and the boxes loftily stacked within wooden shelving, one on top of each other as well as being racked three deep in places.

There is very little order to the layout of the boxes, although a random pick will more than likely expose jewels at each turn. A few brands hold court in their own nooks and crannies. adidas, quite a few Reebok [Omni Zone 4 in White, Black and Mulberry being a highlight] and Puma struggle for space and there's even a women's shoe rack full of pastel colours, aerobics inlay cards and cute sizes.

A second repository uncovers a room full of neglected but unforgotten brands: Avia, Brooks, LA Gear, Kangaroos and British Knights line the shelves. Japanese issues of Reebok Fury 'Jackie Chan' editions take up a whole section, Ewing Concept Hi's, 33s and Guards are just sitting around waiting to be worn. All the Ewing's boxes still contain the plastic lace guards, stickers, product info tags and the famous basketball keyring [was it just me, or did we all get slightly over-excited about the stickers as kids?]. Some K-Swiss Classics in White and Burgundy from before the marketing 'brandwagon' rolled out a year or so ago, and the odd pair of Saucony for the running connoisseur are also to be found.

As a collector and a fan, the enormity of this kind of unchartered territory is very difficult to stomach. In a passionate yet predatory fashion I found myself grabbing at boxes, grasping inside them to expose not only the kicks, but original monogrammed tissue paper lining, promotional product information inlay cards [Jordan Flight Club membership anyone?] and more colourways of anatomical supports than you could shake a shoe horn at.

After speaking with and inviting a carefully chosen number of other trainer nuts to the store, I firmly believe that there isn't another cache of this size in the UK or maybe even Europe. Who knows, this could be a complete one-off world wide!

As I brush the dust off a box with 'Clockwork Orange' coloured Air Trainer 3 SCs inside there's a cry from across the 'Bay of Broken Dreams' [actually it's the bay containing all the Air Max]. Behind the shelves I hear my mate Rixx yelping in elation, 'Holy Fuck, look at these Jordans!' It seems he's uncovered a box of original Air Jordan Xs with the MVP details on the sole, in Carolina Blue. Then he shows me a box of baby sizes and kids' Jordan 1s but my immediate broodiness is overwhelming. Then another whoop and more expletives as he discovers a box full of OG IIIs in white and black, 'Jeeesus, there's more Jordan's here!'

As I return to where I'd been dusting off the top layer of a stack of Huarache Internationals, some Puma boxes catch my peripheral vision. I look with trepidation at the boxes, but sadly I find few styles of note. Then it hits me, a box that says Basket Leather. As someone that has a penchant for and owns a number of Baskets, Super Baskets and Clydes in several colours, I virtually soil myself as I lift the lid. At first it's the grid-pattern gum sole, then my eyes light up as I discover the all leather White on White Puma Baskets with White laces and a perforated flash. Perfection.

At one stage I thought to myself, 'Wait a minute, I haven't spotted any Uptowns.' Within seconds I've peeked behind a bank of Mowabb's [in that recycled box] and there they are: a pristine pair of Canvas White Air Force Ones with Black trim. This is heaven. I locate a wall of really old Chuck Taylors too, sadly some of these have seen better days – remember kids, these are perishable goods, glue doesn't stick forever!

At virtually every turn is something of note, Nike Air Accelerator in Night Purple and Black [an exquisite shoe for balling, I remember, I had 'em first time round], a selection of Hi-Top Fila FX100 in a variety of colours as well as several colours of Air Bounds. Black and Orange Air Max BWs, a few women's Pegasus and Air Mad Max with Purple trim hold our collective attention span for just long enough until another unearthing occurs, some OG Air Raids. "The straps!" Rixx hollers again. "This is too much!!"

I stumble upon some Air Flite Mids in Lakers colours from '91 [worn originally by Cedric Ceballos], then in Navy and Red I find the same design in a High. There's a small stash of 'Big Window' designs from the late Eighties and early Nineties; I uncover a pile of unblemished and almost faultless White and Fluoro trimmed Duellist PR, several Infrastructure Plus and Air Huaraches in a plethora of colours and models as well as one solitary OG pair of Air 180s [That were delicately handled like a new born baby].

Black Magnum Force, Air Escape in Black or Green Leather, Agassi's, Air Uptempo, Nike Baby Sport and literally hundreds more designs have been in this basement since they were purchased not long after the store opened in 1991. Either that or they were picked up at bankruptcy auctions across the US during the mid to late Eighties. All the stock along the way being purchased from a reputable source each time, no variants on these shelves!!!

The staff of this popular local footwear specialist are possibly some of the most obliging and knowledgeable in the game right now. If there's a shoe they don't know, they'll dig hard for it, they may take a while [there are thousands of boxes here remember], but they'll check for it. As they admit themselves, it may take a while cos they still use a number of paper files with dog-eared pages for inventory [this is true school], but every single pair is listed, so hope is kept alive. If they do unearth one of the gems you might have in mind, it's a guarantee you'll pay a fair price for 'em, they have been on ice for some years remember.

The location of this remarkable family-run shop is in a gritty area of South London, a sleepy parochial neighbourhood at times, but certainly a far cry from the pretentious re-issue-wearing and no history-having wanna-bes or the hustle and tussle of the central business district.

There may be a tad bit of mean-muggin' goin' on, but it's expected round these parts. The majority of kids that shop here are from Brixton and Streatham [areas of some social and economic deprivation], with some travelling from further afield for this truly original retail experience. The staff say they used to get the Japanese kids coming in every few months, but they've found something else to spend their money on. The amount of times people have queued at this store overnight for a 'quickstrike' you could count on no fingers!

The guys here do things at their own pace, they rush for no man. 'Junior' is bright, friendly, sharp and savvy for a 21 year old. Despite his tender years, the store owner's 'progressive youngster' son could school more than most on his specialised subject. Between my pals and Junior, I didn't know whether I was in the basement of a sports store, on the boundary line of a 'Knicks' game or a fly on the wall at a marketing meeting in Oregon circa 1990!!

SPORTS & THINGS

"AS SOMEONE THAT HAS A PENCHANT FOR, AND OWNS A NUMBER OF PUMA BASKETS, SUPER BASKETS AND CLYDES IN SEVERAL COLOURS, I VIRTUALLY SOIL MYSELF AS I LIFT THE LID..."

The 'Boss' is an erudite old boy, he's a mindful sneaker magnate, a reserved, yet quick-witted gentleman that doesn't need to move too fast. He has other people do that for him, namely his comedic younger brother, also staff at S&T. As well as being aware of turning trends, Boss still makes regular trips abroad and at his age, [he ain't no whipper-snapper, more of an elder statesman of sneaks] that's quite an accomplishment.

Far too often, the fashionable [and let's face it, a lot of the activity in the world of re-moulds over the last five years originates from the fashion glitterati's passing interest] independent boutique owners are unaware of the 'vintage/deadstock' game cos they're more concerned about where their next over-priced rent check payment is coming from. Sports & Things is no more interested in eBay shenanigans, launch parties, quickstrikes, free bars, finger food and shoes produced specifically for the consumer to part with their hard-earned fold, as you are in chewing on your own feet!

If you do have any enquiries for the guys, don't expect a reply within 5 minutes, or even 5 days, they like to take their time and do things the old-fashioned way. There really is no preset price structure for a lot of these items so you need to know your shit before you go asking what they're gonna charge you. The lease on the property is up for review in 2011, so that's how long you got to save up and just get yer asses down there.

Alternatively, get your negotiation hat on and make Junior a serious offer he just can't refuse at www.sportsandthings.co.uk. Or phone them on 0208 6773810. The fax number is 0208 696 9751.

CRAIG LECKIE
[craig@oldboyentertainment.com]

With many thanks to Boss, Junior, Brad Farrant, Rixx Firth and Mr. Rek-Shop ['The Raiders of the Lost Ark'], without whom none of this would have been possible.

VIVA LA SNEAKA!

VIVA LA SNEAKA!

VIVA LA SNEAKA!

PARIS

Wine, Women and Sneakers!

Well, here we are in Paris, where everyone and everything is beautiful and just a little bit gay! Sneakers are not as big here as you might think, after all, Parisians still like to dress up fancy style, even in summer. But we did manage to find all the best stores for your convenience. Be warned though - prices are pretty steep here, with the best shoes around the 120-180 euro mark. Fortunately we were in town at the end of June which is SALE time - everything was half-price! And that's better than a poke in the eye with a baguette!

CENTRAL

For the purposes of our tour, we will begin at the superchic **Colette** store. Colette certainly isn't a sneaker store per se but they do have exclusives from time to time like the Kitsune New Balance and Nike also designed an awesome window display of the Futura/Armstrong project during the Tour de France. In any case, try getting in and out of **Colette** without buying something from their book collection - easier said than done. Colette sell Sneaker Freaker and it's also where we had the launch for issue 6 so we love them longtime! They also have a hand-picked line-up of electronics, high-end fashion, toys, gadgets and real cool stuff. Incredible store and a good enough reason alone to visit Paris.

From here we walk further up the street to **Starcow**, where you may meet Fred, a very laidback and amiable Parisian. Starcow is a super friendly shop stocking all sorts of stuff: toys, kicks, tees and modern accoutrements. From there it's only a block or two to the weirdest building in central Paris, Les Halles. Basically it is a massively grotesque, semi-underground mall (it certainly sticks out like dogs nuts in Paris) which is packed with kids just hanging out being delinquents. Underneath, there's 4 or 5 floors of clothing and other crap you don't need but there is a great electronics shop down here. Perfect if you need mini-cassettes, headphones or stuff like that which can be hard to find in Paris.

In the immediate vicinity of Les Halles you'll find a massive **Footlocker**, plus **Courir**, **Athlete's Foot** and all sorts of crummy touristy sneaker shops. They don't seem to have Nike accounts but they all have the same proddy which will make you giddy. There's so many you'll start to go nuts after a while.

I did find one store out of all these lookalikes that had a sweet selection of vintage and parallel import stuff called (would you believe) **Hip-Hop Neo-Shop**, it's on Saint-Denis which is full of hookers and porno stores a little further along. The store is full of hideous XXXL throwbacks but don't be put off, there's a sneaker selection at the back that is worth finding.

On the north side of Les Halles is the well known and highly regarded **Opium Crew**. They only sell Nike so don't go in asking for adidas or NB - they ain't got it! Opium is *the* destination for all your quickstrike needs, and they have a great selection of Huaraches, 180s, Air Max, Air Force et al. Opium is also the home for an amazing collection of vintage sneakers - all Nike again. See our interview for more pics of this incredible collection. When we were there they had a brilliant series of Air Trainers on show.

COLETTE

adidas	148 rue de Rivoli :: 01 58 62 51 60
ADN Snkr Lab	27 rue de la Ferronnerie :: 01 42 33 19 96
Aimecube	7 rue Vauvilliers :: 01 40 26 55 83
Colette	213 rue Saint-Honoré :: www.colette.fr
Courir	www.courir.fr
Decathlon	www.decathlon.com
Made in Sport	33 rue Quincampoix :: 01 44 61 80 41
Neo Shop	133 rue de Saint-Denis :: 01 42 36 71 32
Puma	22 Boulevard Sébastopol :: www.puma.com
Onitsuka	22 rue de Halles :: 01 55 35 30 10
Opium	9 rue Du Cygne :: 01 42 33 55 83
Ozone	52 rue du Roi de Sicile :: 01 42 78 74 38
Quarterback	21 rue Vieille du Temple :: 01 40 29 02 30
Shenkine	5 rue du Renard :: 01 48 87 11 67
Sneaker Fashion	115 Faubourg St Antoine :: 01 43 47 06 56
Sneakers Gallery	4 rue de la Ferronnerie :: 01 42 33 14 21
Starcow	68 rue St Honoré :: 01 42 21 07 51
Street Machine	6 rue Bailleul :: 01 47 03 64 64
The Tube	2 rue de la Ferronnerie :: 01 40 39 99 00

STREET MACHINE

Onitsuka Tiger

SPORT ☆ USA

NEO - SHOP

SHOP

Ozone

PUMA

OZONE

On the south side of Les Halles is **ADN Snkr lab**. There's no signage and it looks like a blacked-out sex shop and that's just the way Thomas and Marc like it! ADN is dark, mysterious, seductive and a little confronting. Basically it is a long black corridor with black walls, a black floor and a black ceiling and a selection of quality kicks bottled in jars. They also have an incredible historic stone vault downstairs which the lads plan to turn into an exhibition space and sneaker laboratory which will be grouse when it is completed. See our interview for more info on ADN.

Walk out of ADN and you have sneakers on both sides. On the left, you have the **Tiger** store. They have some nice Onitsuka kicks and a sleek range of apparel. To the right is **Sneakers Gallery** and **The Tube**, both totally commercial, but you'll want to take a look because you love sneakers right? I might point out that the dude with the frizzy hair in The Tube is a major knobhead. Best bet is to heckle him as you walk past. Pity the FOOL!

Somewhere between Starcow and ADN are a few smaller stores which are worth a squizz. We found a really cute store called **Aimecube** with quite a few vintage kicks (Jordans, adidas and Nike running) mostly in small sizes. Strangely, the store was wide open but the owner was not around - we could have racked the lot but we were with Thomas from ADN and he told us not to! A stone's throw from here is the skate store **Street Machine**. A great range of decks, clothing and skate kicks. And they were friendly as well... amazing for a skate shop. This would be your best spot for Nike SB.

The big brands have a retail presence in Paris as well. You'll find a **Puma** and **adidas** store in the same vicinity as **Made in Sport** and **Sports USA**. There are no major surprises in any of these stores but you'll want to go all the same.

THOMAS G

Street Machine

J'AIME MON QUARTIER

JE RAMASSE

RÈGLEMENT SANITAIRE DÉPARTEMENTAL ART. 99-2
INFRACTION PUNIE PAR UNE AMENDE
POUVANT ATTEINDRE 3000F (457€)

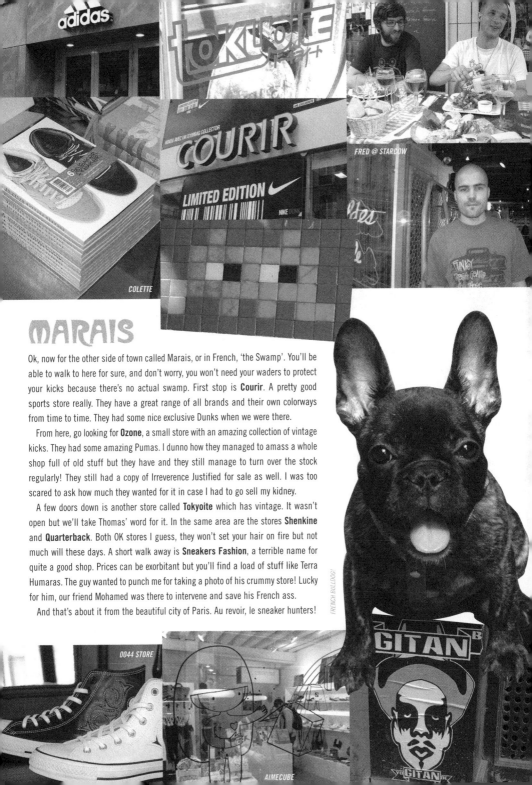

COLETTE

COURIR
LIMITED EDITION

FRED @ STARCOW

MARAIS

Ok, now for the other side of town called Marais, or in French, 'the Swamp'. You'll be able to walk to here for sure, and don't worry, you won't need your waders to protect your kicks because there's no actual swamp. First stop is **Courir**. A pretty good sports store really. They have a great range of all brands and their own colorways from time to time. They had some nice exclusive Dunks when we were there.

From here, go looking for **Ozone**, a small store with an amazing collection of vintage kicks. They had some amazing Pumas. I dunno how they managed to amass a whole shop full of old stuff but they have and they still manage to turn over the stock regularly! They still had a copy of Irreverence Justified for sale as well. I was too scared to ask how much they wanted for it in case I had to go sell my kidney.

A few doors down is another store called **Tokyoite** which has vintage. It wasn't open but we'll take Thomas' word for it. In the same area are the stores **Shenkine** and **Quarterback**. Both OK stores I guess, they won't set your hair on fire but not much will these days. A short walk away is **Sneakers Fashion**, a terrible name for quite a good shop. Prices can be exorbitant but you'll find a load of stuff like Terra Humaras. The guy wanted to punch me for taking a photo of his crummy store! Lucky for him, our friend Mohamed was there to intervene and save his French ass.

And that's about it from the beautiful city of Paris. Au revoir, le sneaker hunters!

FRENCH BULLDOG!

0044 STORE

GITAN

AIMECUBE

Here's some happy snaps from the launch of Snkr Frkr 6 in Paris at the Colette store! Special thanks to Sarah, Nadaje and Linlee at Colette and Thomas G and Marc from ADN for all their help and a great lunch. An incredible effort also from Philipe at +41 who not only flew in from Switzerland - he also brought his insane chocolate Vandal sneaker along!

Big shouts to everyone we met in Paris... Nails, Josh, Pascale, Opium Crew, Guillame at Clark Mag, Julian, Vincent, Nike iD, Daniel, Mohammed & Charles from sneakers.fr. We drank all the Tiger Beer and we had a bloody bewdy of a week in Francais. Vive le croissant!

Bonjour! When in Paris we like to do what Parisians do - have a massive lunch with plenty of smelly cheese and a few apperitifs to wash it all down! And who better to dine with than Marc Le Blond and Thomas Giorgetti, two friendly guys behind the freshly minted ADN Sneaker Lab. Situated in the heart of the popular Les Halles district, ADN is a refreshing oasis in the Parisian sneaker scene. As you will read, Thomas and Marc sure like to have fun, but they know what time it is. Bon appetit!

So Thomas, how's Paris these days?

T: Ah, we are in Summer and the weather is so nice. All the ladies...

All the ladies...

T: Yeah.

Ahem, but we're not here to talk about the ladies.

T: I was sure this was an interview about the ladies in Paris. [laughs]

So, amongst other things you do the ADN store. Tell us about how long it's been going and what your concept for the store is.

T: Hmm, it's a kind of a quick story, because we start working all together maybe six months ago now — at the beginning of 2005. Marc is a journalist and doing some reporting for Tyler magazine.

M: Then we met a guy called Sam. We were talking about some Japanese stuff, some other things. And we were talking about the idea of a black boutique or a black store. So then he checked out Tyler. 'I like the stuff you do with this,' he said.

T: At the same time as Marc was working with Sam, I was in touch with Nike who called me and said a guy wants to open a shop that's a little bit more high-end. He's a guy more into the mainstream sneakers culture, but he's got dope knowledge. He's working in the sneakers shops since he was fifteen years old, so he knows the business, he knows how it's done.

And downstairs you have this amazing crypt, or tomb. I don't know, it's hard to explain, but it's a beautiful temperature on a hot day. What are your plans for down here?

M: We're doing some kind of an office showroom and we'll have a two-level downstairs. We want to do a gallery and maybe some street art, some graffiti things, some painting and stuff. Maybe do some exhibitions. That's what we've planned for the next few months.

T: I think we'll do launches for sneaker culture. So, here is a place where you can have a dialogue and a nice time talking about sneakers as we can talk about wine or cars, you know what I mean? We'll go down and have a coffee. You want a Darjeeling? Ok, then go for a Darjeeling. If you want an au lait, then go for an au lait.

M: Go for au lait then.

I was a little surprised that in a city the size of Paris there's only really such a small number of sneaker stores...

M: You've got Colette. Opium is more focused on Nike, more into historical stuff, but they have a really good edge, you know? At ADN we're more about testing the new stuff. In my opinion, the object is to invent something new with the same kind of spirit as the Footpatrol, or Union, and all the different shops who make the craze of the sneakers. That's what we wanted, you know? Go back to the core of the thing.

T: I think it's a nice evolution and we're here to make some crossover because now the look is part of the fashion industry. It is about using a kind of street knowledge, and all the sneaker knowledge, and actually using it into the fashion. Not so establishment, you know what I mean?

Oui! Variety is the spice of life?

T: Yeah, it's against the rules, you know? The designers who want something new, they like the way of sneakers, but they do not like the logo type on it. They like the shape of the sneakers, they like the quality of the sneakers, but they are a little jaded about the swoosh or the trefoil or the logo in different brand, like BAPE.

Did you say BAPESTA?

T: To be honest, I like the BAPESTA. I find it very clever and smart. But when you are looking in terms of product... put your feet into a BAPESTA then put your feet into a Nike Air Force One and you will see the difference. In a BAPESTA, at one hour's span your foot is warm and hot. It's only for the trade and not for the technical part of the shoe.

The Air Force One is not a real technical shoe, it's a lo-tech actually, but the technology, the shape and the manufacturing is a little bit more interesting. After all, they're using only the Air Force One because they see you can print dollars with it, and so they print dollars with the BAPESTA. So I find that, in terms of business, those guys are very clever.

M: It is pretty wise, but in terms of authentic stuff...

How would you describe Paris in terms of the way fashion and sneakers go together? We've been here for three days and I've seen some guys in Air Force who're very influenced by American hip-hop: they're wearing XXXL Tees and Fubu and things like that...

M: Paris is very influenced by what is called the Dirty South because people like to pretend they're in New York. But if you go to New York you see that it's not the same. When you go to Les Halles you see them in the centre of Paris wearing big baggy stuff like that. They're influenced by MTV, VH1, all that kind of mass-marketing. The main influence in Paris is hip-hop, mainstream hip-hop.

T: More this season, Marc. Of course, some people will focus on the Crunk kind of style. The worst is the R&B stuff. It's too borderline.

Commercial.

T: More into Justin Timberlake, or maybe Oosher?

Usher?

T: Usher. This is very fashionable stuff in mainstream Paris. All the kids, yeah...

M: Real cheesy, real cheesy stuff, and now it's all the fashion brands like Diesel and stuff like that. They think it's a look that's getting good. It's not, man.

T: All the guys focus on MTV, that's the main problem. Every kid now with a private channel at home with special network.

Is the Puma Mostro big here?

T: It's massive.

M: It was massive.

I haven't seen it so much here this summer.

T: The Easy Rider from Puma was a real hit with the cammo and all the retro colourways five or six years ago. It was hard to find some retro running shoes in those days. In 2000, not a lot of sneakers looked like the Nike Metro. It was very good outside of the country, not right here. That was the beginning of a new fashion.

Me, I was into this kind of fashion for a long time. I was looking for all those sneakers from Nike and Converse from the mid '80s. Then, in 2000, it was the talk of the high-end guys in the fashion world. Now mainstream stores are using vintage shades and graphics. Back in the day, you had to go to a flea market to find these kinds of products. It was a real quest, you know? It was a quest.

M: Yeah. People like Thomas and me, we were freaks at the time. And even now, all the sneaker freaks, the sneaker community, we are little. We used to meet on a Thursday night here with some friends with something like, in the max, we are 10 to 15. And when you go to parties and stuff, you see always the same people, you know? We want

to educate the people that you can look good in a good jean, a good clean jean – like, vintage stock, but with no marks on it – you know? Always like, you want to get some rust on your jeans?

T: It's a more interesting thing when you do it yourself.

M: 160 Euros, man! 160 Euros, that's 180 bucks. 180 bucks for Diesel fucked up jeans. How crazy it sounds.

They make them all new, then they spend a lot of money to pay someone to make them look old.

M: But the movement has got to keep moving, man. It's 2005, I think it's a good year. You've seen that we've opened.

When did you launch here?

M: We launched here on the 12th of May. And there was, like, 200 people outside, man. It was amazing.

T: Marc does not lie about it. [laughs]

M: We had an open bar and stuff. All these alcoholic mixtures.

T: We put some money on the table to get a real party. People came and said, 'Oh, it's a good place. Come, come, it's free.' And everybody enjoyed. Actually, at this time, I still receive some congratulations and thanks for the party from outside of the country. People come from London, the guys from Recon in London came to be here. And all the press from Paris and all the French magazines who are into lifestyle or fashion stuff were there.

M: It was a good mix. Like Thomas was saying, there were people from the press and people from the corporate. Big people from Nike and from adidas. And there was the sneaker freaks. And the people from

MARC

THOMAS

the streets. And the people who don't give a fuck about sneakers and were just curious: 'Ah, what's that? It's a black thing, you know? A black shop.' That's what I find interesting: this melting of people.

T: That's our main point, to make something where all the kinds of people who consume sneakers: high-end fashion guys, music… where all the different kinds of people come together. We are very close to the hip-hop and the street cats for sure, but if you want to have an evolution you have to be open. And you have to show your knowledge and bring that knowledge back to other people.

What's the reaction been to painting the shop black?

M: Darth Vader. Darth Vader shop.

Have people found it a little intimidating?

T: Yes.

M: Yes, quite disturbing. Some people will stare and sometimes, when I keep the door closed, some people will walk in and are like, 'Is this a sex shop?' [laughs]

M: It's funny, you know, but that's cool.

I think every teenager goes through a period where they'd like to paint their bedroom black as well. But, of course, they're never allowed to do it.

T: Lots of kids into the…

M: Revenge! Revenge!

T: …Black Sabbath and stuff want to paint his room black. No, I find the black on black is… I find it very smart and somehow addictive.

M: It gives a focus to the product. It's a classic, you know? I think black is a very good thing.

What other scenes are there in Paris? I've noticed a lot of flat-shoes, people seem quite influenced by soccer boot style.

T: We do the fashion stuff, as I told you. Now there is the trend that is more like a mix between Paris and Milan. Here, when you're more trendy, you go Italian. I think it's a variant from the old Gucci and Chanel shoes and stuff like that, you know? And people want to get trendy and get some flat shoes, because in France it wasn't trendy when you have a pair of sneakers to go out clubbing.

You couldn't get in wearing kicks?

M: You couldn't get in. Now it's very different, because now sneakers are getting trendy and stuff. It's more of a suburb kind of thing. In the suburbs it's trendiest to be with the Diesel jean with t-shirts two sizes too small, that kind of trend you know? It's kind of a cliché.

T: It's a European style because, in Europe, our main sport is football. So, at this point, people are looking for the jersey soccer and they are looking for some shoes which look like soccer boots. That's why you are looking in the street and you have some borderline sneakers. You don't know if it's for boxing or street soccer, and those people right here love that because, as Marc told you, they like the specific shoe for a sport like boxing or martial arts. Back in the '70s in France, a lot of the people were mixed between two different movements. There was those that walk with the Americana who were into the heavy metal and stuff. And then there were those people who were street cats or listen to some funk music (because the funk was so amaze right here) were more into the Stan Smith or the Tobacco.

Which shoe is that?

T: Tobacco.

Yeah. How do you spell that?

[Thomas shows the shoe]

Oh, this one. Tobacco! I'm not familiar with this one. adidas has so many shoes that are more or less kind of the same.

T: Keep in your mind, Stan Smith was for the street cat listening to funk music and living in the suburbs, and Americana was for the white boy with the long hair listening to heavy metal or punk stuff for adidas. Nike was not available right here. adidas was the main label in terms of sneakers. Nike had just arrived in the middle of the '80s.

How about the '90s?

T: I know people who came back from New York or a different country outside of France, with some Jordans in '90, '91 or '92. You were obliged to watch your back then because they were a kind of Holy Grail for those cheap cats, a very, very Holy Grail.

M: In the '90s in Paris people would come to you and say, 'What's your size?' And you might say, 'Yeah, my size is 8.' And if he was 8 he'd take yours, and you'd go home in your socks.

Parisians are still quite formal, aren't they?

M: Yeah, but... I don't know for Thomas, but when I was young I wore some Wallabies Clarks in the '90s. And people would stare at me in the street and say, 'Man, why are you going out in your slippers?'

[laughs]

T: People prefer to follow the line than cross the line. That's it! You can cross the line. If you want to have a red hat and a green shoe: do it! You don't care, it's your own personality. And if other people do not like you, you do not like them. That's it! Everybody knows you can't love everyone. Follow your way. Follow your word. Your friend: follow your word. Your family: follow your way. Your work: follow your word. Your personal evolution: follow your way.

In Paris, no-one knows why they are wearing Air Force One. The Air Force One comes from Harlem, and Jay-Z was the main ambassador for the Air Force One, it's the Jay-Z touch. But here, nobody knows. Nobody knows. Nobody knows the Air Force One is called Uptown because it comes from Harlem. Here, nobody knows that. They prefer to wear the shoe that's baby blue with a little bit of pink and a thing under your hat and that's it!

What's your Holy Grail now?

T: My Holy Grail? What I'm looking for?

What is the shoe you want?

T: I'm looking for the Pythons from Nike from '87. It's like an AJII in the shape and this shoe is using the snakeskin. I find the AJII, for me, was like a revolution in terms of design and marketing. No swoosh.

Mark?

M: For myself they are the Air Tech Challenge. The black and hot pink and grey one with the shading.

Do you think there's too much choice now, too many sneakers? All the shops in Paris are on sale and they all seem to have the same shoes....

T: I find it's too much, actually. Go inside the mind of the consumer who is not a sneaker addict or someone who particularly loves sneakers. Go in a shop and look at the display and you have so much information that you can't understand any choice. You can't understand: 'Why this one?' Now we put some product on the display and that's it. Maybe it's one of the bad points of the market because, when you are looking around the sales in Paris - when you are looking at the Foot Locker - some prices are very less, so less, so less.

50% off.

T: Yeah. It starts at 50%. I think that's a big problem. Foot Locker was running some radio spots to tell the people they are on sale. I think it's the beginning of something. It's a big problem worldwide. We are living on the last year and I'm sure the next is a conclusion of our period. Should be no good in one or two years.

In this area there's Sneaker Gallery across the road, ASICS is around the corner, quite reasonable shops, but also around here are all these touristy sneaker shops. How hard is it for you to run your shop and get the product you want for your customer?

T: We'll keep our main idea about sneaker culture and try to develop our interest, our shop, our love, with our knowledge. We've got the knowledge about sneakers, we can tell a story. It's interesting when you can tell a story about a sneaker: about the designer, about the choice of colour, about it's development. I don't want to be in the mainstream society, I don't want to be like anyone. I don't want to have a shop like everyone.

So, have you got any special plans for ADN shoes?

T: Actually we have appointments with some different brands. And maybe we will receive a special make-up from Nike with a Nike iD. They will run for us 10 models in our colourways. And they will make a special set with second laces and sneakers inside with a special box with Nike iD. We have lots of calls with them. And after, we will get in touch with Puma. That's the only thing I can tell you right now.

Next stop is Opium! The Crew have been running for a while, but they've been friends forever and with a solid education in the street, they know their sneakers back to front. They only sell what they love which means one brand only - NIKE! And they have a collection of vintage that would make your eyes water - OG Olympic 180s, Escape Series, all sorts of Jordans, tonnes of runners, heaps of Air Trainers, Air Max - you name it and they just might have it! Plus they got all the new school stuff covered as well. Time to smoke it up with the Opium Crew…

So, tell me about the Opium crew. Who's in the crew?
The crew is us three guys, Yace, Mounir and myself who all used to make graffiti and tags together here in Paris.

Have you guys been friends for a long time?
Yeah, maybe twenty years.

When did you open the shop?
We opened the shop in 2000.

You've always been in this spot?
Yeah.

How's Paris these days? Would you say it's happening place for sneakers?
Now it's starting to be a very, very happening place. A lot of people are starting to collect sneakers around here now.

You guys only sell Nike. Is that because you only like Nike?
Yeah. We like only Nike so we sell only Nike.

When you started off tagging and doing graff, what shoes were you wearing?
Windrunners.

Safaris as well?
Yeah. Some limited edition Windrunners and Jordan IV.

One of the other features of your store is this amazing collection of vintage shoes you have in your vault. I didn't know when to stop. Is this your personal collection?
Yeah, this is our personal collection. We started in 1988 when we were buying sneakers for graffiti or tag. We particularly like the limited editions with the colour on the leather, very special.

You've got a great collection of the vintage Air Trainers. Have you had all this since you were kids?
No, no, no. When we were kids we didn't have a lot of money so we had to make trades, or some kind of business, to buy the shoes. We bought a lot of these when we were older, you know? So, the collection starts in '88, but I think it's not finished yet.

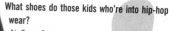

Of course. Same for me, I'm still buying shoes that I remember from when I was a kid. There was no way you could convince your mum to buy five pairs of shoes at the same time. **What's your favourite of all the vintage shoes that you own?**
Personally, my favourite shoe is the Jordan '89 in White/Military Blue.

I saw you had a pair of Jordan I as a low.
Yeah.

That's a pretty rare shoe.
Yeah, yeah. Very nice and hard to find.

I saw a pair for $9000us.
I think so, yes. But I think it's not the same colour. Theirs is metallic blue.

Maybe you have a very valuable shoe there...
I think so.

...If you wanted to sell it.
We don't sell our collection.

Otherwise you don't collect. Have you guys done special make-ups with Nike?
Maybe we'll do a special make-up next year. I think it's a very good make-up, but it's a bit secret right now.

This is for iD?
Yeah.

Which shoe did you do?
Nike 180 Runner.

Sounds great. Tell me, what sneakers are kids mainly into in Paris. What's the hot shoe right now?
I think, for the kids, SB shoes are very popular. Some limited edition shoes, co-brandings with artists, these kind of shoes make young guys crazy in Paris.

So where can you buy Dunk SBs in Paris?
When the SB started in Paris only our shop and another shop were selling it. Now the politic has changed and every skate shop in Paris has them. The SB is a very popular shoe in Paris right now. So, except for special co-brandings with artsits and the like, we've stopped taking SBs.

Hip-hop is very big here, from what I can see, with the kids.
Yeah, very big.

What shoes do those kids who're into hip-hop wear?
Air Force One.

Anything else?
Nothing else.

What other scenes are there? I've seen a lot of low profile, very flat shoes.
That style of shoes is just a fashion.

Paris, or French society, is very formal. You often see people in a proper shirt and proper pants.
On working days it's very formal. After people finish work they wear anything they like, you know?

Do you see things changing in the sneaker scene?
It's hard now because a lot of people want to make a business with this, you know? So they find some sneakers they would like to sell at 2000 or 3000 Euro. I think this politic is not good. I've seen many people sell sneakers on eBay at very crazy prices. Personally, I don't like this system. Everyone wants this Dunk SB because Futura made it, or Zoo York, or whoever else made it, and to see one SB at $700-$800 is amazing, you know? Crazy. At the same price you can get a Jordan I original in box and, personally, I prefer to buy vintage. I think for young people they're thinking differently.

They're also quite wealthy as well if they've got that much money lying around.
Not like us when we were young guys, we didn't have $500 to spend on one shoe.

Is everything a lot more expensive in Paris since the Euro?
Yeah, yeah.

So shoes went up in price as well?
Yeah. It's very expensive to buy in Paris. I think the Euro is not a good thing for it. I think the cost of living is the same as like, maybe, in Tokyo. If you want to rent an apartment or little room it's very, very expensive. Very expensive.

But it's a beautiful place.
Yeah. We are lucky.

Okay. Anything else you want to say about Opium?
We just hope to make our best for the sneaker community in France and for the world.

Co-presented by Snkr Frkr & Provider Trainers, **THE ULTIMATE SNEAKER SWAP MEET** was held in Melbourne mid-2005. A super snazz crowd of 400 heads rocked Swanston Street and whether they came to buy, swap or just ogle the bogle, the event was rocking cuz the Tiger Beer was poppin! The meet featured stalls by some of Australia's best known collectors including Hans DC, Kickz101, Rare Air, Jazz and Mike Cola. There was a load of quality pick ups on offer including OG Jordans, a full set of Le Bron AF1, SS35, a fair bit of vintage and a series of customs from local kid Astoria who is definitely worth keeping an eye on. Look out for further Snkr Frkr endorsed Swap Meets in your area!

Here's the photos from the SF6 launch in Amsterdam. Thanks to Ivo and Remko from Endorsed and Ido from 90sqm for all their help in launching the magazine, you guys did us proud. It was worth the price of a last minute return flight from London just to see the look on Remko's face when we turned up unannounced! Lexflex was also in the house painting up a storm and Dr J posted some very sweet paintings of his favourite shoes. Shame we had to jet out in the morning with a very sore head, would have been great to see a little more of the city. Next time...

PHOTOS :: Simone

SNEAKER
FREAKER DOES

NEW

YORK

I like to keep them on ice and defrost at just at the right time...

If you have four or five then you can keep some on ice and you can wear some so you're always fresh and it confuses people when three years later you pop up and they're like 'Where the hell did you get that?' I love clean sneakers so I don't buy pair one pair, I buy two and three and four pairs so that when they get dirty I give them away and I go and get new sneakers. I always wear new sneakers all the time, rain sleet or shine, it doesn't matter.

What are those ones you've got on now?

These are European exclusives and I got 'em like the day they came out. They have never done a colorway like this in New York and these are ill, I bought 20 pairs of these when they came out!

You bought 20 pairs?

20 pairs, that's why I wear them in the rain, I don't care...

Have you got anything else in the cupboard?

FIRST THING you notice when you get to New York is how the whole damn city is dominated by one shoe - the Air Force One. I reckon one in four people are wearing them! (slight exaggeration) So anyway, I'm hanging around Broadway looking at this rare shit behind glass and I ask the manager 'Can I take photos?' and he says, 'Ask that dude over there' and so I ask and the dude says, 'Sure, my name is DJ Clark Kent, so how many pairs have you got' and I say (slightly cocky), 'Over thirty' and he mishears me and says 'Three thousand?' and I sheepishly say no, 'Nah, just thirty.' And just then the penny drops and I remember exactly what Clark Kent is famous for - his absolutely monster collection of Nike Air Force...

I have never seen a town so dominated by one shoe...

I think what makes it so dominated is the fact that they are very simple. There is nothing confusing about them, they are the easiest to wear, they are very comfortable and they can either be dressed up or dressed down.

You can't beat something when it's too perfect!

They are the most perfect, most simple, most perfect, most simple sneakers. That's why I got 1400 pairs.

1400 pairs?

I get more every day

Do Nike just send a truck round?

Nah, I hunt. I don't do what everybody else does, I don't go to Nike and try to get them to do any big favors for me, I've got people in every country that go to sneaker stores every day and tell me what is coming out.

Maybe I can get you some stuff from Australia?

I would appreciate that, we got to keep in contact.

How do they know what you are missing...

I buy anyway so even if like I have two pairs I buy three more just because it's not really about what I'm missing. Size 12 is my size and I'm buying, it doesn't matter.

What do you mean?

Sneakers wise I mean - not like tinned food or anything, just sneakers?

Oh yeah I got a couple of pairs of Air Maxes, the Air Max '87 those are another pair of my favorites. You name it, if it's ill, I got em! I go back, way back...

Have you got a big house?

Yep I got a big house and a three car garage full of sneakers, got a walk in closet full and my Mom's garage is full of my sneakers.

You can't stop can you?

Na, I don't stop and it's not because I want to have more than anybody else. I am not collecting just to have everybody on my back about it, if it's a good color I'm buying it. I buy every color AF1. If they are low top, I buy them if they are high top I'll buy em.

In general what is it with New York and AF1? Is it a Harlem thing or a Brooklyn or a Queens thing? What?????

I think it's a good lookin' nigger thing, it's not about where you from or where it started, it's that the b-ball players back in the days of the street wore AF1 when they came out so it was a New York street ball thing - it was uptown playing at (indecipherable) and if you went to b'ball camp they gave you AF1. That's what made them popular on the street, everybody wanted to dress like b-ball players. AF1s were so ill that it just couldn't stop and that's what it was, I think that's where it really came from and since they were playing uptown that's what changed the name to Uptown.

You probably have to get back in the mix, thanks for your time!

For Airs, I'll do whatever...

Without doubt, the most distinctive sneaker store in New York is the Alife Rivington Club on the Lower East Side. The doorway is totally anonymous, entry is by buzzer and the fitout is all deluxe timber, much like a Men's Club where you might go for cigars, cognac and a chat about pork-belly stocks. Alife also has a sister store in nearby Orchard St. We had a chat with the lively and entertaining owner of these fine two stores, Mr Tony Arcabascio.

What's Alife all about Tony?

We're more of a creative agency, company, whatever you want to fucking call it and these two stores are only part of what we do. We created these like faces for the company. Orchard Street is a little bit more of a roundabout of I guess who we are and Alife Rivington Club is like a segment from that. We're all down with sneakers, I think everybody around our age grew up on this shit…

Yesterday when I came in it was quiet but today there was 20 kids in there going crazy and I could smell the excitement.

I know, so it's fun to see that but I mean we really, I'll be honest, we had the other store first and Nike came in. We were basically more of a casual shoe type of store. But we started seeing the trend a couple of years ago that it was more towards the hardcore sneaker more than the casual shoe. Kids were wearing sneakers with suits, you know. Nike came by our shop and they basically wanted to use us more as like their, I guess the word they used was a 'probe' account…

Does that mean they bend you over and…

Nah, it's more like a trial shop and at that point they were trying to launch the Air Woven and we were pretty much the first store in the US to have that and we saw the craziness that went on, I mean, we couldn't believe it. There were kids waiting out, we opened up at 12

and there were kids at like 8 in the morning and that's when I got there. God knows how long they were there for and it was like a concert, you know. We were basically selling out in 15 minutes, every time we got a new colour. As soon as we saw that we knew we gotta do this, there's something that… you know, something that's gonna start up again and we opened Alife Rivington in 2001 and we've just gotten a lot of love from everybody in the area ever since.

Yeah, that's, I mean it's a big sneaker area isn't it?

Yeah, now you're seeing a lot of more specialty sneaker shops popping up, especially this year, there's been like 3 or 4 of them. When we came into the scene, we were the only one here pretty much in New York and our business hasn't really changed because of all the new shops. I guess we have a clientele that wants to actually come here for the atmosphere as much as the special shoes, you know.

It seems like some of these kids have endless supplies of money…

You know, we can't pinpoint our customers, sometimes we have limo's and shit coming from the upper east and west, we've also got people from the neighborhood, you know the guy that deals shit on the corner and then we got like celebrities like from Missy Elliot to Fat Joe, people like that, Robin Williams, you know, so it's like…

Alife, NewYork

What did Robin Williams buy? I bet he's into Rifts and Reebok!
I'm actually not sure, I know that he always comes into the other shop and I know he always comes here too coz once in a while I see him with a bag from here but I never really actually saw…

I wouldn't have pictured him as a sneakerhead.
I tell ya, he is a mad collector of everything. He goes around, from Supreme to Stussy to Alife to 360 Toys and it's crazy. I never expected any of the shit. He's a real mad customer.

I suppose everyone's kind of trying to predict when the bubble's going to pop but no-one can see it coming. Is it going to wind down or…
I don't know man. I mean I'll be honest with you, this whole retro thing, I mean it's still cool and everything but I feel like people are starting to exhaust their back history you know and…

Nike still has a ton of stuff in the vault though I guess?
Well, I mean so does adidas, they actually have an even bigger history, you know they probably have even more to grab but I think the real test is going to be to see who starts bringing out the new shits, you know. Changing up colourways, changing up leathers, changing up whatever materials, that's the easy part. The test is gonna be when it's time to move on…

How many collaborations did you do with adidas?
We did three. One pair I'm wearing right now, these are the Top Tens. We did 'em in kangaroo skin and silver leather inside and all that.

It gives you a bit of credibility doesn't it?
Yeah, I mean they're great to work with. It was like a no-brainer for us. You know, we approached them, they totally went for it and they were excited to do it and we got mad press on it. It worked out for both of us, it was an easy, stress-free experience. Puma has also given us some special stuff where they actually, if you could see in there we had a couple of hi-tops, suedes, a bunch of stuff…

Were they exclusive to you guys?
They're gonna be out to everybody soon but they gave it to us just a little bit beforehand and they stitched the Rivington ribbons inside so we got a special lot exclusive to our store. A lot of people have really been coming forward and we've been holding back, you know, just coz we wanna do it the right way. We figured if we sit around and think about it a little bit we'll figure it out, you know, but we don't wanna just jump into anything, but adidas was an easy thing to do.

New York does seem to be obsessed with the AF1, I know it's almost a cliché but I've never seen a town dominated by one shoe alone.
And Dunks, man, it's crazy. I mean, that shit's like, it's like a drug. People will come in here every other day just to see if we have anything new. We get stuff so randomly and we sometimes showcase a cool collection, like there's a lot of really avid collectors here in New York City. I'm learning a lot just by having a shop like this, you know… Just the extent that people will go to keep up with their collections. From having separate storage areas just for their sneakers so that they can keep the boxes so they can have everything kept in mint condition.

New York's probably not far behind Tokyo in terms of lack of space. Where do people put this all this shit?

That's right, that's what I'm saying, I mean everybody's got their thing. Some people come in here and they automatically don't want the boxes coz I guess it's easier and they don't have much space. They're more fanatics than collectors, coz most collectors wanna keep the boxes. These people who don't want the boxes are rare and everything but they buy mad shoes, like they'll come on a Friday and ask us to put everything in size 12 aside. They'll call before they come and it's pretty incredible.

And, what was the blackout like? You know the next question I'm going to ask... I know you got robbed.

We had a problem with that. We were probably the one store that really got hit the worst in all New York City. I think there was a couple of other stores that got hit or were attempted to get hit but not to the extent that we were. They actually had a little more time in our store because they were able to break through our landlord's door and once they were in the building they were able to come though a side door so they didn't actually break through from the street. Once they were in the building they were able to sit there and work on our big metal door and once they were in there they were out of the public eye. So they were in our store and it looked like it was still closed, you know. Once I found out it was being looted, I ran over here, we were near the other store on Orchard Street, I came over with like whoever was with me, it was one employee and his girlfriend and my girlfriend and another one of our friends...

Far out, you must have been freaking ?

We just came here, we saw everything was already wrecked and there were people outside trying to get in while we were here and, I mean that's how the whole shit went down, we ended up getting into fights with all these kids... yeah, local kids but you couldn't really tell, I mean everything was pitch black, all you saw was shadows and I mean pretty much, long story short, my girlfriend ended up getting 16 staples in her head, one of my boys ended up getting a bottle smashed across his face and a whole bunch of stitches on his face and lacerations and we had problems with the police, they didn't want to help us. It was just a nightmare man. We are just trying to get over it, forget about it and move on. Business as usual, you know.

It's business but it's also your heart and soul isn't it?

It just sucks because I've always got that feeling, especially when you walk around the neighborhood, you're looking at everybody's fucking feet wondering if those are your kicks or not.

I shouldn't laugh but I guess you've gotta...

I gotta laugh about it too, otherwise I'll fucking... I'll get too fucking upset, you know.

Alife, New York

What about the future, like you got anything juicy you can tell...

In Alife style you don't talk about shit, you know, so as far as juicy I'm probably not gonna give you what you want to hear, but we're definitely back in business. We're getting a lot of support from the sneaker companies, from Nike, Puma, adidas just to name the top three right now but they're sending us really great products ahead of time to help us get back on our feet. So we're gonna have a lot of product that no-one else is gonna have in the world. I can't say thank you enough to everybody, from the people that work for me to the sneaker companies, to our customers. Everybody's coming through. I've gotten calls from everybody and just as an example, Stash from Nort, he wants to donate part of his earnings you know while we were closed coz he thought that he was picking up a lot of our customers that we were losing and he was just basically offering to give us a percentage of what he was earning.

Is it hard when everyone wants something that no-one else has got? That's kind of the crux of the whole thing isn't it, I mean how do you...oh, I don't even know what my question is.

Something else that we're actually working on and you have to see, we just finished doing our whole new Spring 2004 Alife NYC line. It was Rightfoot, now we're switching it to Alife NYC. We're bringing back part of that Argyle stuff that sold out and was crazy when we first launched it, when we first started our own shoes. I don't know if you ever saw the slip-on Argyle ones that we that we got sued by Vans for. **I never heard that!**

Yeah, that was a whole big fucking fiasco...

You never hear about anyone getting sued for copyright infringement which is surprising I guess because there's so much plagiarism in the industry.

Well, you know what it is, when Vans sued us, it wasn't for the actual shoe, coz I mean a slip-on is a slip-on. They got that shit from keds, you know what I'm saying. They weren't suing us for that, they were suing us for the pattern which they were saying they had a patent on checkerboard. We were doing Argyle so I don't even see where the connection was. A long story short they were just trying to put us out of business coz they felt that there was a threat coz they saw that when we launched those Argyle slip-ons it was like a craze throughout the world, I mean, we didn't have enough pairs to sell. Then we had to stop it because of this whole legal bullshit so we were never able to capitalise on that. So now, we're not bringing that particular style back not exactly but we are bringing back the Argyle pattern but we'll make it a bit different.

Those original ones must be kind of collectors' items now...

Yeah, we have a couple of pairs left in storage but we don't know exactly what we're gonna do with them yet coz the sizing is a little bit irregular. Anyway, we are launching some really great styles coming up beginning of next year so keep definitely a lookout for that.

I will, thanks Tony, good luck with your slip-ons.

Supreme New York

How's New York these days?
New York has been pretty fun, I'm enjoying the Indian summer, it always hits hard around September/October.

How was the New York blackout?
I wasn't here for it but I heard it was chaotic, everyone was having fun in the street like it was mardi gras or something.

How did the relationship with Nike start?
We'd been doing combination shoes with different companies like DC, Vans and now we started this thing with Nike and it's been an amazing ride. Definitely been a good thing for us - and for them!

Do you get nutters who come down and don't understand the fact that they can't always get what they want?
So many kids are trying to get our sneakers in every way possible. They offer us bribes, they send a gang of other kids inside to get sneakers for them... it's insane, the scene is very strong.

What else do they do?
They always find all kind of weird ways to try to get through, like masking their voice on the phones, calling the shops like five times a day...

Really, how do they mask their voice? Do they have one of those machines they use on television to disguise witnesses?
Nah, but you can just tell it's the same person on the phone, it's pretty funny, I mean there is always a good story to get us through the day. Always.

How many did you sell through the shop?
It was only a limited edition run. We only sell them through our shops - nowhere else...

I think we've got 40 pairs in Australia so I'm not sure...
I don't know how they do it but they do it, I guess everybody got their ways...

Well anyway, it's been a massive success, you timed it perfectly.
Yeah, everything happens for a reason.

Do you know how many pairs were released? Everyone's always talking about how many it may have been - is it 500 or 2000. Do you wanna set the record straight?
We really don't let out the numbers.

Was it more than people say?
I dunno, I'll just leave it at that (laughs).

Go on! Just settle a few arguments cause we've got all the kids wondering out there...
That's our little secret!

Have you seen any of the fakes?
Yeah, definitely.

Were they close?
Close, but you could just rub it off with your thumb.

Were they painted on?
More like printed on, like a bad screenprint.

Rubbish?
Yeah.

Thought so.
Pretty funny.

What do you think about all this fake bizness?
No matter what, there is always going to be a fake something like Louis Vuitton or Burberry or Gucci.

Supreme, New York
ALEX CORPORAN

With all the craziness that you see down at the shop, do you think the sneaker thing is healthy at the moment or is it a bit over-cooked?
It looks like it is getting over-cooked but something will always jump off. Out with one thing and in with another you know, out with the old in with the new.

Can you anticipate what it will be or does it just pop up?
Right now the next big thing is our shoe, the second, which is the hi-top Dunk. Other than that, right now it's hard to project what's going on.

Who put out the anti-Dunk tees? They went round the world really quick, I was thinking it's funny how something can be super cool one second and then all of a sudden all bets are off.
I don't know.

You don't know?
I don't know (laughs).

Why did the new pictures get put up up on the Nike SB site and then taken down.
Nike just put it up on their site and we just pulled it off you know. It was too soon to put it out. I don't know, probably some kind of like a mistake or something?

You think it was a mistake...
Yeah.

You don't want to say?
Uh huh.

You don't give much away do you?
No (laughs).

Who is responsible for the actual design of the second shoe?
James Jebbia, the owner, he was responsible for putting it all together.

Well I like it. I really like the detail, the little gold bar on the new Dunk, it's grown on me. It looks better in real life.
I'll tell him.

Reaction was kind of a bit mixed do you think?
I'm not sure yet, you know...

That didn't come out right, I'm thinking of a really directional design, take the Safari for example. Sometimes the best stuff takes a while to be truly appreciated.
We just try to do something different you know...

What's next for Supreme? The new Dunk drops in October 2003???
Yeah, we have the Dunk and our fall line is what everyone is waiting for. We shut at the end of Summer for a few weeks and then we drop the new shit.

I heard you come down to Australia every year?
Yeah, yeah, I come down every year actually, I love it out there.
Sydney?
Sydney. I also went to Byron Bay actually this time around. It's always fun. You know I am going to have a photo exhibition over there as a matter of fact.

Well I'll probably see you then!
Thanks Alex.

Righto, you've finally booked your trip to Japan. If you're like me, you've probably got a few ideas of what it's like. You've watched *Blade Runner* and *Lost in Translation* and asked a few buddies who've been and now you have it sussed. Wrong! Tokyo is everything and nothing like you think. I can say from personal experience having just visited for the very first time. It has been something of an unfulfilled dream for me for the past decade, so I was determined to make the most of my 6 days. It is definitely unlike anywhere else. You will spend hours pondering just why and how this is so...

Because let's face it, the Tokyo kids were on it way before anyone else. Their insatiable desire to have the latest and greatest ignited this sneaker boom way back in the early '90s. Fair play to the NYC kids, but I think Tokyo takes the World Title Belt by knockout. Remember when the Air Max '95 came out and sold for insane prices in Tokyo????

The following pages will give you a guide to everything you need to know about shopping for kicks in Japan. We also get the whole nine on the Nike HTM project from Hiroshi Fujiwara and examine new wave Japanese label Visvim. Steve Sneddon from ace Harajuku shop Jump also gives us the lowdown...

Once you're there it isn't nearly as nuts as you might think. The first thing you will notice is that there is *more*. More people, more shops, more people, more noise, more craziness, more people, more brands, MORE OF EVERYTHING! Peak hour trains are pretty rammed but once you get the hang of the subway you'll get around no problems. Strangely, it isn't as prohibitively expensive as you might think. Food, alcohol, public transport, kicks etc are all comparable with most big Western cities. I think London is probably $$$ worse. Drinking all night in a club and catching a taxi home is a different matter entirely.

The best preparation is to go to the site www.superfuture.com and print out the maps. **THIS IS ESSENTIAL.** You will now have a brilliant guide to all the cool areas of Tokyo. The second is to make sure you change money at the airport. Getting cash out with a credit card is a fricken nightmare. Take it from me. You'll be able to buy most stuff from shops with your Visa (even shops that look tiny), it's just getting cash that is a tuff cookie.

My other advice is to get down low and go, go, go. Tokyo shopping is more about what's going on underground or on the 8th floor than what you will see strictly at street level. Don't be afraid to just get in a lift and see where it goes. Most of the treasures I found were in oddspots, I mean local knowledge helps but you gotta be in it to win it. People are polite and about as friendly as anywhere. Most peeps can't or won't speak English but you've just gotta persevere and find someone who can. You won't be able to read jackshit anywhere but you can't have everything your way in this crazy, mixed up world.

In terms of sneaker hunting, you'll find Nike, adidas, Converse, Vans, Saucony, New Balance et al in more colours and styles than you can poke a stick at. It will literally drive you nuts. I managed to budget myself to 3 pairs only, but I could easily have bought 23, such was the variety. My best advice is to not get too carried away. Get around for a day or two, do your research and then go back and clean up. I came across a fair discrepancy in prices and with so many apples to choose from you won't want to go hard early and not have money in the bank for that killer pick-up later on.

Prices range from around ¥8000 for Japanese issue Nikes to ¥20-25,000 for your parallel imports. Heineken, Supreme, Homer Dunks, Bape adidas, HTM AF1 etc are available in many shops but with limited sizing. Prices for that type of stuff ranges from ¥40-60,000, depending on supply and demand which is the law of the jungle here like nowhere else.

As far as sizing goes, anyone US11 and under will be fine. While it's certainly true that most Japanese dudes are small, there's enough big guys around to suggest that this sizing policy will have to change soon. Must be all the hormones in that teriyaki chicken! If you're size 12 and above, life will be difficult...

One of the more bizarre aspects of retail in Japan is that shops are able to parallel import from the US and Europe and still have local accounts. I'm thinking this is the only place in the world where you would get away with it but maybe I'm wrong. Either way, it certainly adds a supreme level of choice to the shopping experience. In fact it is probably what makes Tokyo so unique. I guess as long as they are roughly twice the price of the local stuff it can't hurt local sales and only adds cachet to the brands.

You'll probably spend most of your time wandering the back streets of Harajuku, the heart and sole of Tokyo cool. You won't be able to swing a cat in here without hitting some Bape, Dunk, Supreme, AF1, Bounty Hunter, Head Porter-packing munchkin. It's an oasis in the heart of a heaving metropolis - no cars, low-rise, low-tech, hi-fun, super cool, trendy as f%#k! It's a rabbit warren but that's half the fun and in any case after 3 laps you'll be an expert just like I thought I was.

It is the best place in the world to go stare at Tokyo fashion. And to go shopping. You know those great books with kids dressed as punks, mods, goths, ravers, sex fiends etc - all those people hang out around here, which is why pervert photographers swarm the joint on the weekend.

My other advice is to give summer a miss. And probably winter as well. Temperatures in May are perfect. About 22-28 degrees celsius and muggy as dog's balls! The nights are warm as well, so no need for your furlined Carhartt jacket during this time. You might need an umbrella though! It pisses down pretty regularly which is something you would be advised to avoid.

Peas! (wasabi)

WOODY

Thanks to everyone who made time and space for us - especially Hiroakiki Nakamura, Steve Sneddon, Miyagi, Ben Frost, Chris Gurney, Andrew Wu, the yank who lent me 1000 yen, Takuro Kawase, Dennis Yuen, Hiro, Hiroshi, Shinjuku Park Hotel, Nic A, Michele at visvim, Simon P, Nikki Hudson and everyone who let us take photos of them... arigato and sayonara!

atmos

NIKE AD21 GALLERY

JUMP

ATMOS AIR MAX

SNKR FRKR MGZNE

kino

CHAPTER SNEAKER STORE.

Realmad HECTIC

Limited.edt
www.limited-edt.com

HARAJUKU (PRON. HAH-RAH-JUO-KOO!)

Take the train to Harajuku and get ready to rumble. Opposite the station is a sports store called **Oshman's** which is boring but if you're like me, you wont be able to help yourself - there might be some cheap pickups! Next step is to walk downhill on Takeshita St with all the schoolgirls. It's junky but fun and you'll end up walking down here loads of times anyway. Halfway down is a store called **GarageFine** which is not very cool, but worth a look.

Eventually you will come to a major road called Meiji Dori. To your right will be the flagship **New Balance** store. They have a big range including the Sakamoto collab but it was always quiet when I went in which was really odd - NB are huge in Japan!

Across the road you will see the huge gated entrance to Harajuku proper - now let the good times roll! With your **Superfuture** map you'll find all the stores easily but for argument's sake we'll start with Jump, probably the first store you will come across.

Jump doesn't have the biggest profile but it does have the best overall range, especially for things like Puma suedes, Saucony, SPX, Nike euro imports, JB brand, New Balance, Reebok and of course the big 3 - adidas, Nike and Converse. The staff are very friendly and the shop outfit is simple but one of the best. We'll give it 10 out of 10 - one of our favourite shops in the world.

A few doors down is **Chapter**. If you want mad Nike this is numero uno. They have everything, inc HTM (cost a fortune), Jordans, orca pack, old stock AF1, loadsa Dunks as well as locals like Madfoot, Visvim etc. The attitude of the staff and the music are a bit more aggressive in here but you would have to say they have the shit so we'll give it perfect marks as well...

Many people will know the store **Atmos**. Their collabs with Nike (like the AM Safari) have been top notch and well sought after. Surprisingly we found the range in Atmos rather disappointing but we understand that they are in the process of altering their product mix to include more of their own brands and design. They have no signage so look for the building shown above...

Further along you'll find **Underground, Stussy, Bape, Prohibit** and **Recon**, not exactly sneaker shops but all worth a look.

In the next street you'll find the Nike concept gallery/store called **AD21** which was promoting the Speed event when we went. We heard it might be closing but if it's still open, press the button and the doors open, just look confident and lurk around til you see how it's done. Directly underground is **Real Mad Hectic**. The staff are way cool here and although they don't really sell shoes they have done some notable collabs and so, you gotta go take a look.

Also look for a sign for a shop called **Breakthrough**. They had a ton of stuff, some of it on sale and some stuff I didn't see elsewhere. It is down a lil laneway and out the back of a shop so you'll have to look hard. Another funny joint is **Limited Edition**. They aren't really a store so much as a sneaker wall on the street with a metal door. Their pisstake Footlocker stickers are a giggle.

Elsewhere you will also find fashion shops like **Beams, Bounty Hunter, Head Porter, Hysteric Glamour, Fresh Jive, Haze**. There are also quite a few shops that specialise in vintage clothing, both American and Japanese. Many stock bits and pieces of second hand old sneaks and some have pairs of Supreme, Heineken, Homers etc on display at crazy prices, just depends on the day....

Another road you'll come across is 'Omotesando'. Apart from being very beautiful, very European and chockablock with super-expensive labels, it is where you'll find Citibank, one of the few places you can get cash out with a visa card. It is also home to a couple of chain stores like **Asbee** and **ABC Mart**. Nothing sooper dooper but they are worth a squizz. The **Puma** store is also down here. They had a few unusual things and some weird gaijin store dummies that freaked me out! The **DC** store is also just off the main road hereabouts, as is **adidas**, which I forgot to go check out, maybe they have some Y3 gear, who knows...

Supr[eme]

DAIKANYAMA (PRON. DIE-CAN-YA-MA!)

Situated somewhere between Shibuya and Daikanyama subways lies one more strip of coolness. Officially the street is known as Daikanyama-cho, Shibuya-ku. I almost had a heart attack trying to find it but then I walked from Harajuku and thought I knew where the hell I was going. First stop is the **Bathing Ape** store - **Footsoldier**. Famous for it's sushi-like conveyor belt that transports shoes around the shop, Footsoldier only sells a very limited range of Bape shoes like their lookalike AF1 and shell toes. Despite what you may hear, on the day I went I was able to choose between one or two Bapestas in a size 11. As you can see here I went for the minimal snakeskin - 15,000 yen. Not too bad!

Across the road is the **Silas** store and **Supreme** is just down the road along with a few small sneaker stores like **Monotone** and **Top to Top**. This area is sure to grow so I wouldn't be surprised if it changes pretty quick around here.

Footsoldier - 03 5784 1660
Supreme - 03 5456 0085
Silas - 03 5459 0608

DOWNLOAD THIS REPORT FROM
WWW.SNEAKERFREAKER.COM

UENO (PRON. WAY-NO!)

Take the subway to Ueno. It's about a 20-30 minute trip from Shibuya/Shinjuku on the JR line. I'd suggest going on a weekday because it gets super busy around here!

Walk down the ramp and you'll find a labyrinth of market stalls selling everything from fake watches to pink squids and denim like Evisu.

In amongst it you'll find a few good sneaker spots. One of the best is **Mita**, who've done special make-ups with Nike including these rad aqua, black and white Alpha Force! A good pick-up for 17,000 yen. Things are a little cheaper here and it pays to keep an eye out for old stock on special, I found a few bargains in amongst the usual stuff.

There's one other store around here called **Footmarks** which is run by a real cool kid. He had a load of rare shizz plus a ton of secondhand kicks like this Stussy NB. Like elsewhere in Japan, you'll just have to keep pounding the pavement til you find it - good luck!

Mita Sports - www.mita-sneakers.co.jp - 03 3832 2227
Footmarks - 6-10-3 Ueno Taitou-ku - 03 3833 0003

FOOTMARKS

STUSSY NEW BALANCE

Looking at today's sneaker culture, there are three obvious global hotspots that lead street trends around the world: London, New York and, of course, Tokyo. The first two are quite similar. Tokyo however, is a land of its own with its traditional design and Asian lifestyle mixed with a healthy dose of Western coolhunting. Since Issue 4 of Sneaker Freaker is a special issue on Asia, I think people might like a quick overview of Japanese street fashion and culture.

Although it is one of the world's richest countries and the home to many famous brands, Japan has a surprisingly recent and low-key fashion industry. During the 1960s, the economy started to boom. With disposable income increasing and a void of home-grown designers, people looked overseas for inspiration.

However there was one person who blended the craftsmanship of Japanese tailoring with the latest in euro-style. Rei Kawakubo founded Comme Des Garcons in 1973 and revolutionised Japanese fashion. Her first Paris collection in 1981 was reviled for its bleak and austere outlook and was dubbed 'hiroshima chic'. By 1987 she was honoured as one of the leading women in 20th-century design.

Since that time, Kawakubo has influenced and inspired other talented Japanese designers such as Yohji Yamamoto, Mihara Yasuhiro and Junya Watanabe who are all well known internationally. Yamamoto now works with adidas on his Y3 range and Yasuhiro is now famous for his range of distinctive Puma shoes...

The early '80s was a time when many teenagers desired a more relaxed and 'free' lifestyle. Shops like Beams, United Arrows and magazines like Popeye seemingly popped up every month. Amongst all this progress stood two individuals: they absorbed all of the knowledge and style on offer and would define Japanese street culture for years to come. They were Hiroshi Fujiwara (the H in the HTM) and his personal assistant, Nigo (head of A Bathing Ape which incidentally means 'to bathe in lukewarm water' in Japanese).

Hiroshi was originally a hip-hop DJ and music producer. He is known as a solo artist and also for his work with Major Force. He was the first to bring Stussy to Japan and is also the originator of a labyrinth series of brands including: Electric Cottage, GoodEnough, FCRB Bristol and Gravis. He also designs HeadPorter, a premium luggage, accessories and clothing collection manufactured by the Yoshida/Porter company. They have shops in NYC and Tokyo.

Nigo met Hiroshi whilst working at Popeye as a stylist and became his assistant. The pair were so close that 'Nigo' is actually a nickname which means 'Number Two' in Japanese.

In 1991, Nigo, Hiroshi and Jun Takahashi (head of Undercoverism) started a monthly column in Popeye magazine called 'the Last Orgy 2'. In 1993, they formed Nowhere. Ltd, the parent company for brands like A Bathing Ape, Undercoverism and agent for Supreme.

1990-96 are regarded as the 'childhood' years of the so-called 'Ura-Hara' trend (named after the back streets of Harajuku where most of the trendy shops are located). Inspired by the success of the So-Cal brands like X-Large and Stussy, many other brands started to infiltrate this area such as Devilock, Neighbourhood,

Number (N)ine, Bounty Hunter and realmad HECTIC. BAPE was gaining more media attention and expanded its store network around Japan. Then in 1997, it all blew up.

Takuya Kimura, acclaimed as the most handsome Japanese actor and singer from the J-pop group 'SMAP' (Sports Music Assemble People - a Japanese version of the Monkees) was the culprit. He shot one of his many TV ads in a BAPE Gore-Tex Camo jacket. When it aired around the country, BAPE skyrocketed and the same jacket has since been reissued in 4 different variations whilst the original one can easily fetch $2000 AUS. Later he was seen wearing brands like Neighbourhood, Number (N)ine and Wolf's Head.

Nike were quick to see the huge potential in the Japanese sneaker market so they teamed up with stores such as realmad HECTIC, Atmos, Chapter, Mita and Hiroshi himself to release special editions.

In 1999, Nike Japan opened up its own design division called 'co.jp' which was responsible for Japan-only shoes. The division created classics like the Atmos AF1/AM87/Dunk Low, Coca AF1, 3M Snake AF1, Viotech (Rainbow) Dunk Low, Halloweens, smurfs, putty etc.

Meanwhile BAPE had grown to include hair salons, a record label, two cafes, a children's clothing line, a TV show, a sneaker store and a range of sneakers called BAPESTA which lookaliked Nike AF1 and adidas Shelltoes. Hiroshi, on the other hand, collaborated with Nike on special colourways like the recent Orca Pack (supposedly AD21 and Head Porter exc in Japan) and of course the HTM series! As a matter of fact, Hiroshi was also the person behind the popular rising in Japan for Gravis in 2000-01 and Visvim in 2003-04.

What does the future hold for Japanese street fashion? Who knows, but times are tough! Things still haven't quite recovered from the popping of the economic 'bubble'. Imported fashion, particularly skate stuff remains huge - labels such as Haze, Recon, Prohibit and Supreme and Silas for example. Many established brands like Super Lovers, Hysteric Glamour and BAPE are struggling to find new ideas. In fad obsessed Japan, this can spell DOOM!

With Japanese society undergoing radical change, perhaps the biggest change will be political. So called 'freeters' - youths who have rejected traditional 'salaryman' careers in favour of western style 'freedom' remain a potential social and economic loose cannon in the years ahead.

But in the middle of all this, new players are enjoying a modicum of success. Revolver, W)Taps, Whiz, Nexus 7, Quench and Rebirth are doing fine amongst the big names in Harajuku. Undercoverism just attended the Paris Fashion Week in 2004 with its 'Twins' series and Number (N)ine is opening up a new store in NYC.

The boom has peaked but Harajuku remains a vibrant shopping destination, albeit out of economic reach of most small labels to enter the fray. Who knows, maybe a few years down the track we'll see a new-wave of style and talent? Perhaps Tokyo will find room for a 'neo' Harajuku? One thing is for sure - there is always something new in Tokyo, it is a city unlike any other...

IORI

with additional reporting by S.Y. and S.W.

{INTRODUCING}

HIROSHI FUJIWARA

{HIP-HOP DEEJAY & MUSICIAN}

{HTM DESIGNER FOR NIKE}

{CREATOR OF BRANDS LIKE GOODENOUGH & HEADPORTER}

HTM AIR FORCE ONE
FIRST SERIES

HTM COURT FORCE
2005 RELEASE

How's Tokyo?

It's good, it's busy...

It's always busy! You've had an amazing career...

Well I was originally a DJ and I brought hip-hop here more than 20 years ago. Maybe not only me but I was one of the first guys. Then I started making domestic little brands like Good Enough which was maybe like 15 years ago. It was the beginning of the fashion generation for Harajuku. And I kept producing music. I work with Nike doing design, some clothing designs and I do Head Porter...

And you were in Major Force as well!

Yeah I was.

Electric Cottage?

Electric Cottage is finished.

What was Harajuku like when you first started?

There was a lot less people and more property so you could do your own store. Now it's three times as expensive. I don't think young guys can come here and start their own store anymore. I think it is the same as New York in Soho.

Well it's still very beautiful, I have spent most of my time here...

Uh-huh. When we started the Harajuku scene, there was the end of the bubble and the Japanese economy was going down and property was getting very cheap and we then found our place. But now it it's going up again, so it was a nice gap in between for us...

Do you prefer music or fashion?

I think both. Sometimes I get bored with fashion, I do music. Sometimes I get bored with music, I like to do fashion and so on.

Well my sister is a big fan, she asked me to pass on her regards...

Oh, thankyou. I should give you a cd.

Yeah she would like that - thankyou...

Where do you live?

Melbourne? Have you been there?

No. I have been to Sydney maybe two times.

Oh, Is the sneaker scene in Japan very strong at the moment?

Yeah, I think maybe two years ago it was more. Now it has calmed down. Prices were much higher for special things...

Are you a collector yourself?

Not really collecting, I like to wear them, I don't keep them in a box or anything.

Well you also have the luxury of making your own special pairs.

Yes.

Do you think sneakers are just another part of fashion or do they mean more than that?

I think they are just fashion. Not only athletes can wear them.

I was wondering, Japanese kids buy so many sneakers and have such little houses - where the hell do they put them all?

(laughs) I don't know. I think their whole house is packed with records, with sneakers and toys.

I saw the HTM crocskin Air Force Ones yesterday for 84,000 yen.

Oh really? WOW! I don't know how they sell it?

Will people buy them for that price?

I don't think so. We haven't started selling them here yet, so they imported from somewhere else.

Maybe from Australia.

I think they were released there first.

お客様へのお願い

型くずれ、汚れ防止のため、つま先部分を持たないで下さい。

CHAPTER

HTM AiR FORCE ONE ~ 2004 RELEASE

{HiROSHi FUJiWARA}

Maybe. How about in Australia, are people crazy about sneakers?

Yeah! We have diehard kids like all big cities. But in the last two years things have completely changed. For example, Mark Smith came for the launch of Laser. It was always hard to get product but now it's really good, we get most things like HTM...

Right! Have you bought any shoes while you are here?

Yeah, I bought some pink and white Air Force Ones from Jump.

Uh-huh (Laughs)

I liked your Orca pack as well. Simple but a nice change up..

Yeah, thankyou.

Going back to HTM, how did it start?

It started three years ago I think or maybe more than that. I was talking to Mark Parker about doing a project together and then it started.

What was the first product?

I think maybe this? (shows me his foot)

The Wovens...

The original concept with HTM was kind of customising. Like better performance, or better design, or premium materials, beautiful leathers. That was the concept.

I have the first HTM Air Force One in black.

Yeah.

So how does a HTM shoe get designed?

I go to Portland three times a year, and we do some samples...

Do you think you will do a HTM Dunk?

I don't know maybe for the future. Our next shoe is a Court Force.

Do you know it?

Yeah - when is that coming?

Maybe this year. I have a sample in my office, we can take a photo.

Yeah. (excited) That would be good? Will you do HTM Clothing?

Yeah we are talking about it. It hasn't happened yet.

ORCA PACK DUNK
2004 RELEASE

Is that the only work that you do for Nike?

Yeah - Orca Pack. If I have some ideas I just tell them and then we decide, this is HTM or this is Quickstrike. For example I am not sure if the Court Force will be a HTM product.

Do you work with other Japanese sneaker Companies?

Not really. Only VisVim.

Do you design for them?

Not really design but I know the guy who started it and I help from the beginning. I just offer ideas, he is a great designer so he can do it all himself...

I watched Lost in Translation and I thought I noticed you...

Yeah that was me. I am friends with Sofia, she asked me to come.

Did you like the movie?

Yeah, it was beautiful. It seemed a little unfair, I think Tokyo is not as unfriendly as they made it seem... but then after I came here I realised it wasn't about Tokyo, it was about being lonely.

Yes I think you can have that same kind of feeling anywhere, if I go to London and stay in a hotel by myself, maybe I get lonely and the same kind of feeling.

What other projects are you working on?

Well, I'll just keep doing the same thing - music, actually I have a new CD. I am making a photo book with Vivienne Westwood which should come out soon. And I was in Portland two weeks ago and I gave a few new designs and ideas - we should have the samples for those pretty soon. They will be HTM I think...

Well I'll be looking out for them.

Thanks for your time Hiroshi...

HIROSHI
AIR FORCE ONE
(SPECIAL MAKE-UP)

AIR

STEVE SNEDDON AND MIYAGI...

JUMP HARAJUKU

So! As you have read, Tokyo is a mysterious place in many ways! To break it down a bit further we spoke to Steve Sneddon who has lived in Japan for the past 15 years. He is also the owner of 'Jump' - one of our favourite sneaker stores in downtown Harajuku. Also present was Store manager, Miyagi who gave us a local's insight into the peculiarities of the Japanese sneaker scene. We put Steve's answers in black and Miyagi's translated answers in cyan so you know who said what - aren't we clever?

How's Tokyo?

It's getting better actually. There's new buildings, the economy has picked up a lot in the last 12 months. A lot has to do with China, its booming so much there and we are riding their wave really.

And the sneaker scene?

Not as good as it was I think. Too many limited editions, before it was really cool but now there's new ones every week so it's just not as exciting as it used to be.

You've been here for 15 years. You must have seen some great footwear fads in Japan?

The first was the Northwave, that was massive and lasted about 18 months. Retail price was ¥8000 and they were selling for ¥35,000 so that was good business. After that the Nike parallel import was very big for several years, from the US and Europe. In-line from Japan was ok, but it was different. Redwing shoes were really big here as well and the last big one 2 years ago was Gravis.

Why was that?

Snowboarding was very big here and their link to Burton was strong. Also their product placement was crucial, they placed Gravis with Hiroshi and some very cool people. They were careful with distribution, now it's everywhere...

What happens to a brand that has been through a boom like that?

They usually disappear! Gravis has hung on, not like it was, but its OK. Northwave, Redwing are done. Nike are still number one which is amazing really. So unless it has a lot of history like Vans or Converse it will come and go... It's a very, very fickle market.

Converse is really big here isn't it?

Yeah it's Number 3. Nike is Number 1 and adidas is Number 2. Both sell around about eight million pairs here a year...

I remember when the original AM95 took off, were you here then?

Yeah, that was nuts. I got into the shoe business in '93. The AM95 retail was ¥15,000 and they were selling like hotcakes for ¥60,000, you'd see them for ¥200,000 but they weren't selling. It was crazy...

You have the same colour right now in Jump!

Yeah I know, same price as well. And you can't get more than that! It's nice that they reissue them and its great for the young kids but I think it's sad for the collectors who spent so much money.

There are so many brands here it is the best place in the world to shop isn't it?

Yeah I agree. Choice here is beyond anywhere. So many brands, so many styles. They are maniacs about getting exclusive product. The prices aren't as high as they used to be. It's hard for retailers because every time a new Nike comes out your customer expects you to have it. They look in mags and they know there's 12 new limited editions coming and they want to see them all. It's very hard.

Especially in Harajuku where there are 20 cool stores...

Yeah it is hard to make a point of difference. It's great for the consumer but it makes life very hard...

I haven't seen any fakes here..

No there isn't. There were a ton of fake AM95s. A lot of companies were importing them because it was such a high value shoe but it's stopped now. They cost a lot of money to make and unless you have a shoe that is hot enough to make it worthwhile it won't happen. There's just too many new shoes.

OG 1996 Air Max 95 - ¥60-200,000

You mentioned that women have stopped wearing sneakers?
Yeah I think so, it has become a lot more feminine, same as in Europe. Kitten mules and sandals, high heels, it's just not the same as it was a few years ago. In Harajuku it's still strong but I can see the waves come and go.

What is gonna be hot for the next few months?
I mean Nike are always huge, the HTM has been a big hit. Saucony does well, Hurley (Nike owned) has a new range, I'm interested in seeing them. Will they sell? I don't know. But I think Reebok have some good shoes going forward... great quality.

What did you think of the HTMs being ¥84,000 in Chapter?
Crazy, they will sell but they should be ¥60,000 - so who knows?

What about the local brands?
There quite a few domestic brands like Visvim and Madfoot. The kids really like them, you don't see them everywhere. If you're looking for a point of difference it's good. Euro and US retailers are picking up on it, Visvim might sell for 300 dollars in Europe...

What about Jump - what are you known for?
We're in the heart of Harajuku which means we're often one of the first stores sneaker heads come into. We are probably best known for our wide choice and also for sourcing new items quickly. That and not asking silly prices. With so many sneaker shops in Tokyo it is important to differentiate yourself, so we do try to pick up on new projects which we think may be of interest. Things like the JB shoes and the Dave White Tees, both of which went down really well with our customers. Jump is also #1 for Saucony and Puma suede in Japan. We sell the 680 New Balance really well...

New Balance did a Ruichi Sakamoto collab - has that gone well?
For people interested in shoes it doesn't mean anything. For ABC Mart and the family shops it might be OK... he is very famous after all.

They seem to only have one style of shoe - would you agree?
To the general eye, yes I agree, but there are hardcore New Balance fans in Japan who don't think they look the same. Even the slightest difference to them is huge. Their main market is guys in their late twenties to forties, they are the hardcore. They have the 'Made in USA' and 'Made in UK' shoes and they have the Offspring collection which has had a good reception. They've done JD Sports shoes as well, but they don't do too many so they keep it fresh.

What is it with Japanese kids and fashion? Is it because most people are the same shape, roughly the same height, black hair...
Yeah I think so, it is true. A lot of self-esteem is involved, it makes people feel good, so they are always looking for the new hot thing. They always move on very quickly. Fashion is the way to stand out. There are so many magazines, so much product, the kids are very, very good at it. Ten years ago they were looking at the West but not now. Big brands are always coming here to see what is going on.

In terms of sneakers, how does Japan differ from the West?
A lot of sneaker colours are influenced by childhood but people don't realise. Take Gundam for example - red, white and blue with yellow accents. Same with Pooh Bear - orange and red and caramel. A while back it was Pokemon so blue and yellow were hot. Dragonball is quite popular in Japan so shoes in these colours are ingrained in the consciousness. Some understand it but most don't. Designers use these colours to emotionally appeal to kids.

Like the Homer Dunk?

Yeah exactly...

Hey thanks for your time Steve and Miyagi, thanks for supporting Sneaker Freaker and thanks for showing us around Tokyo...

HONG KONG PHOOEY

Well if you've survived Tokyo you should find HK a piece of cake! Quite frankly we didn't really need to go figure but in the interests of the Magazine and you, the reader, we thought we better go see what's what in this neck of the woods! Actually that's not quite true - it was on the way home to Melbourne and the stopover was free, so we thought bugger it - may as well stop over for a few days R&R&SS.*

Aside from sneakers, HK is a pretty snazzy joint. I'm not writing a guidebook here but it's got a lot to offer. The best part is that you'll probably only need 3 or 4 days max to get around and see it all. Compared to the overwhelming sensation that is Tokyo, HK is far less confronting. Although it's definitely Chinese, there's plenty of hangovers from the colonial days to make everything easy peasey. Heaps more people speak English, it's a lot smaller, the subway is brilliant (less crowded and verbally bi-lingual), the cabs are cheap, the weather's humid and the food's great. On the other hand, the pedestrian overpasses are trickier than a Rubik's Cube.

There are some oddball things about the HK sneaker scene. First, all shops love to shrinkwrap their sneaks. I guess it keeps them spotless but it adds a plastic, slightly surreal level to sneaker sightseeing. You can't tell what's what - suede, patent, nubuck, leather - it all looks the same! You'll just have to wait and see til they bring out a pair to try on. The other thing was that all the best shops in the arcades and plazas open somewhere between 3 and 4pm and shut around 10 at night. Which is fine by us - HK by night is really cool. Once darkness falls and the neon is switched on you'll be completely lost all over again. In a nice way.

In terms of sneaker shopping, the scene is still fairly small but there are a growing number of hardcore heads. Most kids are obviously influenced by Japan - the Harajuku look is very 'in'. All the usual labels covered in the Tokyo section are to be found in abundance here. Strangely I was hoping to find more fakes! I found a few weird ass ones but they wouldn't fool Blind Freddy. Perhaps I didn't get too far into the nitty gritty market scene but it seems like there may have been a police crackdown if newspaper articles are any guide.

There are two main areas to go see - Mongkok and Causeway Bay. Here's a shopping guide and an interview with HK skate guru Brian Siswojo who is doing his best to put HK on the world skating map.

WOODY

* That's Rest, Recreation and Sneaker Shopping...

MONGKOK

Yep, it's officially crazy. There must be 30 sneaker stores in this area which is probably why its unofficial name is Sneaker Street. The actual name of the streets you're looking for are Fa Yuen and Nelson St. Take the subway to Mongkok and keep walking around in circles til you find it. That's how I did it. Asking people for directions seemed to draw blank idiot faces - I shoulda had a map!

Now, take it from me, I checked 'em all out for you - prices are fairly consistent here. It is mind boggling that so many stores can survive and (theoretically) prosper in such a small area. Prices are generally identical, product lines are identical - a lot of stores are obviously owned by the same outfit. That's why you get Toronto Sports, New York Sports, Chicago Sports et al all in a row. Weird!

I did find a few things on special so you should be able to find a bargain but you may take pot luck with sizes. For example I saw OG Safari's anywhere from $600-1299нк - a fair gap. As with Japan, US11 seems to be about the biggest you'll find in anything...

I missed out on a few styles I was after, inc the Notting Hills in orange/black and the white/red/black Trainer 3s that I think came out of Europe. Other notables include a pair of Tokyo White Dunks on view at a shop called **World Sport Gallery** (67 Shunting St, Mongkok 2390 3507) They'll set you back a cool $12,000нк but it's

the closest I'll ever get to a pair so it was nice to see them, even if they were behind glass. I also came across a pair of Char Aznable Air Max (Gundam) for $2100нк. Not my style but cool all the same. adidas also have a store over here (or at least a store that just sells adidas) and you can pick up cheap shelltoes in a million colours, including the switcheroo colour ones for $400нк.

The other place in MK you should visit is the **Sino Centre**, or in chinese, **Shun Wor**. It's about a 5-10 minute walk from the nearest MTR exit. On the ground floor would be all the major sneaker stores you would want to see. But beware of the one next to the watch shop near the elevators - I heard they sell fakes. You could ignore all the other levels, unless you're into Japanese anime, comics and weird porn. You'll also find a few stores here selling Japanese vintage toys and figures.

Second place is called **King Wah Centre**. It's located about two streets away from Sino Centre and the 2nd and top floor are packed with sneakers. Some of the more well-known shops are located here, but beware - customer service is poor and price tags are way high - try $3000нк for a pair of Supreme in black/red or $3500нк for the white/blue. If you see them for any less you can bet your bottom dollar they are fakes.

銅鑼灣
Causeway Bay

LOOK FOR THIS SIGN!

with additional reporting by Ivan

CAUSEWAY BAY

Causeway Bay is on the HK side of the water. It's a 15 minute ride by subway from Mongkok with a very simple changeover. It is home to a load of Plazas and malls and is quite a fun place to wander around, especially at night when it really comes alive.

Actually locating some of these places can be really difficult. Street signage is about as piss-poor as Japan - virtually non-existent except on major roads. Plus, being from Australia, where we are so conditioned to snooping around at ground level - it often never occurs to look up or down. We spent an hour trying to find a plaza only to realise that it was downstairs behind a grotty doorway!

First stop is the skate shop **852** - 506-508 Jaffe Rd, Level 2. On the next page you'll find Iori's interview with Brian, the owner. The beauty with finding Brian's shop is that directly opposite is the **Ginza Plaza**. Just walk downstairs and you'll find a maze of really tiny shops run by young kids. I bought a set of 12" 1990 Gundam from an amazing toy store down here. You'll also find Bape, Neighbourhood, Good Enough, real mad HECTIC, Supreme and Stussy. Reports suggest that it is all legit product. The best shop was called **AD**, the guy seemed to own several spots down here.

Further up the road and around to the right is a plaza called **Upfront**. Go up the escalators, it's a 4 or 5 level joint. There are several sneaker spots in here, one of the best was **Hamlet** who had a pretty amazing collection of stuff including Pharrells, Supreme, and other bits and pieces. It's a pretty cool plaza and although more focused on teenagers, it was a good place to hang out.

There is also the **East Station Walk** or what used to be known as **New Face By Sogo**. It is located behind the **World Trade Centre**. The exit should be around the corner, a few blocks away from the Baleno shop and next to a big shop that sells cosmetic stuff. Go up to the 1st and 2nd levels and you'll find a few sneaker spots. The one on the 2nd floor is called **Monogram.**

There is also **Causeway Bay Walk** which is located infront of the old Mitsukoshi centre, opposite The Body Shop and a Swarovski crystal store. I can only remember seeing 1 or 2 shops in there, but it's always worth a look.

Besides these places, you'll find CPU, Catalogue, Marathon Sport and Royal Sporting House. Sometimes they have a few surprises. If you're interested in adidas Y3 product, I found a shop called **J-01** (57 Paterson St - 280 80 501) while I was walking around...

Julius Brian Siswojo 852

DATE: 18/6/2004 :: LOCATION: 852 SKATESHOP, HONG KONG :: TIME: 8:30PM

It wasn't a good day to go out shopping in Hong Kong. It was raining, it was windy, and man, it was warm. In the middle of this bad weather, I found myself sitting inside a skate store with a mate of mine, Fung Jai, listening to whatever he has put into the CD player. Suddenly someone walked in wearing a pair of Haze Dunk Hi and I thought, 'Is he crazy?! Haze Dunk Hi in pouring rain?' Before I could say anything, he held out his hand and said, 'You're lori right? I'm Brian'. Julius Brian Siswojo, born into an Indo-Chinese family in 1976, migrated to Hong Kong in 1984 along with his family to learn English. In 1986, he took up skating and hasn't stopped ever since. And boy is he tired!

Brian, tell us a bit about yourself and the store...

Well I started up 852 Distribution in 1999 and the first brand we distributed in HK was alphanumeric (a#). Within one year the chain grew to 12 stores. I was a member of the a# skate team in Asia and the Asia Marketing Manager till I left the job in 2001. After I left I started this shop since I love skating, and I really want to promote this sport and the culture in Hong Kong.

I see, I see...that explains why you have two pair of a# Dunks!

I'm also a big sneaker head - started collecting Nike in '86-87. I remember my first pair of Nike was Vandal Supreme, and I skated in OG red/black AJ1s. Always a big fan of Nike, but also Converse All Stars and Weapons, adidas Campus/Shelltoes and Wallabies. I think I have over 400 pairs at home. I still kept about 55 pairs of Prestos in different colourways.

55 pairs of Presto?! Wow... So aside being a sneaker head, what are you trying to achieve with the 852 store?

The main aim of 852 is to push skateboarding and to re-educate people that skating is a healthy form of sport. We want to provide the best equipment for our local skaters, and we promote the sport, not the money aspect where some other shops are heading.

How do you see the current skateboarding scene in HK?

Generally the scene has improved a lot over the past few years, but if we compare it to the US, it's still a bit low. Hey, at least we gave it a try in HK - there ain't many who tried this before.

Ok, now getting back to some sneaker related questions: what has made you to decide to import Nike SB shoes into Hong Kong?

Well this has to go back a long way in time, just about when the first SB series came out in the US. I saw the catalogue for the new SB range when the first series came out and instantly I went straight to the heads at the SB department about bringing it into HK. The response we got was that the HK market wasn't ready for the SB range yet, so they kept it within the US only. Fast forward to June 2003, they suddenly approved the sale of the SB range in HK and their request to Nike HK was that 852 must be one of the stockists, so you could say we were in it from the beginning.

So what do you see in the future of the SB range?

I reckon the outlook for the SB range is great! But I do feel that the Dunks are overplayed, because whenever people talk about the Dunk SBs, they look at it at the fashion point of view. Nevertheless it's still an amazing shoe. I think people also need to concentrate on the other shoes in the SB range – in my opinion, FCs are the next big thing...they are HOT!

What about the future of the SB range in HK? How do you see that?

We're currently negotiating with Nike to form our own HK skate team. We believe that if we support the skaters, the skaters in return will support Nike SB. 852 have been sponsoring a few skaters already with the SBs and the response has been great. By getting more skaters to wear them, hopefully it'll get more media and word of mouth.

I've been reading on the forums that the SB shoes in HK were sent off to the Japanese resellers in one big batch. Is there any room for improvement in this area? And what's your take on resellers?

Resellers are good! They boost image and create the awareness (hype!) around the shoe which benefits the retailers. But they are also bad in the way that they lift the prices and make Nike look like they're in it for the money rather than the passion to support

skateboarding. As long as they don't sell fakes, then we won't interfere. As for the distribution problem, we are talking to Nike about it as well so hopefully they'll be improved when the shoes come out in the future.

You've got some pretty good shoes on the racks. Can you tell us something about them?

Well, all of them are from friends. Much props to Haze for giving me five pairs or else I don't think I'll be wearing the Hi's as a rainy day shoe! Also big shoutoutz to Jesse from Nike (featured in SF#3) for the a# Dunks, Alyasha and Tabo of Fiberops for the Wildwoods, the guys at Suppa in Japan, Futura, Tim O'Connor, the guys at Zoo York skate team and peeps like Danny Supa, Todd Jordan and Brian Anderson. You guys rock!

I heard there may be a HK Dunk - true or false?

Oh, for real! Well, let's see, hope it'll happen and if it happens, it'll be banging, for sure!

I noticed that HK is cracking down on fake DVDs and shit coming in from China, is that the case with shoes?

In Hong Kong, nah, no-one rocks no fake shit out here, I mean, cats out here appreciate kicks, but bootleg DVDs, tonz of 'em are mad cheap! Same as kicks, same shit, that's why for those companies that want to do business - don't make 'em in China, shit can just come out easily, name it, you'll be able to buy KOSTON 8 way before Eric himself designs the shoe! Fake Nike usually only come in size 9 so you have to chop your feet if you are an 11.

What other skate brands do you rate?

Oh, Nike SB for sure, we all have been waiting for a while till Nike makes it right and finally they do - it used to be so wack. The URL is sick, the FC is the dopest skateboard shoe, try it and you'll all understand. adidas is doing the same too, even the Gonz finally realized that all his previous models suckdickbigtime.com

Lakai is doing their thing and they are gettin' doper and doper! I'm feelin' KOSTON 6 for sure, their shit's dope! Eric Koston knows what's up about sneakers. Geoff Rowley from Vans is always the dopest! He brings back the old school, accept it or not. D-3 is ugly and now Osiris is trying to make another ugly version of D-3 in 2004, you know which one I'm talkin' about - the Ali Boulala first model. Another D-3 but I guess it's more sad because ravers dig D-3, that's why he makes paper but now it's 2004, more and more dumbasses know about good sneakers. Sorry Boulala, don't get me wrong. Boulala is a dope skateboarder and I like his skating so much. But the shoe, nah, sorry! Majority of skateboard shoes out there are suckdick.com though!

Last question! What's the big plan for 852 in 2004?

Trying to organize more demos, competitions and parties so we break the culture and make it mainstream. To show people the positive image that skateboarding should have. Inviting more pros to visit HK, and bringing brands such as UXA, Fiberops and Mato (new brand from NYC) into the store and one new Nike SB shoe per month.

Thanks for your time today Brian! Nice talking to ya.

No worries man. Just rock up and chat whenever you feel like!

IORI

★ 852 SHOP ★
2/f, rm3 United Success Commercial Centre, 506-508 Jaffe Road,
Causeway Bay, Hong Kong :: +852 2573 9872 :: www.8five2.com

(pron: MELBURN)

MELBOURNE
SNEAKER HUNTER GUIDE

I read somewhere that Melbourne is one of the most liveable cities in the world. Having lived here for the last 12 years or so, I think I can vouch for that. Melbournites have pretty much everything they could possibly want right on their doorstep. And of course it is home to the world's greatest magazine, Sneaker Freaker!

From the nightclubs to sports, entertainment and shopping, Melbourne is top notch right across the board. The cuisine is grouse as well. Some say meat pies and sausage rolls are the staple diet of Aussies… but I say its more like beer! HA! And fake Japanese sushi bars.

Melbourne is also one of the easiest cities to get around in the world. If you've been here before you'd know what I'm talking about, the entire city centre is on a grid and you can walk it in a day if you try hard. With its network of trams and trains, Melbourne also boasts one of the most efficient public transport systems, so getting around is a breeze.

There are two main destinations in Melbourne - the CBD (City) and Chapel St. If you have time there are a few other places to check out, namely the ugly suburban shopping centres like Southland and Chadstone. You could easily spend a full day just cruising around and maybe even have time for a movie. Late night shopping is on Fridays where shops close at 9pm (normally they shut at 6pm).

There's also a discount store area in Collingwood with factory outlets for most major brands. (Addresses are on the next page for those). You can also take a squizz on the sneakerfreaker.com forum to see what's going on in the outlets and save yourself a trip.

With the major sneaker companies putting time and effort into making sure Melbournites get their share of exclusive releases, the sneaker scene has blown up over the last couple of years. Strangely, it may just be easier to get the goods here than it is if you lived in some other global hotspot like London, (especially when it comes to SB releases). Supremes, Jedis, Heinekens, Rayguns, Homers, Bisons and Dunkles have all dropped locally in quantities adequate enough to soothe the local population. Retailers like Footlocker, General Pants, Dakota and Evolve have also jumped on board and there's been some very social pre-release parties for HTM, the adidas Superstars, McFetridge Vandals and so on. Like any place you can't go to sleep for too long but still, it makes for a lively scene. And a very friendly one as well.

In fact, there are so many sneaker heads around town, you better keep your eyes peeled - but don't get yer necks broken!

HANS DC

Chapel St. Now don't be put off by this place as I'm sure every city has one. It's one of those places where people like to be seen. Unfortunately, it also attracts pond scum. There are two ends to this strip – Toorak (the $$$ upmarket ritz) and Windsor (more of a laidback vibe). Let's then take a walk from South Yarra train station and bring it home as we head towards Windsor and Provider on Greville Street.

General Pants 529 Chapel St. South Yarra +61 3 9826 0115

This is *the* supermarket of urban streetwear in Australia. If you've got limited time and need a new wardrobe in an hour, then this is the place to be. GP's own magazine (Our People) is always worth a look, the staff are super friendly (loads of hot chicks + Paul Garvey) and you can pick up absolutely anything you need from caps to watches to Vans to thongs and denim. They've held exclusive launches for Dunkles, Rayguns, SS35, so you know they value our culture. Make sure you check out the sneaker rack cos you never know what you'll find.

Dakota 501 501 Chapel St. South Yarra +61 3 9826 9596

Back in 1976, a store called 'Jeanmakers' opened shop with denim as its bread and butter. A move down the street in 1989 and a name change to Dakota 501 has transformed it into one of Melbourne's leading shopping destinations. Still an indie store, this place is filled with the latest and freshest streetwear, especially denim brands from all over the world. Dakota also works closely with sneaker companies like Nike and adidas, and recently had all 35 of the 35th Anniversary Superstars on display. It also holds some of the best sneaker launch parties in Melbourne. Have a good look – you won't leave disappointed!

Puma Concept 514 Chapel St. Sth Yarra +61 3 9824 1699

Just across the road from General Pants and Dakota is the Puma Store. Although footwear isn't the primary focus here, it's always worth a visit. Definitely the best place to visit if you're down with the Mihara ranges and old school Puma apparel.

Sports Lords 291 Chapel St. Prahran +61 3 9521 2280

One of the oldest 'hot spots' in Melbourne, Sports Lords is run by two of the most down-to-earth guys I know. Lou and John have been in the sneaker game for longer than anyone and still today remain the most knowledgeable, friendly and helpful retailers in Melbourne. This shop should be the first destination for Nike fans when in Melbourne. The only thing they don't sell are SBs, but that's because they don't skate. Other than that, it's most unlikely that any other store in Melbourne will have the Nikes you're looking for if these guys don't have it.

Provider 114 Greville St. Prahran +61 3 9529 2629

Provider is a great little shop started by an enterprising couple, Chris and Mel, who have gotten off their ample asses to provide Melbourne heads with the most interesting store to date. The carpet is plush and the wall fittings look like something out of the medieval period. Not only do these guys have a cool looking shop and product to burn – they will also try their hardest to fulfill your personal sneaker wants by helping you search for that one thing you've been lusting for. I recommend this store for superior one-on-one service. Also, look out for their cool miniature greyhound named Bruiser.

Evolve 214 Chapel St. Prahran +61 3 9529 5466

A must-see for all SB fanatics and skaters alike. Evolve satisfies its customer with Nike SB, adidas, DC and pretty much every skate shoe brand out there. There's a million tee shirts (from Recon to Obey to Bape) and they also support local designers with a selection of sweats, hoods and accessories. The window displays are always interesting and full of the latest product and there are always some rare hard to find sneakers and toys on show in the display cabinet. Great shop!

KICKZ101

DAKOTA 501 SAPATOS SALE

carhartt ★

DAKOTA 501

adidas

MATT & LE BRON
KICKZ101

ARGENTINA

HERE'S SOME
OTHER PLACES
OF INTEREST!

PAUL AT GENERAL PANTS

carhartt

FEIT ™

PROVIDER

trainers

SNEAKERS

Nike Factory Outlet
416 Smith St, Collingwood +61 3 9419 9655

Converse Factory Outlet
U1-3/397 Smith St, Fitzroy +61 3 9417 4966

adidas Outlet
377 Smith St, Collingwood +61 3 9419 4499

Trigger Brothers
2/1 St, Kilda Rd, St Kilda. +61 3 9537 3222
Small chain of skateshops around Melbourne that
has an SB account. No one thinks to go there for
new releases so these guys always seem to have
stock months after they've sold out elsewhere.

Sole/Platypus
417 Chapel St +61 3 9824 1377
Melbourne Central +61 3 9654 5900
After an ownership change, this company is currently
undergoing a facelift. It's fairly commercial but the
super knowledgeable staff make it worth a visit.

CARHARRT STORE

Melbourne City

I love Melbourne. Not only is it small enough to navigate on foot, it's gotta be the friendliest city in the world, and almost European in looks and temperament. There are countless cool little stores tucked away in tiny laneways all over town. As far as sneakers are concerned, there's the usual suspects but there's a handful of places you should check out. Let's start from the top of the town!

Carhartt Shop 58, Melbourne Central +61 3 9639 6870

Carhartt is located in the LaTrobe St side of Melbourne Central and is surrounded by G-Star and General Pants. But you know it's the coolest store in the building when you hear the drum&bass pumping outta their more than decent system. Not only do they have all the Carhartt product you would ever want and a decent range of Nikes, they also have an exclusive on a new line of shoes called FEIT. Check these puppies out in the future if you haven't already, they are definitely worth a look - www.joinfeit.com

Kickz101 63 Elizabeth St, Melbourne +61 3 9620 1101

GENERAL PANTS

This is a cool underground store (literally) that will make any basketball freak, freak. They have everything related to basketball and the kids that run the place live the damn game. It's awesome for Jordans! They also have a chill out area in the store with beanbags equipped with DVD and Playstation facilities. Big Matt will tell you all about what you need to know regarding the game. Ask him about his sneaker collection. You'll be impressed.

Nike Town 1/246 Bourke St. Melbourne +61 3 8660 3333

I don't think its officially called NikeTown as such... the official name is Nike Melbourne when they answer the phones. But either way, this two-level multi-section store is located in the heart of the Melbourne CBD. You just can't miss it. With lifestyle, soccer, basketball, tennis, outdoor, kids and lifestyle sections, you'd think there wouldn't be a need to go anywhere else would you?! And you're right.

PSC 121 Swanston St. Melbourne +61 3 9639 7121

This is the local skateshop where all the kids wanna hang out. It's somewhere I feel comfortable and all the staff are skaters. Managed by Anthony Mapstone (XEN Skateboards), this is THE SB destination in the city. They also stock all the top skate sneaker brands like Vans, Es, Emerica, DVS, I-Path and a host of other skate-related sneaker brands. PSC is easily the biggest and best skate shop in Melbourne. Ask for Ben in the sneaker department. Oh, and make sure you don't get punked with their remote-controlled fart machine...

EVOLVE

DAKOTA 501

Prime 191 Little Collins St. Melbourne +61 3 9650 5344

Known as the only place to buy Fred Perry gear in Melbourne, Prime has a pretty cool collection of adidas, Puma and assorted clothing to boot. Small store but Josh will sort you out. They also have branches in tourist destinations like Brunswick St, Fitzroy and St Kilda.

Foot Locker 125 Swanston St, Melbourne
166 Melbourne Central +61 3 9663 7919

You always need to check out the Foot Locker stores no matter what city you're in. Always worth a look, especially when hunting for different colourways as they often have exclusives on things like NB 574s.

CAN YOU REALLY 'KEEP IT REAL' & STILL GET THE JOB DONE?

I have lived in the city of Melbourne since 1994. In that time, I have come to love and appreciate Melbourne as one of the most liveable and exciting cities in the world. Having being lucky enough to travel the world, Melbourne also happens to be a city that offers the most opportunity in everything you want and desire. It's safe, it's entertaining, and for those who have been to the rest of Australia, it has the friendliest and the best dressed people in the southern hemisphere. It offers entertainment next to no other capital city in Australia and is regarded as one of the dance capitals of the world. As for hip-hop, one of the best turntabalists in the world, DJ Dexter (of the Avalanches) hails from here. Not to mention all the sports talent, and of course, Kylie. The cultures and sub-cultures are also prevalent in everyday life in Melbourne. Think a mini-Manhattan Island!

With all this in mind, the sub-culture of sneaker collecting was bound to explode right here in the land down under. Sneaker collecting has been rife in Melbourne for as long as I have lived here. And I'm sure its roots stem from the time the first basketball shoe was ever imported into this country. I guess I would have to be a third or fourth generation sneaker freak in this town. Ones before me would have to be dudes like DJ Peril (of 1200 Techniques) and Mr. Rekshop.

Back in the day our hobby was a little different. There were no 'special' releases or collaborations then. The local stores couldn't care less about limited editions. The internet was there but we were all too busy hanging out and hunting for sneakers at markets and secondhand stores. The Salvation Army and Savers were THE place to meet sneaker collectors. Scavenging through other peoples unwanted stuff was an art. A relative or mate who went overseas was usually bombarded with shopping lists of shoes that were not even heard of in Australia.

Then it started to get popular. Demand increased, so supply grew to accommodate. Soon places like Foot Locker would experiment with retro releases. High-end streetwear stores started to capitalize on the '80s look which was making a revival. All of a sudden, it was fairly easy to walk into a shoe store on payday and walk out with something you would be proud to have in your collection.

In just a few years, the next generation of sneaker collectors has emerged. This generation will be a threat to some, but a welcome sight for the more enterprising of us all.

Overnight, Australia was noticed as an important account to the major sneaker companies overseas. In the last three or four years this country has been a destination for all the amazing product that was thought never to be available. Little did we know that whilst all of us were bathing in our new found blessing of sneakers, this had been the norm for the rest of the world for a long time now. The internet was a superhighway of communication and commerce for shoe dealers specialising in collectable sneaks. There was eBay and it was a cyber auction house not only for shoes, but for everything you can think of. Limited editions seem to get released more frequently than regular

styles. Collaborations with artists, celebrities and sportsmen seem to go down every week. On the rev meter, it would have to be redlining it. Shoes sell for in excess of $1000us. And people are buying.

The Japanese are known to be the biggest buyers, offering ridiculous amounts of money for a sought after pair of sneaks, closely followed by Hong Kong.

The impact of all this on Melbourne seems to be gains and losses. The most obvious gain is that the suppliers and the retailers are set to make a handsome and prolonged profit if they keep coming up with the goods. With more availability, the growth of our sub-culture has been astounding. Australian based websites specializing in hard to get sneakers will start popping up. Specialized stores will emerge. And how long have we been waiting for something like the exclusive Sneaker Freaker Magazine? Too long!!!

But the bad news is that with change, there is usually a loss of culture. Many people will bypass their morals at the sight of money. Retailers sell entire shipments to overseas buyers who put them on the net for a healthy profit. Customers are not even given a chance to smell the product because it never even makes it to the shelves. Fakes are becoming a major problem. And most of all, local collectors will miss out on what they thought they had been included in.

How long will it be before it is just too difficult and costly to keep up our hobby? Will our subculture suffer because of this so-called evolution? I dunno, but I guess at the end of the day, business is business. And who is to stop anyone from anywhere coming to Melbourne to stock up and make a profit elsewhere? You could say that it's that 'old-skool' attitude that we have to break out of to make way for the progression of sneaker collecting... but does this mean we have to compromise the very values and morals that hold this culture together? If you are a retailer – do you knowingly sell to overseas dealers to move stock, or do you service that long time customer that always has and always will stay true to your store because of a shared interest? If you are a supplier – do you flood the market with accounts just because you need to make quotas, or do you try your hardest to establish a fair distribution with longevity in mind?

More exciting things are yet to come for this beloved hobby of ours. There will be changes and shakeups. And we will accept most and live with the rest. I guess I'm a little sentimental when it comes to sneakers. It pisses me off when a retail store defeats its own purpose of being there in the first place. But I (along with many others) have been spoilt with the availability of so much new product as of late. Spoilt kids are always the worst.

There is no right or wrong here, it just is. As for me, you'll still find me at Camberwell market on the odd Sunday morning looking through other peoples stuff...

HANS D.C.

SYDNEY FOOTAGE

THERE ARE LOADS OF COOL SNEAKER SHOPS IN AUSTRALIA, BUT ONE STANDS OUT IN OUR BOOKS AND THAT'S FOOTAGE! RUN BY SUPER NICE TEAM, PHIL AND KARIN, FOOTAGE TAKES THE BEST FROM ALL ROUND THE GLOBE AND SERVES IT SUNNY SIDE UP. IT'S NOT EASY, BUT THEY SOMEHOW MANAGE TO BRING SOMETHING NEW TO THE AUSSIE SNEAKER SCENE EVERY SINGLE WEEK. WE CAUGHT UP WITH THEM BOTH IN THEIR DARLINGHURST STORE...

Hey guys, how's Sydney these days?

K: Things are good in Sydney. We'd seen a couple of new shoe releases this year, notably the 180s and the HTM Court Force.

How did you both get into the shoe game?

K: In terms of collecting, I got into the shoe game through Phil. He used to drag me with him to flea markets and op shops to look for the vintage shoes and jeans. I guess that sorta rubbed off on to me after a while and I developed my own style and collection. With the business, we used to go away on holiday or to visit family and come back with some new shoes. We'd get people coming up to ask us where we got our kicks. Before long, we started hooking friends and their friends and soon people were asking us for shoes. That evolved into a full time thing and we would make appointments to meet people to show them what we had in the shoe department.

P: When I was a kid, mum would only buy me Batas and some Panda branded white ones. I missed out on the Jordans, the Maxes, the Suedes and the rest of it. Having a shoe store now is SWEET REVENGE. Muahhhahaha! On a more serious note though, I got into collecting vintage some years ago and my interest in older style Nikes and adidas shoes gave me a few ideas for a shoe store.

OK - now I heard stories before I knew you — you used to drive around Sydney and sell shoes out of your car — is that true?

K: Phil can't drive. Haha! So I had to be the designated driver. We started selling out of our old gym bags (you know those old adidas ones you got from the '80s). Soon there wasn't enough room to fit more styles, so we had to put the shoes into our car boot.

Things were different then! Australia has been awash with awesome sneakers for the past 2 years. How come things changed so quick??

K: Well the whole sneaker market worldwide has boomed in the last few years. Take the Dunk for example. These days you'll find 3-4 different colours on the shelves at any time. 4 years ago, you'd be lucky to find 3-4 colourways a year. The big companies have realized that there's a big market in Japan and the States with so many collectors after shoes from the late '70s to early '90s.

P: 2-3 years ago, the scene was different, sneaker lovers had to turn to Internet purchases/orders or friends to buy shoes for them while they were on overseas trips.

You did a Dunk with SBTG, tell us about that hook up?

P: We got to know SBTG some time back through an introduction and our appreciation for vintage Nikes struck a chord. We started talking about the whole shoe collecting business.

K: Late last year, after he won the competition on Niketalk, he started customising shoes for stores like Atmos and Chapter (Japan). We approached him about doing a shoe for us. He's supported us from the start and liked the idea. That led on to talks about doing a SBTG x Footage Dunk for the sneaker faithful down under.

Do you think we'll see a collab shoe between an Aussie store and a major label?

K: Well we've seen a fair bit of collaboration going on overseas in the last 2 years. With the sneaker market growing in Australia, I think it might just happen soon. After all, weren't the Homers supposed to be an Australian exclusive?

SBTG x Footage Dunk

You are probably the only sneaker store in Australia that has different stock, how the hell do you manage that?

K: We keep good relations with our suppliers overseas. It takes time to build relationships and we did that for quite a while before starting the store. It's hard to work out what comes out in Australia. There's only so much you'd find out from local sources, so occasionally, it's hit and miss. We're constantly online for hours searching for the latest releases around the world.

P: Yeah, a mix that includes shoes that sneaker lovers don't see in other local stores. It's about sorting out the clientele with a wider choice of product.

What do adidas and Nike think of Footage, since you guys don't technically have local accounts?

P: The kicks are merchandised in a manner that projects these big players in a good light. We are trying to offer an add-on service to the good work the big boys are already doing in Australia. I believe we have an amicable relationship with Nike and adidas, albeit without local accounts.

What is it about Asian kids and sneakers?

P: I can't say what it is, but the Asian heads seem to have a serious take on what shoe they'd like on their feet. A real sense of pride in the foot department, I guess.

K: My take on the whole thing with Asian kids and sneakers is that it started with the Japanese. Some 10-12 years back, there weren't many retros of most of the original sneakers. So, they'd hunt for vintage in flea markets. After a while, the big companies started bringing out retros of the styles having realized the true potential

of the retro market. People started switching from buying vintage to buying retros to keep. Furthermore, most Asian kids use Japanese influences on style and pop culture on their own fashion style. Sneakers are huge in Japan and thus its influences have rubbed off onto Asian kids. The funny thing is, Japan got a lot of its initial influences from American pop culture but these days it's a reversal of roles.

Which shoe would you like to see retroed?

P: Would love to see an AJKO, Yum! Perhaps the Dynasty too.

K: That would have to be the Big Nike or the Nike Team Convention.

Loads of kids are wanting to start shoe stores, what do you think?

K: Its not easy starting a business. Footage was a steep learning curve for both of us and we're still learning by the day. In retrospect, it will be encouraging to see some new blood in the local sneaker market. The increase in good sneaker joints can only contribute to sealing Australia's place permanently on the global sneaker map. At the same time, it keeps us on our toes...

It's a golden oldie, but tell me your favourite sneaker and why?

P: Nike Vandal Supreme (Black/Gold), gotta love the Velcro strap. There was something about the old materials used on vintage Vandal Supremes that really give them a glow. I like that.

K: Nike Delta Force Hi in white/purple. Like the Terminator, it had the Big Nike at the back. Would love to see Nike retro that beauty along with the Nike Dynasty and Legend.

✴ FOOTAGE ✴
13c Burton St, Darlinghurst, Sydney
+ 612 9332 1337

Vintage Corner!

WITH

DELUDED MONKEY

A little while back we came across **www.deludedmonkey.com** and marvelled at some of the rare and abstract deadstock kicks on the site. In fact, we were so impressed, we asked him to put together a bunch of his favourite vintage sneakers for us. And here it is... how about those Guams and Alohas!

All photos :: Brian Findlay

ADIDAS FLEETWOOD
Mid 1980s. Made in France. Deadstock.
Part of the adidas range endorsed by RUN DMC.
The different variations of the grey actually
give this model quite a subtle
feeling despite the snakeskin effect!

PUMA BEAST LOW
1987. Made in Taiwan ROC. Grade 1.
This is one of the most valuable and collectable Puma models.
A model very much of its time and apparently the first time that fake
fur was used on a sneaker. Puma should really feel very proud of
this amazing and important fact.

NIKE TERMINATOR
1985. Made in Republic of Korea. Grade 2.
With models like the Terminator, Air Jordan I,
Big Nike, Dunk, Dynasty and Team Convention
all released in 1985, it would be safe to say that
1985 was a pretty good year for Nike
basketball sneakers!

ADIDAS JEANS
Late 1970s. Made in Austria. Grade 1.
A highly collectable model for football casuals and an expensive
model when released, at approximately double the price
of an adidas Superstar!

NIKE ATTACK
1985. Made in Republic of Korea.
John McEnroe wore this model and hence it acquired
the nickname 'Mac Attack'. The colour scheme
is nice and it's somewhat surprising that
it wasn't used more.

NIKE ROADRUNNER (HUSKERS)
1980. Made in Taiwan. Grade 2+
A special make-up for the University of Nebraska,
whose athletic department is known as the Huskers.

ADIDAS METRO ATTITUDE
Mid 1980s. Made in France.
If it could be argued that the adidas Fleetwood
shows some subtlety, the Metro Attitude certainly
does not! This colour version, in particular, is
unadulterated 1980s gaudiness at its best.

PF GOODRICH MEN'S SANDLOT
1950s. Made in USA. Deadstock.
Although this may only appeal to the more hardcore vintage sneaker collectors, it is still an interesting part of sneaker history. And to think that some people consider something from the mid 1990s to be vintage.

NEW BALANCE TRACKSTER II
Early 1970s. Made in USA. Deadstock.
This is the second version of the Trackster. The first was originally introduced in 1961 and was New Balance's first foray into running shoes. NB only introduced the 'N' on the side of their sneakers in the mid 1970s, so pre 'N' models are hard to find. If anyone does find any, please email!

ADIDAS SAN FRANCISCO
Mid 1970s. Made in Yugoslavia. Grade 1.
Part of the adidas city range.
The reissues of this and the adidas Jeans, pale in comparison to the originals.

PUMA UNIVERSAL
1950s. Made in Western Germany. Deadstock.
A very early Puma model produced not that long after Adi and Rudolf went their separate ways and way before the Puma stripe was created. The old treatment of the leather gives quite a different feel and look.

NIKE ALOHA
*1984. Made in Republic of Korea. Deadstock.
Infamous model with many different stories
surrounding it. One of the most collectable and
sought-after Nike models around.*

NIKE GUAM
*1984. Made in Republic of Korea. Grade 1.
The women's version of the Aloha
Also a very collectable and
sought-after model.*

NIKE UNKNOWN
*1971. Made in Taiwan. Deadstock.
Possibly called the Nike Flyte, this is one
of the very few models made when BRS was
first able to subcontract its own sneakers.
This is more or less as early as it can get
with Nike. Bear in mind that BRS actually
launched Nike in the US Olympic
Trials of 1972!*

NIKE DAYBREAK
*Late 1970s. Made in USA. Deadstock.
Popular mid range running shoe from
the late 1970s to early 1980s.*

IS ANOTHER MAN'S...

A SPECIAL REPORT BY VETERAN VINTAGE SNEAKER HUNTERS...

Gola 'Viper'

adidas 'Edberg Pro Club'

Quick 'Saffier'

Quick 'Ottawa'

Reebok 'Shaq Attaq'

EVERY SNEAKER FREAK WILL AGREE THAT AFTER SEARCHING FOR MONTHS THERE IS NOTHING BETTER THAN FINDING A REALLY NICE PAIR OF VINTAGE TRAINERS IN AN OLD STOCKROOM.

The experience of opening a box and looking at something that has been stored for 10-30 years or sometimes even longer is indescribable. It's loving every part of the hunt, it's the box, the way they smell, the place you found them and the history. It might sound strange for somebody who is not into vintage the way we are, but the vintage freaks out there know what we're talking about, it's love at first sight!

When we are talking about a booming sneaker hype, Amsterdam is one of the better places in Europe. Because of this hype it's hard to find a nice pair of vintage trainers. We decided to go out and look in other cities and even small villages have proven to be a good source. Sometimes you are lucky, but it takes a lot of time and most of the times the trip ends in a disappointment.

Once somebody tipped us on a ridiculously filled stockroom we immediately checked it out. We talked to the owner of the sports shop for a while and he took us upstairs and showed us his storage room. It was a huge room about three meters high and filled with boxes of a variety of brands, especially adidas. We are talking about 500 pairs in mint condition! We had never seen a place like this before - he stocked vintage soccer, tennis, basketball & running shoes. Most of the pairs were really nice old soccer models which would be great for a collector. We found brands like Converse, Hi-Tec and Reebok, but the nicest things we found were trainers from Puma, adidas and Quick.

Most of you will probably say 'What the hell is Quick'? Quick is a really old Dutch brand (1905) that re-entered the trainer market about two or three years ago. They were famous for their soccer shoes and people like Johan Cruijff played in them. From adidas we found things like the Edberg (two different styles) and a lot of nice running shoes from the mid '80s, like the adidas Squire, Tulsa and Melbourne.

Diadora 'Leopard'

Saucony 'Blaze'

Puma 'System XS 7000'

Max Miles

Quick 'André V.D. Ley'

Last month in Denmark another great thing happened. We checked out Copenhagen and after walking for an hour we bumped into a crazy store by the name of Sneak Freak. When we came in we were speechless, because the store was filled with vintage stuff. We are talking about models from Nike, adidas, Puma, Reebok, Hummel, Pony, Onitsuka Tiger, Gola etc. The owner of the store has a lot of love for vintage and really knows his stuff. He told us about different models and that adidas had been in buying old models from him to reissue. He also told us a lot about Hummel, an old Danish brand and showed us old collabs between Pony and Hummel.

Just to let you know that not all hunts are successful, we once got tipped off on a spot in a little city in the Netherlands, we were told that this sport shop had a storage room that went beyond imagination. They were stocking a wide variety of brands and models with a total of more than the 500 pairs we found earlier. After taking days off and planning to make the trip to the shop,

we heard in the news there was a fire in a sport shop in a very small Dutch town. Our worst nightmare

EURO TREASURE!

came true, the shop had burned down to the ground and all the shoes and their history were gone.

We have talked about a couple of our sneaker hunts. Some have been successful and some haven't been successful at all, but isn't it the greatest thing to find beautiful stuff you never knew existed?

We will keep searching and never give up, because when we are looking at our shoe collection on a rainy day or when we are getting dressed in the morning, we look at 10 to 30 years of sneaker history and a story of a successful hunt. Keep on hunting...

REMKO NOUWS & IVO FOKKE
www.endorsed.nl

Straight Sets Winners!

Anyone for a spot of French tennis then? As you might remember, this is how we ended our article in the fourth edition of Sneaker Freaker. We think you are not only ready for a spot of French tennis in this issue, but for a spot of tennis period! Because most of us know Ilie Nastase, Stefan Edberg and Stan Smith were great players who won most of the Grand Slam tournaments, we decided to make it a bit more interesting by creating our own game. What if tennis was not about the game itself but about the shoes these great players ENDORSED? *Close your eyes & imagine how these shoes would beat the competition!*

☺ Ilie Nastase

First on the court would be the signature shoe of the man who was also known as the Bucharest Buffoon, Ilie Nastase. The shoe you see here doesn't have the original colourway (White/Satellite), but this one is the adidas Nastase Super. The Nastase was also released in leather, but we prefer the mesh edition. We like the Nastase because of the used materials, the chunky outsole and the signature logo of the master himself on the tongue.

Nastase was one of the original tennis bad boys. He has singles and doubles victories in tournaments like Wimbledon, but he was more known for his humour as well as his hot-tempered character, which made him so popular with the audience. We think adidas rewarded him with one of the most beautiful tennis shoes ever made, definitely a shoe for a tennis hero.

We will call this a set, 1-0!

☺ Stefan Edberg

For the second set we have the shoe of the ideal Swedish son-in-law, Stefan Edberg. This tennis shoe was made in France and has some great details like the signature Edberg logo on the perforated tongue. Other great details are the holes on the toebox and the green eyelets. You can also find the green/yellow colourway they used on the famous three stripes at the back of the shoe.

Edberg was especially known for being a nice guy and won the ATP Sportsmanship Award five times. The fifth time they honoured him by renaming this award the Edberg Sportsmanship Award. But don't think this guy was a dull player, because he had some kick ass skills and fought like a true Viking. He had great anticipation and deadly backhand volley. He won tournaments like Wimbledon, the Australian Open and the US Open. In other words, adidas made him a shoe that resembled a true champ.

That makes it 2-0!!

☺ Stan Smith

For the third set we have the most famous signature shoe ever made in history! It was first endorsed by French tennis player Robert Haillet, but then renamed Stan Smith in 1971. Stan was an American who won a lot of different tournaments including Wimbledon. He was a part of the American Davis Cup team for a long time and was also very successful in doubles.

The Stan Smith is a classic design and has proved to be timeless and more popular by the year. The saying 'less is more' does appear to be completely true in this case. The perforated pattern instead of the three stripes and the colourway (white/grass green) really makes the difference. We personally think that everybody should have a pair of Stans, but just try to get a pair with the famous signature on the tongue as this makes the shoe so much more special. Check the special leather, the sole and the special embroidered signature logo. You got to love them.

A definite third set winner, 3-0!!!
Game, Set and Match!

Even though we already called it a Match, we do think there are other shoes that can come a bit closer to our personal favourites. We found some other pretty nice other tennis shoes in the past we would like to share with you.

☺ Andre Agassi

Before Andre Agassi even won a single tournament he was well known for his long blond hair and his dirty denim outfits. Agassi started his professional tennis career in 1986 at the age of 16 and is still playing on the highest level. In 1999 Agassi won the French Open at Roland Garros and because of this victory he was the first player since Rod Laver to win all four grand slam tournaments in his career and the only player besides Steffi Graf (now his wife) to win all four and an Olympic gold medal for singles.

The Air Tech Challenge wasn't the first Nike shoe endorsed by Agassi, but it is probably a favourite of all sneaker freaks. The shoe was made in 1990 and has some funky details. Let's start with the colours of both shoes. Neon yellow /green and purple/orange. Next to this we like the shape of the Air unit and the large Agassi logo on the back of the shoe.

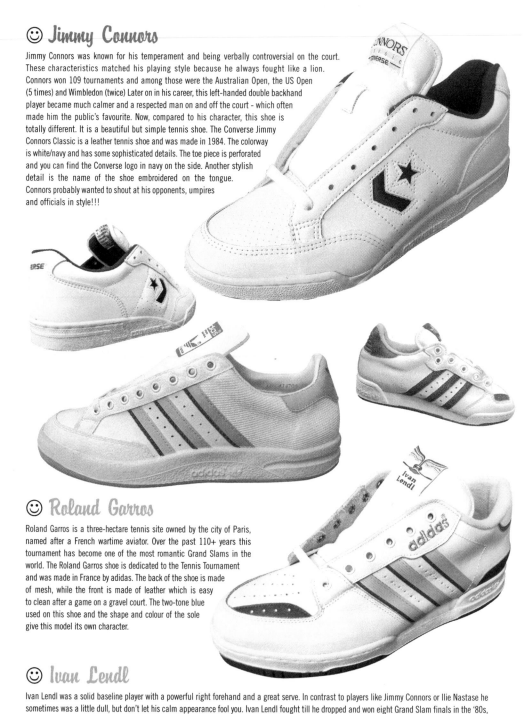

☺ Jimmy Connors

Jimmy Connors was known for his temperament and being verbally controversial on the court. These characteristics matched his playing style because he always fought like a lion. Connors won 109 tournaments and among those were the Australian Open, the US Open (5 times) and Wimbledon (twice) Later on in his career, this left-handed double backhand player became much calmer and a respected man on and off the court - which often made him the public's favourite. Now, compared to his character, this shoe is totally different. It is a beautiful but simple tennis shoe. The Converse Jimmy Connors Classic is a leather tennis shoe and was made in 1984. The colorway is white/navy and has some sophisticated details. The toe piece is perforated and you can find the Converse logo in navy on the side. Another stylish detail is the name of the shoe embroidered on the tongue. Connors probably wanted to shout at his opponents, umpires and officials in style!!!

☺ Roland Garros

Roland Garros is a three-hectare tennis site owned by the city of Paris, named after a French wartime aviator. Over the past 110+ years this tournament has become one of the most romantic Grand Slams in the world. The Roland Garros shoe is dedicated to the Tennis Tournament and was made in France by adidas. The back of the shoe is made of mesh, while the front is made of leather which is easy to clean after a game on a gravel court. The two-tone blue used on this shoe and the shape and colour of the sole give this model its own character.

☺ Ivan Lendl

Ivan Lendl was a solid baseline player with a powerful right forehand and a great serve. In contrast to players like Jimmy Connors or Ilie Nastase he sometimes was a little dull, but don't let his calm appearance fool you. Ivan Lendl fought till he dropped and won eight Grand Slam finals in the '80s, the French Open (three times), Australian Open (twice) and the US Open (three times.)

If there would be a tennis shoe to replace one of our favourites, it would be one of the shoes from Ivan Lendl. Lendl was probably next to Edberg the player with the nicest tennis gear. The distinguished signature logo made his clothing line so popular. The shoe we are presenting to you is the Ivan Lendl Champ 2. We really like the purple/grey/white colour way and the purple arch support. adidas used the same purple on the toebox where you can also find a creative perforated pattern. And just to make us happy, adidas came up with the beautiful signature Lendl logo on the tongue.

☺ Martina Navratilova

In between all those gentlemen, we also have one lady and her beautiful tennis shoe. Navratilova loves to play enjoyable tennis which you can find in her energetic, athletic and attractive serve and volley style. Navratilova returned in 2002 at the age of 46 (if we are correct) to play doubles and has been very successful. Martina won the US Open, the Australian Open and at Roland Garros more than once. What she did on the court of Wimbledon was not human: Martina won Wimbledon nine times!!! Maybe somebody can make sure she isn't from another planet???

The Puma Martina pictured was made in Italy and looks a bit like the Puma California, which we love. There are not a lot of special details on this shoe, but we really like the chunky sole just like the adidas Nastase. The shoe is a classic white and grey colourway, with a perforated tongue and toebox pattern. The gold Puma sign on the tongue and on the side of the shoe is a very classy detail. Martina we definitely think you have to be proud of a shoe like this!

☺ Boris Becker

Boris 'Boom Boom' Becker was a true playboy known for winning Wimbledon in 1985 at the age of 17. Most people thought he was just lucky as the big players of the moment did not make it to the finals. The year thereafter he proved it had nothing to do with luck as he won Wimbledon again, by beating Ivan Lendl in the finals. This was just the start of a long trip down victory lane.

The Puma shoe made for Boris Becker doesn't look like anything traditional. The pairs pictured are the black and the white releases with the Boris Becker signature on the side. Great detail on both pairs is the lining around the Puma stripes and the eyelet panel. Next to this we really like the coloured line on the midsole. We would love to 'Rock' these shoes like Boris, so anyone with a spare pair in a 9 or a 10, give us a call!

☺ Arthur Ashe

Last but not least is this humble Arthur Ashe shoe by Le Coq Sportif. Simple, plain white and strikingly slender, the shoe was as simple as Arthur was complex. A magnificent sportsman, Arthur Ashe was a pioneer African-American in the 'whitest' of sports. He was also an activist for players' rights and won Wimbledon in 1975 aged 31. Arthur had an amazing career but sadly, he is also remembered for contracting AIDS from a blood transfusion. He died in 1993.

We would like to thank: Remco Korf for the Ivan Lendl Champ and 2Bootsy from Harputs [San Francisco] for the Air Tech Challenge, the Stan Smith Supreme and the Boris Becker

Remko Nouws & Ivo Fokke for Endorsed - www.endorsed.nl

adidas Spirit of the Games

Made in 1984 in Taiwan. We truly can say that we are very proud to have this pair in the Endorsed collection! The Spirit of the Games was made for the Olympic Games in Los Angeles in 1984. Look at the great details of this shoe, for instance, the Spirit of the Games logo in the United States colourway and the sophisticated thin adidas striping on the side of the shoe. The partly red mid-sole is the finishing touch on this slept-on collectors item.

Karhu

In the late '80s and early '90s, Karhu was a very popular brand among youngsters in the Netherlands and especially in Amsterdam. In fact, they were just as popular as Nike at that time and that's why we wanted to introduce Sneaker Freaker readers to Karhu.

Karhu is the only Scandinavian sports brand from Finland and dates back to 1916. Karhu has always been the technology leader in running shoes. In fact, they claim to have invented the technology, now called Air, in 1970 and had it commercialized in 1976.

Karhu is still one of the players when it comes to functional running shoes, but they also brought back the Karhu original collection in which you can find models from the '70s and '80s.

A funny thing to know is that there is a rumour about a well-known sports brand that carries the three stripes buying their famous trademark from Karhu in the '50s for two good bottles of Whiskey and 1600 euro. Hmmm, which brand would that be???

adidas Squire

Made in the '70s or '80s in Taiwan. Not much information on this one but we can tell you this, the grey, black and silver colourway is just beautiful and the Squire is definitely one of our favourites. Nuff said, just look at it!

This issue's Retro-Fest comes direct from Mr Remko Nouws, representing the Netherlands. Remko has an insatiable appetite for old sneakers and spends some of his spare time out and about with his girlfriend looking for them in unusual positions. Most days however, you can find him shooting the breeze with his great friend and partner in www.endorsed.nl, Mr Ivo Fokke. What these two guys can tell you about the old stuff is not written down any place I know about.

So sit back, crack a tinny and enjoy the fruits of their past few months of vintage hunting. Ciao!

ENDORSED

Written by **Remko Nouws**
for www.endorsed.nl

Thanks to LEXFLEX 81 for the photo clipping!

Nike Air Structure

Made in 1990 in Korea. The Air Structure looked totally different on both sides and it almost felt like you were wearing two different shoes on one foot. There were two different colourways and shapes of air units and only a Swoosh on one side of the shoe.

The Nike Air Structure will probably be in the top 3 of favourite Nike trainers from the '90s for a lot of trainer-wearing kids of that time. Those kids, probably now in their late 20s and early 30s, will tell you without a doubt that the Air Structure, Air Stab and the Air Span are their favourite sneakers. Everybody loved those three, no matter what colourways. Nike note: has anybody noticed that the Pursuit and Air Structure never had any kind of coverage in the Sneaker books that came out the last few years? What's up with that?

adidas Boston

Made in 1984 in Taiwan. The adidas Boston is another classic. But don't confuse this pair with the Boston Super that has been reissued by adidas, they came some time after them. The Boston is simply a really nice runner from the mid '80s and we just love this navy with light grey colour way. Anybody want to run a marathon in this pair?

adidas ZX 320

Made in the mid or late '80s in France. We have always been great fans of the ZX series, but when we found the ZX 320 we didn't know about its existence. What we do know is that it's definitely a must-have for any ZX collector!

Nike Pursuit

Made in 1985 in Korea. The Nike Pursuit came in a black Nike box and was decorated with the gold Nike logo. The Pursuit is a definite classic and a favourite of collectors across the world. The blue and white colourway together with the silver Swoosh really worked for the Pursuit.

adidas Hot Shot

Made in the late '70s or early '80s in France. The Hot Shot has the original blue and red colourway of the Top Ten and also looks a lot like the adidas Jabbar. They used the same upper and outsole as they did on the Jabbar. Did adidas bring the Top Ten and Jabbar together in one shoe? Well, if this was the case, then the Hot Shot had to be a success!

adidas Campus

Made in France. Originally known as The Tournament, this trainer was renamed as the Campus at the beginning of the '80s. The '90s edition had a different upper and Superstar outsole. The outsole on this (early) version is vulcanised. This edition of the adidas Campus is a definite collector's item.

adidas Newcombe

Made in the early '70s in France. Sometimes you bump into a mystery pair of trainers and the moment you see them you know you've found something really special. This is the adidas shoe endorsed by the winner of Wimbledon (3 times) and the Australian Open (2 times): Mr John David Newcombe. Look at the picture and you just know this is a highly collectable model. The cool thing about this trainer is the gold stamp on top of the tongue which says 'adidas Newcombe, made in France'. Another great detail is the use of the perforated striping pattern, which we thought adidas only used on the Stan Smith. Although the adidas Newcombe and the Stan Smith have the same perforated striping pattern, the two are totally different, just look at the thinner outsole and the toebox on the Newcombe.

Beckenbauer Allround

Made in the '70s in Yugoslavia. Beckenbauer is probably the most famous German soccer player and the only man to have won the World Cup both as a player and manager. The Beckenbauer Allround will be reissued by adidas in July of 2005 and that makes this already highly collectable trainer even more special. The coolest detail on this shoe is the face drawing of 'Emperor' Franz on the tongue and we think the black silver colourway is simply Royal!

We saw this one a couple of years ago at Shoe's Victim in Antwerp. We fell in love immediately, but they wouldn't sell it. Luck was on our side when we found two pairs a couple of months ago, unfortunately it wasn't a 9 or a 10 so again we had some bad luck. But, oh well! At least it's now a part of the private Endorsed collection.

adidas Eddy Merckx

Made in the '70s in France. This is the cycling shoe made for Eddy Merckx who was the five-time champion of the Tour de France and the Giro d'Italia. He is also one of only four cyclists to have won all three of the Grand Tours: the Tour de France, the Giro d'Italia and the Vuelta a España.
The Eddy Merckx has been made for years and there are a lot of different versions of this cycling shoe. It was also reissued in 2002 as a lifestyle shoe. They changed nearly everything on the reissue, but kept the perforated side and the adidas stripes. Probably only for the diehard original collectors!

Spot-bilt

You're probably thinking, 'Spot-bilt??? THAT is definitely a pair of Saucony basketball shoes.' Well, we did some research and we can tell you this, Spot-bilt is the oldest division of Saucony, so you're partly right. They started in 1898 and they still make shoes today. In the past they made, for example, football, basketball and soccer shoes. A very interesting thing to know is that Spot-bilt built the first shoe ever worn by an Astronaut in outer space! Spot-bilt and Saucony carry the same logo and came in the same boxes in that period of time.

Spot-bilt X-press

This Spot-bilt X-Press was made in Korea in 1987. When we found it we didn't know anything but after reading about it in Bobbito Garcia's *Where'd You Get Those?* we found out that this in-your-face basketball shoe with ankle support system came in different colourways like red, green and purple. We think Spot-bilt definitely brought some freshness in a period when brands like Nike and adidas were household names on and off the basketball court.

Puma Buenos

Made in the late '70s / early '80s in West Germany. The Puma Buenos is an all-leather trainer with stitched to upper outsole. The white upper, in contrast with the black Puma stripe and the dark gum sole, makes this beautiful indoor trainer a definite Endorsed classic.

Lotto

Established in 1973 by the Caberlotto family in Montebelluna, Italy, Lotto started by producing tennis shoes. After the tennis shoes became a success, Lotto expanded by producing models for basketball, volleyball, athletics and football. Lotto signed a couple of great tennis players in the '80s. One of them was, coincidentally, John Newcombe who played in adidas in the '70s.

Lotto Brooklyn

Made in the '80s in Italy. The Brooklyn is a trainer with a lot of great details. We just love the perforated toebox and side logo, the padded nylon ankle piece is also a great detail. They used a printed Lotto fabric to decorate the inside and, if you look closely, you can see a little piece of it.

Lotto's People

Made in the '80s in Italy. Lotto signed a lot of athletes in general and named them 'Lotto's People'. This trainer comes out of the collection that accompanied these athletes. Look at the back of this shoe, now isn't that funky!

JORDAN I

This is Mazik from Conveyor in Santa Monica with a very rare purple and yellow AJI. It's hard to see in this pic but the original owner made some 'home improvements' to the side of the shoes with a purple texta! Who knows why or what the real story is...

WINDRUNNER

Fraser Cooke showed us this one. We can't remember what he told us about them but it appears to be some sort of Windrunner with a smidge of Jordan III elephant print thrown in. Did it come out before the Jordan?

STUDIO 54

Posibbly also known as the Night Trax, this is a sneaker of rare beauty. You may have seen a pic of these little disco dancers before, but what is never shown is the sole, which is finished in a glorious deep red glitter and completely flat. I guess this must've come in handy on the dance floor, but would have been a nightmare everywhere else. Super rare and very beautiful.

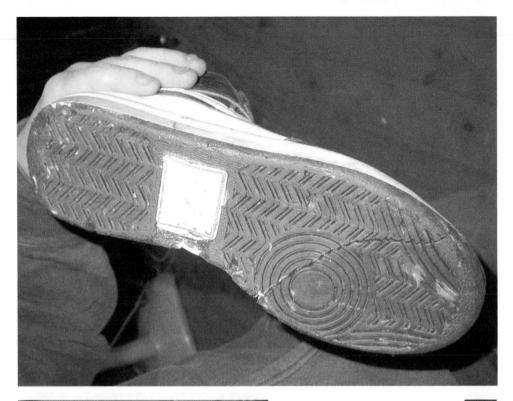

C H I C A G O

You like your sneakers done rare? Well these little steaks came out of the kitchen blue! The Chicago is also known as the Jordan you have when you're not having a Jordan. Note the logo, the red, black and white colourway and the overall effect seems like an amazing premonition. As you can see the sole is totally cracked, a fate which apparently afflicts all known pairs in existence due to the composition of the poly-rubber. So they're not for wearing... but nice all the same. Has anyone else noticed that the sole and midsole look suspiciously like a Puma California? Thanks to Justin Dickens for showing us both these and the Studio 54s at his stall in Camden market...

JOHN DOE?

These were bought in London over 10 years ago and no-one knows their name, not even adidas heads. Some suggest it may be part of a handball range? The hard chunky rubber stripes that sit outside the leather and the thick shelltoe are unique on adidas models as far as I can tell. '90s English brand Acupuncture liked it so much they used this model as 'inspiration' for all their early product. These have been thrashed to death, badly glued back up and worn again. And again. And again.

AWESOME

Puma weren't kidding when they named this bad boy, even if the colour does seem to be vaguely reminiscent of some other famous b-ball sneaker. This pair belongs to DJ Peril.

California Dreaming

THE VANS STORY

A very, very, very long fireside chat with...

STEVE VAN DOREN

I've found there are two common ways most people remember their visits to Southern California. One is tales of smog, traffic, tourist traps, fast food and girls with fake tits. The other is stories of Hollywood, Rodeo Drive, Disneyland and cosmetically enhanced breasts. For me it's always been the simple, everyday icons the locals have grown up with and take for granted: sunshine, Double Double's (animal style), Wahoo's Fish Tacos and great racks.

These were the happy thoughts I had in my head as I strolled down Flinders Street, Melbourne on the way to learn more about another SoCal legend, Vans. I was on my way to interview Steve Van Doren whose father had co-founded the company nearly 40 years ago and who has spent most of his life immersed in the business of sneakers. I was pretty pumped. It's not everyday you get a history lesson in sneakers straight from the horse's, or, in this case, the foal's mouth.

STORY :: JASON LE

ABOVE:. Paul Van Doren, Gordon Lee, Jim Van Doren and Gordon's son Butch cut cake to celebrate opening day, March 1966.

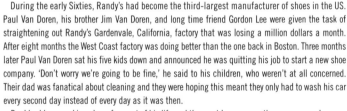

THE BEGINNING
::THE VAN DOREN RUBBER COMPANY

Paul Van Doren was born in 1930 and grew up in the Boston Area. When he reached the 8th grade, he realised he didn't like school and promptly left. He had a passion for horses and, at the age of 14 and a half, made his way to the racetrack. He was known as 'Dutch the Clutch' and for a buck he would give you odds on the race.

Paul's mother couldn't stand that he wasn't working or going to school. She dragged him into the shoe factory where she worked and got him a job making shoes and sweeping the factory floor. This was to define the young Van Doren's future.

In twenty years, Paul worked his way up the ranks and became the Executive Vice President of Randy's, a Boston based shoe manufacturer. Randy's was well known at the time and made canvas shoes for Bob Cousy, the flashy Boston Celtics legend who was later voted one of the top 50 NBA players of all time.

During the early Sixties, Randy's had become the third-largest manufacturer of shoes in the US. Paul Van Doren, his brother Jim Van Doren, and long time friend Gordon Lee were given the task of straightening out Randy's Gardenvale, California, factory that was losing a million dollars a month. After eight months the West Coast factory was doing better than the one back in Boston. Three months later Paul Van Doren sat his five kids down and announced he was quitting his job to start a new shoe company. 'Don't worry we're going to be fine,' he said to his children, who weren't at all concerned. Their dad was fanatical about cleaning and they were hoping this meant they only had to wash his car every second day instead of every day as it was then.

Paul had been making shoes for most of his life and the most he ever saw the company make, even while making hundreds of thousands of shoes, was a dime a pair.

The retailer was the one who was making all the cash. Paul's dream was to have his own factory as well as his own retail stores. He was a great businessperson, his brother Jim was an amazing engineer and their friend Gordon was an excellent manufacturer. They formed the Van Doren Rubber Company with Serge D'Elia, a Belgian friend Paul made in Japan, who had been supplying shoe uppers from Japan to the USA.

The company was founded in 1965. Paul and Serge owned 40% each and Jim and Gordon owned 10% each. Built from scratch using old machinery bought from all over the USA, it took a year to set up the factory at 704 East Broadway in Anaheim. It took a lot of machinery and was a lot harder to do then, compared with today's modern processes. Since 1900, there had only been three companies that had manufactured vulcanized footwear in the US: Randy's, Keds and Converse. And then there was Vans...

Vans Factory and Store 1966

INTERVIEW
:: STEVE VAN DOREN

So when did Vans open the doors for business?
Well they were building the factory throughout 1965 and they had 'Opening January!' painted on the front, but it wasn't ready. This was the year of Maxwell Smart so they had 'Would you believe February?' added to the sign. But it actually opened, I believe, on the first day of March, 1966. The factory, the office and the retail store were all located at 704 East Broadway.

The way they had the company set up was unique at the time, direct retailing shoes from a manufacturer, how did it all work?
The very first day my Dad had probably 10 racks with empty boxes on them. My dad was always a systems guy. Blue boxes were for men, orange boxes were for boys, red boxes were kids' and green boxes were for women. If you're looking for men's shoes, they are in the blue boxes, you don't have to go any further than that.

The first day they opened the doors, 16 people came in and they had a sample of all the styles. We didn't even have names for the styles, we had numbers. Style #44 was our authentic deck shoe. In the 44s my dad had navy blue, white, Loden green and red. We didn't have black at first; it became our best seller in later years.

The women's styles for Vans were smaller styles in the same deck shoes. We had a lace-up, we had a 2-eyelet, we had a slip-on and the styles were called #16, #19 and style #20. Then we had a leather deck shoe, a leather boat shoe, style #46 and a canvas boat shoe, style #45. These were the original styles, with children's shoes called style #15. Women's shoes were $2.29, and men's style 44s were $4.49.

My dad had never been in retail before, so it was new for him. He could basically look at your foot and say, 'Hey you're eight and a half', but they had a stick to make the customers feel good. They would then find out what style they wanted and what colour they wanted. Those first sixteen pairs did have to be made that day, and the people came back the next day to pick up their shoes, just because they wanted to get open so quick. They started filling the boxes in the store and by the third or fourth day they had filled them in.

How did the custom making of shoes come about?

In the women's area, a lady came in and said, 'That's a nice pink but I really want a brighter pink.' And then she picked up the yellow shoe and said, 'That's a nice yellow but it really is too light.' My dad thought to himself, 'For crying out loud I can't afford to carry 5 different colours of pink.' So he said, 'Lady, why don't you get a piece of fabric, whatever colour pink you want, bring it back and I'll make a shoe for you.' So it was almost the first day that they started charging extra to do a custom pair of shoes.

In the Sixties, we had Catholic schools that had uniforms, so we'd make shoes out of their plaid uniforms and stuff. If the high school colours were red and gold, or if their colours were tartan plaid, we would make their shoes. Plus we were making shoes for all the cheerleaders and drill teams all over southern California. It was a big business for us.

What was the original design concept for the Vans #44 shoe?

Similar to what my dad had made before. He was too cheap to spend on marketing and his whole concept was to make, with my uncle Jim, the moulds for the waffle soles twice as thick as PF Flyers, thicker than any shoe out there. We used better canvas, we'd be using 10 duck which is really strong, we'd use nylon thread instead of cotton and the compound was pure crepe rubber on the outsole, so it was going to outlast anything. My dad's whole philosophy was to make shoes like Sherman Tanks. They were really built tough and you'd have to tell your friends about it. We had a sign from the very first day: 'Tell a friend about Vans.' The marketing was my brothers and sisters and I passing out flyers. We did our very first store outside of the Anaheim area in Costa Mesa where we lived. The first manager was my mother.

So from that one store, how many did it grow into?

He started by opening ten stores in ten weeks! Within the first year and a half it had already gone to 50, and my dad's accountant, who was there for 24 years, said, 'Paul, six of those ten stores are losers.' My dad says, 'Well I need ten more losers then.' His whole thing was if he made one pair of shoes and it cost him $10,000 for all the manufacturing, it was $10,000 a pair. If he made 1000 pairs of shoes it was costing him $10 a pair. If he was making 10,000 pairs it only cost him a dollar.

We really didn't sell anything to other retailers between '66 and '76. In the 1970s I remember going to San Francisco, my uncle was on the sales side and moved from Boston, there was always lots of family involved... He moved up to the bay area and put in thirteen stores. In '73 we were stretched too far and the San Francisco stores were bleeding the company dry. At one point we decided to close them down, but people knew Vans and they liked them but it was costing too much. So he stayed and started selling shoes to places like the Oliver Bike Shop and that's how national sales started in the early Seventies. It was the first time we had sold shoes outside of Southern California.

When did the company realise it was developing a following with skateboarders?

Santa Monica and Manhattan Beach is where they started coming in and custom making shoes. In the very beginning we sold tons of the #44 blue deck shoes. Then the custom orders started coming in, and it started with just red and blue. We let that run for a few months then we came up with a stock shoe - navy blue/gold/navy blue and then brown/beige/brown. We would watch the customs and make brown/beige/brown if everybody ordered it as a custom. You had school colours, team colours, skaters and BMX kids who came in the late Seventies and those guys really liked the wild colours. There was no leather around until '76–'77, when we finally came up with the Old School which had leather in the toe and heel because skaters were wearing the hell out of them. Leather would last a long time, longer than anything else. The outsole never wore out, the side wall of the material would never wear out, they could get it down to where there was just a little bit of fabric but the sides would still be good.

Original colour of the first Vans Off The Wall shoe, from 1976

When did Vans start developing shoes for skaters?

In 1975, we had the blue deck shoes, but the guys over in Santa Monica, like Tony Alva and Stacey Peralta wanted us to make customs. We decided to add padded backs, an outside heel counter, and the 'Off the Wall' label. That was our new skate shoe which came out on March 18, 1976. The Skate Hi had padded sides so when the board flew off the pool and into their ankles they didn't kill themselves. That was a big thing. That saved lives for skaters. They loved them.

Did you think at the time skateboarding was just a phase or that it was here to stay forever?

It seemed big because so many of these kids started organizing contests. I remember my dad had no budget so I was driving a van bringing guys from the Valley over to a contest in Santa Monica. Tony Alva and those guys, the board companies looked after them but we just supplied shoes. The first cheque we ever wrote was to Stacey Peralta, I think we were paying him about $300 to wear the shoe and he was travelling worldwide. Each store manager had seven or eight guys that they were supplying shoes to as well. We got our first team manager, Eric, in about '77. He had a van and a plexi-glass ramp and he would travel round, do the demos, and make sure the guys got their shoes. Kids were buying whatever they saw in the skate magazines.

Steve Van Doren 1974

Where did the slip-on idea come from?

The company my dad worked for before made a slip-on. He interpreted it into our own style, number #48. It was actually a slip-on with a non-skid sole for boating. Our 40th anniversary is coming up next year and we are going to be bringing back style #45 which has a blue top and a blue sole designed for gripping.

The checkerboard slip-on is probably the most recognised of all the Vans styles, how did they come about?

In the late Seventies I was now out of high school and I noticed kids were taking the side profile off the shoe, where the white rubber was, and colouring it in checkerboard. So the first thing we did was start making rubber with the checks on it and eventually we made some canvas. Right at the same we had a PR lady named Betty Mitchell and Universal Studios asked Betty for some shoes. So she sent a whole lot of checkerboard shoes for the movie *Fast Times at Ridgemont High*. We had no idea. They liked them so much they ended up on the album cover and then Sean Penn, or Jeff Spicoli in the movie, was hitting himself over the head with the shoes in the movie.

It was magic because we sold millions of checkerboards. My dad didn't really want to sell shoes outside of California and now he had no choice as people everywhere wanted our shoes!

How many times have you seen the movie?

At least 50. Doing 'Dogtown' I got to meet Sean Penn years later and it was really enjoyable getting to say 'thankyou so much for being Spicoli, you made my life a lot easier'.

Has any one in the middle of a sales meeting ordered a pizza?

The theme of the sales meeting about five years ago was Fast Times. Everything was checkerboard and I ordered 10 pizzas and asked them to just barge in the middle of it and bring them right up the front. It was great because after my dad left, sometimes they may have been a little too stuffy. You know, suits and ties and stuff. It was perfect. And I am bit of a prankster.

Sounds like good times, what else do you think was adding to the brand's success?

The thing about Vans is that we had a run from '76-'80 with all the two tones and that rolled into solid colour slip-ons and then straight into checkerboard. We didn't rest on our laurels! We started doing red/white, green/white, two tones, any kind of combination. Because again, we only have a vulcanized shoe. We don't have what Nike has, all kinds of athletic stuff. We had a canvas shoe and we're trying to make it look like a marquee diamond. So how do we do that? With colours and fabrics.

We also used to get kids to draw up what they would like to see on the sides of the shoes. Every month we'd pick a winner, bring them down to the factory and take their family to Disneyland. All of a sudden we had things that had 'Rad' on them, we had unicorns and rainbows. When you get 200 designs with strawberries, we'd do a strawberry shoe. So that's how we would do it and, having our own factory, I could have a new shoe out tomorrow.

Have you ever thought about resurrecting those contests?

I'm proud to say, at least in the States, that we've brought back our custom shoe program nine months ago and it's going sensationally. We do about 2000 pairs every month.

We talked about possibly putting a page in a book with just a silhouette of the slip-on and let kids develop patterns or designs they want and have a worldwide contest for our 40th anniversary. We will actually print the fabric, make the shoes, maybe make 500 pairs and give a royalty to the young person who designed the fabric.

During the early Eighties, Van's diversified and started making basketball shoes, baseball shoes and then you had that Chapter 11 thing. Why did you nearly go bankrupt?

What happened was that my father, who was a great manufacturer and a great business person, was trying to back off just a little bit. Checkerboard was flying, Vans was going great. My uncle Jim was President, and he was doing a magnificent job, but he made a mistake trying to be something that Vans is not. He wanted to be Nike, you know, the next big thing.

He was very talented. We had a 5 star running shoe in Runner's World. We had widths from 4E to 4A, wide to narrow in every one of the athletic shoes we had. We had basketball, baseball, soccer, tennis, skydiving shoes, wrestling shoes... I mean, we had breakdance shoes, we had all kinds of shoes. They weren't vulcanized, they were cold cure which were all made overseas. We were making really nice shoes, but my Dad kept telling my uncle, 'Hey they're costing us a fortune. We're losing our butt.'

My uncle wouldn't listen because, you know, he guided Vans through the checkerboard era and we were flying. We were the hottest thing going. All the money we were making on checkerboard, we were wasting it on all of these lasts, dyes, materials, everything you could imagine on these athletic shoes. And it wasn't selling. People don't know Vans for that. You got big powerhouses like adidas, Nike and Puma and we were just getting our butts kicked on the athletic shoes.

Well eventually the banks, we had a note like when your house is mortgaged, called up and said, 'Hey pay my note back' and we couldn't do it. We didn't have 11 or 12 million dollars. So we filed for Chapter 11. My dad went to court for the first time and the court saw what was happening and asked my uncle to leave. That was a very sad day. My dad didn't know if they were going to ask us to leave or my uncle's side of the family. The courts sorted it out and from that day my uncle has not been involved with the company. They asked my father to come out of semi-retirement, with Gordy's help and Serge as a silent partner, to get Vans out of trouble.

In 1984, my dad got the whole company and told them, 'Hey if you need a raise in the next three years I can't give it to you. We owe probably 15 million dollars. I'm going to pay this back 100 cents in the dollar.' My dad was very proud of what he built and a lot of people get out of Chapter 11 by paying 10 cents in the dollar and it costs millions in legal fees. He said no to that. We have to buy rubber from Uni-royal and US rubber, we buy fabric from this company, we buy the outers from this company, the same people that we owe money to. So we had a plan, it started in '84 and every six weeks my dad would go in with a business plan. He'd come back and say 'This is what we sold, this is what we are going to sell.' He did that every six weeks.

At one point my dad had an extra seven or eight payments and told the bank he wanted to give it to them in case something slowed down. The bank said no but they could take it from the back end. My dad at that point had a piece of land and sold it and the next week he paid the bank fully. He wanted to pay the last $50,000 in pennies but found out he would need a dump truck. He hated them because they were trying to liquidate us at every second. One thing about surviving Chapter 11, I realized everything my dad ever had in his life, he was this close to losing and that wasn't fair.

They sound like tough times, what got you through?
It was back to classics. We didn't advertise one penny from '84 to '87 and that's when companies like Vision Streetwear came through. They started to advertise heavily and we couldn't do anything except just let them go. We couldn't pay skaters or anybody else to wear our shoes, all we could do was give some shoes away. Basically we just put blinkers on and just tried to get the money paid back. Then in '87 we came out of Chapter 11.

You had an ownership change at the end of the Eighties and sold some shares at the start of the Nineties. Was it the corporate changes that forced the end of manufacturing shoes in the US?
In 1988 these men offered my dad $75 million for the company. He didn't owe a penny at the time. With my uncle not being involved anymore, there were politics and we'd never had that in the company before. My dad didn't want to see that happening in the future and he called me up to play tennis. My dad didn't play tennis and he said, 'What would you say if I told you someone offered 75 million for the company?' And I said, 'Sell. You're ready to retire, enjoy life. Whatever happens to me I'll be fine.'

What happened was Black Monday. One of the last deals Michael Wilkin, a famous investor who went to jail, did was Vans. It was 1987 and the market fell and that messed up the deal. It was meant to happen again in December of '87 but the market fell again. The deal actually happened in 1988 for 60 million dollars. The promise was that when they went public they would pay my dad the rest of the 15 million.

California Native Catalogue Shot

Original ad for the first Vans Off The Wall shoe

Californian Kids Catalogue Shot

Steve Van Doren 2004

So in 1988 the deal went through, a company called McConval-Deluit bought the company. The two men behind it acquire companies, grow them and take them public. They owned the company for about the next ten years. They took Vans public in '91 and we were a public company until 2004.

From '88 to '93 everything was going fine. Then things started slowing down a bit. We started buying snowboard boots from overseas and by '94 to '95 we were sourcing everything overseas and people forgot about our classics from about '95 until '02. Trends happen but we just went away from it for too long a time.

We had a factory in Orange and when we were public, we started getting some new management in. They went and built another factory in San Diego all hi-tech, stuff my dad knew for fifty years wasn't good enough. My dad was gone, they thought they knew more, Harvard graduates, and they went and spent a ton of money on a factory that never, ever, made the volumes or efficiency that the old factory did. They kind of screwed it up. That was the point where they shut down all manufacturing and moved everything offshore.

There was also demand for new types of shoes, cold cure. You couldn't do them in California for environmental reasons. So we couldn't do the shoes that our competitors were doing. So we changed the philosophy of the company from manufacturing to being a marketing company.

The Nineties arrives and Vans were getting involved with the Warped tour and skate events, what was driving that?

A guy named Kevin Lyman came to us and said, 'I've got this tour idea'. I said I wanted to do a skateboard contest nationwide and Kevin said his music tour was going nationwide. So we came up with the Vans Warp tour. Well it was the 'Warped' tour year one and then it was the 'Vans Warped Tour' in year two.

Kevin was a hard working guy, but never had the money so we bought 15%. We just had our 10th anniversary. Last year 650,000 kids paid to see the tour in the US. We've been to Australia three times and Europe twice and it's been very successful. During the dotcom era a company bought the tour, but a year later they went out of business. We got it back for a dollar, now we're the majority owner of it and it continues to go strong.

I think it's one the best things we have ever done. Basically, Vans is a company that sells to teenagers, 65% male and 35% female. What did a teenager do before he was 16 and could drive? He skateboards, he surfs, he rides bikes. Then he finds the sheilas and needs a car to go do stuff. But both boys and girls like music, so we tied ourselves into a punk rock scene cause a lot of the guys that were in bands would wear Vans.

Next we decided to do skate events. At first I tied in with the Hard Rock Café and Transworld and did the Triple Crown, which came from my dad because they had the Triple Crown of horse racing. We made a deal with NBC, we won't do horse racing, but we'd like to do a Triple Crown of skateboarding, surfing, snowboarding, wakeboarding, BMX, freestyle motor cross, super cross. So for the last eight years we have done 20 events. We have three different events in three different locations across the United States in each sport.

The very first event we did was in '95 at the Hard Rock Café in Newport Beach. There were 11,000 people, Ben Harper played and Tony Hawk won the skate event. There was an existing Triple Crown of Surfing, so we bought that for a good sum of money in '96. That was the second Triple Crown and the third one was the Triple Crown of Snow Boarding. Then we did BMX, wakeboarding and so on.

Slip On LX

Who owns Vans now?

VF Corporation bought Vans. They are a unique company, they actually researched for a year the Quiksilvers, the Billabongs, the Vans, you name it, any kind of youth culture brand. They kept doing market surveys and Vans kept coming back as a cool company and that's why they bought it for $400 million bucks. When my dad sold the company for $75 million we were doing $40 million is sales. Now our sales are around $360 million.

Vans' big movie experience was 'Dogtown and the Z-boys' which documented the Zephyr teams evolution of Skateboarding. Was it an expensive exercise?

We dabbed into that and put out about $800,000 for Stacey Peralta to buy the rights for the music as well as do the direction of the movie and put that documentary out. We basically got our money back too.

Are you surprised the Dogtown story has become a Hollywood film 'The Lords of Dogtown?'

I am excited about it because I thought the actual documentary was fantastic and it would get to a lot of theatres, but it just didn't. I saw the actual directors cut a few months ago with Skip and Tony Alva and it's going to be great.

The year 2000 saw a massive consumer thirst for retro footwear. It seemed perfect for Vans, but was it easy to re-introduce the classics back in line?

We had different people in charge at that time, the guys at the top now are really behind it. At that time people were saying, 'Why can't you get this?' and, 'Why can't you get that?' I was in charge of events and we had other people in charge of product and we had a problem: they weren't listening. I would just say, 'Fuck em, I'm going to make my own shoes and put them out there.' And you know what happened? We sold a lot of them and people started saying, 'That's what I remember about Vans.' The ball started rolling and we were getting the things back again, the retro stuff.

It's hard to imagine Vans not having things like checkerboard, did you enjoy seeing it all coming back?

I've had the most fun in the last year and a half. It was the first time I'd been over to China and saw where our shoes were made. Before we closed our factories in the States, I snuck out 200 yard rolls of fabric out and hid them in the warehouse. I'd just cut the fabric in squares, go to my cousin and he'd print my material. So when I went over to China I'd have fun and go make a pair of shoes.

I made up a bunch of different ideas and brought them back to show the designers. That's how it was in the old days. You could walk out the back and do a pair of shoes anytime you wanted to. It's harder now. The last trip I went back and got them to make a mould for a size 66. So I actually have a size 66 slip-on now and I'm going to use them to display in stores all over the world. I made up a couple of black pairs, a couple of red checkerboards and some black ones too.

Are they rights, lefts or both?

Right now they are all lefts. The mould was very expensive, so I think I'll stick with just lefts for the moment. I made big, giant shoe boxes for display and the shoe actually fits in. So for the rest of '05 you will see a whole bunch of big shoes everywhere.

Vans Trovata

Ray Barbee SK8-Hi

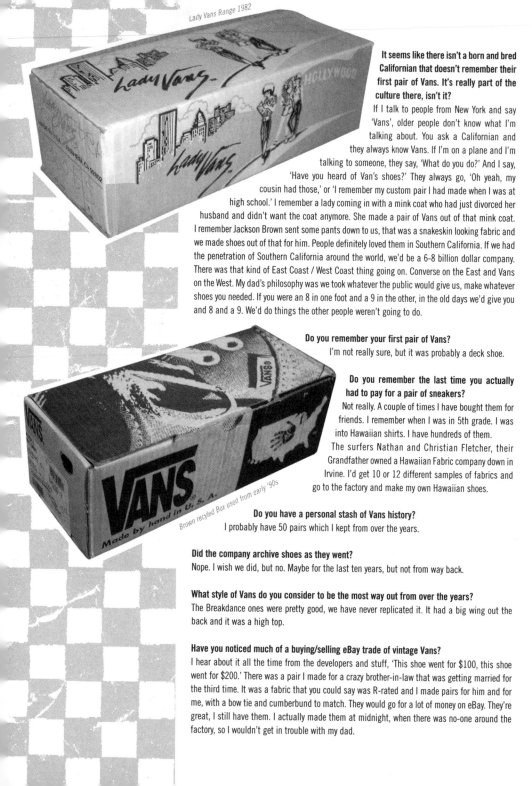

It seems like there isn't a born and bred Californian that doesn't remember their first pair of Vans. It's really part of the culture there, isn't it?

If I talk to people from New York and say 'Vans', older people don't know what I'm talking about. You ask a Californian and they always know Vans. If I'm on a plane and I'm talking to someone, they say, 'What do you do?' And I say, 'Have you heard of Van's shoes?' They always go, 'Oh yeah, my cousin had those,' or 'I remember my custom pair I had made when I was at high school.' I remember a lady coming in with a mink coat who had just divorced her husband and didn't want the coat anymore. She made a pair of Vans out of that mink coat. I remember Jackson Brown sent some pants down to us, that was a snakeskin looking fabric and we made shoes out of that for him. People definitely loved them in Southern California. If we had the penetration of Southern California around the world, we'd be a 6-8 billion dollar company. There was that kind of East Coast / West Coast thing going on. Converse on the East and Vans on the West. My dad's philosophy was we took whatever the public would give us, make whatever shoes you needed. If you were an 8 in one foot and a 9 in the other, in the old days we'd give you and 8 and a 9. We'd do things the other people weren't going to do.

Do you remember your first pair of Vans?

I'm not really sure, but it was probably a deck shoe.

Do you remember the last time you actually had to pay for a pair of sneakers?

Not really. A couple of times I have bought them for friends. I remember when I was in 5th grade. I was into Hawaiian shirts. I have hundreds of them. The surfers Nathan and Christian Fletcher, their Grandfather owned a Hawaiian Fabric company down in Irvine. I'd get 10 or 12 different samples of fabrics and go to the factory and make my own Hawaiian shoes.

Do you have a personal stash of Vans history?

I probably have 50 pairs which I kept from over the years.

Did the company archive shoes as they went?

Nope. I wish we did, but no. Maybe for the last ten years, but not from way back.

What style of Vans do you consider to be the most way out from over the years?

The Breakdance ones were pretty good, we have never replicated it. It had a big wing out the back and it was a high top.

Have you noticed much of a buying/selling eBay trade of vintage Vans?

I hear about it all the time from the developers and stuff, 'This shoe went for $100, this shoe went for $200.' There was a pair I made for a crazy brother-in-law that was getting married for the third time. It was a fabric that you could say was R-rated and I made pairs for him and for me, with a bow tie and cumberbund to match. They would go for a lot of money on eBay. They're great, I still have them. I actually made them at midnight, when there was no-one around the factory, so I wouldn't get in trouble with my dad.

My favorite Vans are the Full and Half Cabs. Steve Caballero has been involved with Vans for a long time, can you tell us about the relationship?

Stevie, I got to really know well in '87. He's been riding for us for 17-18 years. He's my favorite athlete, we do a lot of things together. The Half Cab started because everyone was taking the Full Cab and cutting it off. The shoes are still around today too. It's not a big number driver but it's more successful now than it has been in the past ten years.

Are there any other interesting special make-ups that you have done over the years?

Our Skate Hi. We had the guys from Pearl Jam say, 'Hey we remember that rust colour, can we get some?' So I made 10 pairs of those.

Four years ago MTV called and they wanted to do a surprise band at our skate park, it was the Red Hot Chilli Peppers. Nobody was to know until a half hour before the show. In nine days the art department made up a bunch of Chili Pepper designs. I had twelve pairs of shoes made between Skate Hi's, Lows and Old Schools. They were red and when they came to play I gave each guy a pair of shoes. I kept one pair and gave a pair to my daughter.

'80s boxes

What does the future hold for Vans?

We're never going to have air pockets like Air Jordans and stuff like that, so we have to get creative with the materials. The thing that hasn't come back totally yet are all the fun, crazy things we did with prints. That's an area that still has a long run for us.

It seems hard to get support for a new idea unless it's retro inspired. Is it hard to come out with something fresh and original in sneakers?

I know Grant, who is our head designer, has a really great idea but I'd have to kill you if I told you. He's got something that's not that easy, that he's been working on for a year and a half. If he comes through with it, it's really going to be cool. There's also a new line called Syndicate. We just showed it at ASR, it was on a corner parking lot under a big army tent. It's got four or five different styles, the Half Cab is one, the Old School is one. There is tattoo art on an Authentic, it looks great. These are packaged really cool and it's a special brand just for our best, core skate shops.

Original boys box from 1966

Just to finish off, what shoe would you pick to sum up what Vans is all about?

The Checkerboard Slip-on. People buy them to go do their weddings.

Authors Note:: I'd like to thank Steve Van Doren for being so generous with his time and would like to wish him all the best for his 50th birthday in October. I have a feeling he know's how to throw one heck of a party, so don't miss it if you get an invite. (Even if you happen to be a well known business leader that shares the same birthday, you will have more fun at Steve's Party.) *Jason Le*

VIRGINIA CUMMINS

GOBO

So how's Singapore?

It's hot, humid, clean, safe, one of the cities with the best looking Asian girls, strict, great place to skate in, great food, great clubs, nicest airport in the world, proud of and love to be here.

What's your background in art and design?

I graduated locally with a diploma in visual communication, majoring in electronic media design. Basically I did boring stuff like web design and interactive design which I couldn't catch up. I was taught by great mentors though.

Is this a full-time thing? Or are you moonlighting in another job?

Yes, it has became full-time for me. Well I still do design and so on...

So what made you start painting your shoes?

I had this thing for products right from when I was a kid. I always wanted to add my personal touch to it. It's in the blood, I got it from my dad, Max. At first it was just minor adjustments, like swoosh painting, then it started to get more complicated and involved scissors, needle and thread, paint etc... Then I started modifying shapes and total reinterpretation. Which is what I am doing now.

During my research for the story on fakes, I noticed a pair of Air Force Safari hybrids that look suspiciously like something you designed a while back. Was I right????

Yes, you're right! I was kinda shocked when I stumbled onto a Yahoo Taiwan auction. My boy sent me the link! They weren't cheap...

I guess that is the ultimate flattery - a bootleg custom!

Yeah exactly, it's amazing how these cats work. I only made 2 or 3 pairs for friends. I assume they worked out the copy from Milk magazine (HK). There was a full 2 page spread on them and I received that bootleg as a present last Christmas - the ultimate flattery!

So how did your career start?

It actually started with the Air Force One Safari. There was this itch in my head asking me to paint the craziest, most detailed thing. I call it 'Ant fucking' - I'm talking about the safari print. I loved the Safari colorway, but I didn't like the shape of the shoe. So the challenge was to transfer that into an AF1. The thought scared me, but I did it anyway. It had mad response on Niketalk. That gave me the drive to create more till I started planting my own graphics into a shoe. It isn't just a custom, it is a whole new transformation process and re branding of an existing product. The shoe is Sabotaged!!!

It's taken a while but we finally caught up with Singapore based sneaker customiser whizz kid Sabotage. His handiwork caught our eye a while back but he really shot to fame when he won a comp on Niketalk! Since then, his rep has gone vertical - how many kids can lay claim to the fact that their custom designs have been mass bootlegged in the factories of Asia? We also asked him to be a judge in our Kustom 99 comp! Read all about it...

When was that?

My very first custom that I did when I was a kid. I got a pair of Nikes (I forgot what model, looked like the Agassi shoe but I'm sure it wasn't) that were mostly white with poison green sole and details. The uppers were all white and I just thought that something was incomplete about 'em, so I painted the swoosh. I thought they were the illest joints in the neighbourhood. Then came the skating days like 1991-92 when skaters were dying for midcuts. Cats cut their Vans full-cabs to mid-cuts. Until Vans finally half-cabbed 'em.

I had my electric blue Airwalk Velocity Hi's, ripped the lace savers (wrong move), cut it to a mid-top, painted the base black and the Airwalk logo yellow. The best part was, instead of duck taping the top to hide the revealing sponge inners, I stitched it. It was sealed like an OG. That broke some necks.

There was also the vintage OG era in 1996-97 where I got myself a pair of white/grey Legends. At that time, if you had OG Nikes with colour, you were the shit. But I could only afford whites. I was at a sneaker repair store and I came across this black leather dye, I copped it and my Legends became Team Convention lookalikes.

Did your mum laugh at you?

No! My parents have always been supportive in whatever I do. (not that they could do a thing about it :) Ha ha, kiddin! They are proud of me.

From a technical point of view, how difficult is it to get the right result with the right products?

Everything is right there. You just can't be lazy, anything can be obtained with some homework done.

Are you happy with the durability of your work?

It gets better everyday. Something new is discovered on every new pair painted. It gets stronger and stronger, but there's nothing I can do if you skate in them! The shoes have survived drunken nights out in a crowded club. If you ever come to Singapore, visit Zouk. You'll see what I mean.

How did you go from doing it for fun to making it a business?

Let's put it this way, it was for fun till it became a business venture. Doing what you love at ya own pace is one of life's greatest gifts.

There's loads of kids out there doing it, any other advice for them?

Aesthetically, everyone is entitled to their own style. Do what you love for the right cause.

How do you generate publicity and hook-ups?

I have been lucky so far ever since I started, all the hook-ups sorta came knockin on my door.

Can you make an honest living from kustom shoes?

So far I have been very comfortable doing just 'customs'. The bills are paid, I eat well, shop well and best of all I get to give my parents some money... but I work really hard. So far, more than 12 hours a day when I have a project in hand.

FOOTAGE

DESERT MAYHEM

UNTITLED

Is it important that it's done by hand for you? Given the nature of what you are doing, I guess you can't automate too much of it?

Yes it's all painted my me. I get very anal when it comes to this aspect. I get some help here 'n' there aside from the painting.

Yes the nature is as such but the returns are priceless. I can make the most outta this and still do something else.

So you paint shoes but there's a lot more to it than that isn't there? Now you need a crazy box, embroidered tags, lace lockers - do you ever think it might be easier manufacturing rather than customising sneakers?

The direction I've taken is to 'sabotage' existing product and turn it into mine. As much as I can, I take away almost all of the Nike labels except of course the swoosh. Customising has a whole different touch to it. A very personal touch and at the same time zero restrictions in terms of colors and message. There are of course several restrictions but I guess that's what makes it more exciting rather than painting a black flat canvas. Evolve beyond your surroundings.

We saw the series you did with Phil at Footage in Sydney.... what other collaborations have you done?

Yeah that was in the beginning of 2004. I have done a good amount of collabs for the past year. It kinda scares me that it has only been a year. But I'm glad I've done it in a global span. Namely from the start till now: AMBUSH (SG), ATMOS (TKO), CHAPTERWORLD (TKO), FOOTAGE (SYD), ADFUNTURE WORKSHOP, FRESHNESSMAG (NYC), LIMITED EDITION'S RANK EXHIBITION (SG) AND PACKER (USA). Right now I'm doing a collab with UNKLE and there are several stores here and there on the waiting list. Namely Nom De Guerre, Ubiqlife etc.....

I know you just got back from the States, what did you get up to over there?

I visited NYC during a good week. Peter from SNEAKERPIMPS was nice enough to fly me over (Thanks!!!). It was tax-free week, there was SNEAKERPIMPS, SoledOUT, ALIFE x Levis launch party and of course the DESERT MAYHEM launch at PACKER. It was insane considering that it was my first visit to NYC. Got to hang out with the mad cats like Futura and Kostas and visit their studios. Visited all my friends and people that I only know by their screen names that I've never met before. It was a fruitful trip that made me wanna go back. One word - MADNESS!

UNTITLED

URBAN MASSACRE

RTHQ

DESERT MAYHEM AF1

CASABLANCA

I saw the pairs you gave to James Lavelle - nice work. What was so special about that design?

There were 2 pairs that were sent to him knowing that he has bought the Chapter Vacuum Tracers before. One was the Apocalypse, an early sample of the Adfunture Boulevards. Those had lesser detailed buildings and a slightly different colour placement.

The second one was my latest work, the Desert Mayhem Dunks. Those were my new experiment with different mediums, a combination of screen-printed on fabric and regular paint on a Dunk.

What were your impressions of America?

Nothing like the movies. There is much more realness to it.

I saw your work in Chapter while I was in Tokyo. How did you hook up with those guys?

Atmos and Chapter got hold of me through my fam here in Singapore. My boy Earn from AMBUSH hooked me up doing a 3 store run. There were 72 pairs involved - 24 pairs each store. That was my first job.

Why only Nike? Why not any other brands?

Nike has made the perfect canvases for me plus I am familiar with their product. The shoes have clean lines and great spaces or segments to apply my art to its fullest potential. Secondly, I guess it's the nature of this business with regards to the demand.

Have brands approached you with a view to producing a real shoe for them?

A company from New York has approached me. Can't name anyone just as yet but all are still in the early stages. I'm pushing for a Converse Chuck Taylor deal at the mo.

What's next for SBTG?

Aside from sneakers. ROYALEFAM CLOTHING is in the works - bomb drops early '05.

Anything else?

Yeah - how about an old school shout out!

Nah - don't think so... we haven't got room!

OK then! CHWEN & AZZIE FOR THE GOLDEN SCISSORS, BLTX FOR SINGIN TO METALLICA TO ME, OL CHARLY FOR BEING HIMSELF, EARN AND BIG AL THE AMBUSH FAMILY + HOWY, HAS FOR THE RAWJAK TUNES, SHI, ANTHONY, WAYNE FROM JUICE, KIT, PATRICK FROM MILK, PETER AND MAE(THE OG SNEAKERPIMPS), YUMING FROM FRESHNESS, PACKER, FOOTAGE, ATMOS, CHAPTER, ADFUNTURE, RIFTTROOPER FOR THE GOOD BEGINNINGS, LIMITED EDITION ETC...

Yep, that kills it! Thanks SBTG!

On the next page you'll find the Sabotage Step by Step Guide to Kustomising!

SNOWTROOPER

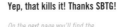

DIPTYCH

SABOTAGE'S

STEP BY STEP GUIDE TO SNEAKER KUSTOMISING!

 +  + +  +

1. SCOURER (SCOTCH BRITE)

2. ACETONE

3. SNEAKERS

4. PAINT

5. MUSIC TO KEEP U GOIN!

1

NOW WE CAN START PREPPING THE SHOES.
CUT UP THE SPONGES INTO LIL SQUARES SLIGHTLY
SMALLER THAN THE COTTON PADS. PLACE THE COTTON
ON TOP OF THE SPONGE. SOAK THE COTTON SIDE
WITH ACETONE. ENUFF TILL U FEEL THE COLDNESS
ON THE SPONGE SIDE.

2

FOLD THE SPONGE IN HALF. START
DEGLAZING THE LEATHER WITH THE
SPONGE. DO NOT RUB TOO HARD AS
U DONT WANNA LOSE THE OG
TEXTURE OF THE LEATHER

 3

THE ACETONE WILL DISSOLVE THE PAINT. THERE
WILL BE A CREAMY RESIDUE OF WET PAINT ON THE
LEATHER. USE THE COTTON PADS TO WIPE THAT OFF.
THE SPONGE AND ACETONE ACTS LIKE LIQUID
SANDPAPER. CHANGE A FRESH SET OF SPONGES
IF THE OLD ONE GETS TOO COATED WITH PAINT.
THE LEATHER SHOULD FEEL LIKE SUEDE...

4

START MASKING THE SOLES.
IT IS EASIER TO MASK THEM
FROM THE MIDDLE AND WITH
THE SOLES FACING AWAY FROM YOU.
(U WILL SEE WAT I MEAN).
MASK EM AT ONE GO.
ONE FULL ROUND.

5 GET YOUR STENCILS
(IF U WANT TEXT
OR GRAPHICS ON IT)

 6

MIX YA PAINTS AND
STORE THEM INTO LIL
AIR TIGHT CONTAINERS.

 7

PAINT YOUR BASE COATS FIRST....

8 PLACE YOUR STENCILS ON THE SHOE. U CAN USE TWEEZERS OR A PEN KNIFE TO HANDLE THEM. FINGERS ARE TOO BIG. POSITION THEM ACCURATELY, THEN LOCK EM DOWN BY PRESSING REAL HARD INTO THE SHOE, U WANT SHARP CLEAN LINES WITHOUT ANY PAINT SEEPING THRU.

9 *PAINTING!*
USE AN ANGLE SHADER (BRUSH WITH A ANGLED TIP) DIP GENEROUSLY INTO THE PAINT, DONT BE A FAG AND SCRAPE OFF SOME AT THE SIDES. ALWAYS START BY PAINTING THE STITCHINGS. THE TIP OF THE BRUSH SHOULD BE FACING THE EDGE OF THE SEGMENT THAT U ARE PAINTING. PAINT BACK N FORTH, THIS WAY U FILL UP THOSE DARN HOLES OF THE STITCHES VERY QUICKLY CREATING A PERFECT STRAIGHT LINE. PLUS, IT REDUCES THE RISK OF GETTING PAINT OVER TO THE OTHER SEGMENT. TRY IT, BELIEVE ME. PAINT WITH LONG STROKES.
SPREAD WHATEVER AMOUNT OF PAINT U HAVE ON YA BRUSH AS FAR AS IT CAN GO. THIS MEANS THIN COATS. THE FIRST COAT WILL NOT LOOK EVEN, DON'T PANIC AND HAVE ITCHY FINGERS AND TRY TO FILL IT UP. KEEP COATING TILL U SEE AN EVEN, OG LIKE FINISH WITH THE LEATHER TEXTURE STILL THERE. PAINT FAST, SPREAD, EVEN OUT THAT SEGMENT AND DONT TOUCH IT. PAINTING/TOUCHING UP A SEMI DRY AREA WILL CAUSE BRUSH STROKES AND THE OG TEXTURE OF THE LEATHER WILL BE LOST. U WILL ALSO FEEL RESISTANCE IN PAINTING, AS SEMI DRY PAINT IS STICKY.

10 THIS IS FOR METALLIC COLORS. THESE SEGMENTS ARE SUPPOSED TO BE SILVER. BUT I'M PAINTING A SAME HUE OF GREY AS A PRIME COAT FIRST. IF U DONT U WILL END UP PAINTING A ZILLION COATS OF SILVER TO GET IT EVEN. THIS APPLIES FOR ALL METALLIC COLORS.

11 I PAINTED THIS SILVER IN ONE COAT. I DIDNT BELIEVE IT MYSELF. PERFECT!

12 THE TIGER CAMMO CONSISTS OF 4 SHADES (INSANE WORK). ONE BASE COAT AND 3 SHADES OF GREY. USE A SMALL/TINY ANGLE SHADER DIP AMPLE AMOUNTS OF PAINT JUST ENUFF TO COAT THE HAIRS OF THE BRUSH. PAINT THE FIRST SHADE OF GREY. SECOND AND FINISH THE SHOE UP.

13 THE MOMENT OF TRUTH. PEEL OFF THE STENCILS BUT NOT WITH YA NAILS. U WILL DIG OUT THE PAINT. USE A PEN KNIFE/NT CUTTER TO CAREFULLY DIG OUT THE VINYL. PULL EM OUT SLOWLY IN THE PROPER DIRECTION. U WANT TO BE 100% SURE OR IT'S BACK TO PASTING EM AGAIN.

14 OK SO NOW U CAN HAVE A NICE FROSTY MUG OF GOOD OL TIGER BEER AND A MARLBORO LIGHT AND STARE AT THE SHOE FOR LIKE A GOOD HALF HOUR. YES U ARE TIRED.

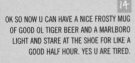

15 *TOUCHING UP THE EDGES.*
I HAVE MY GOOD OLD CUSTOMISED HOOKED BRUSH (IT GOT INTO THIS STATE FROM PAINTING HUNDREDS OF PAIR OF SHOES WITH THE SAFARI PATTERNS) FACE THE BRUSH AS U SEE FROM THE PIC. THE BRUSH LOCKS ONTO THE EDGE NICELY MAKING SOME NICE CLEAN EDGES.

16 SO BEFORE U LACE EM UP, U GOTTA COAT EM WITH SOME VARNISH FIRST. I USE KRYLON MATTE VARNISH. SPRAY FROM A DISTANCE. IN MODERATION. NOW LACE EM UP AND GET READY TO BREAK NECKS.

THE END!
AFTER RECEIVING TONS OF EMAILS EVERYDAY, I HOPE THIS GUIDE HELPS U BIG TIME. EVERYTHING WAS LEARNT FROM SCRATCH WITH ABSOLUTELY NO EXPERIENCE AT ALL. SOME TECHNIQUES ARE GAINED BY CHANCE. JUST TRY IT, DONT HESITATE OR ASK. YOU'LL LEARN FOR SURE!
SABOTAGE.

SPONSORED BY **Tiger** Beer

KUSTOM 99

WORLD TITLE SHOOT OUT!

ARE YOU THE KUSTOM KING?

WINNER TAKE ALL!

Sneaker Freaker Magazine World Championship
Diy Sneaker Customising Competition

Well, we didn't call it the World Championship for nothing! Cheers to everyone who responded to the challenge - we received over two hundred entries from all 7 continents (alright, except Africa and Antarctica!). As you will see, the standard was exceptional. It is quite a powerful sight to see 99 amazing examples of sneaker art. No doubt it is the finest and biggest collection ever assembled in one place!

Amazingly, the competition was almost a deadheat. Two entries polled above and beyond all others and were clearly the outstanding sneakers. In the end Nick Kailola who hails from the Netherlands won in a photo finish. His work, entitled 'CYBERNETIC-ORGANISM, MODEL:T-800' was a stand out for several reasons.

Nick's work showed a high degree of skill and ingenuity, not to mention wearability, durability and feasibility. Obviously the judges had their funny bones tickled as well. It's the sort of in-joke that only sneaker heads could ever hope to understand. Who would have thought such a shoe would land him the World Title?

As I said, it wasn't a one horse race. INSA also polled spectacularly well. So well in fact that we felt it was only right to acknowledge the work of this London-based graffiti artist. The two entries were very, very different which just goes to show how broad a church sneaker customising is!

Other notable entries include Justin Daly's blatant attempt to suck up to the judges by painting a pair of Tiger sneakers and having Tiger beer in the background. C2 also did well, especially considering the fact that he is only 14 years old. Jor One can probably consider himself a tad unlucky as he has an amazing portfolio of work already completed.

For lateral thinking, Dream One's entry on a pair of lawn bowls shoes (including painted soles) really stood out. Excellent entries also came from Martin Ng, Ovelia Transtoto, ST0404, Team Blak-Out, Dvate, Alex Nash and Oliver from DRP.

In case you were wondering, the judges were Phil (Footage, Sydney), Dave (Rare Air), Hans DC (OG SF contributor), Nikolai (Rift Trooper) and Mark Ong (Sabotage). I also seconded my wife as a judge. She was able to bring a certain amount of detachment and artistic objectivity to the judging table (and she's a hot potato). Besides, I thought we needed a ladeez touch!

Who can say for sure how the judges' minds were working? All we asked them to do was choose the shoe that they loved the most. Neck snappin' potential was the prime criteria. Originality was another. Craftsmanship would also be a factor, as would sheer aesthetics.

We had so many entries, some peeps are bound to be disappointed. I'm afraid we just couldn't get everyone into the best 99. Several entries failed when it came to the standard of photography. Many were unsuitable for printing in a magazine for various reasons - low resolution, out of focus, too dark, too light... So, here's a big tip for everyone, do your work justice by having it properly photographed! And follow the competition instructions to the letter - it's not that hard...

So, anyway, that's about enough out of me. Except that I have to thank all our sponsors, especially Tiger Beer! And Deuce Laces, the judges, and most of all, to all the kids out there who love to paint their shoes!

THE JUDGE

CYBERNETIC-ORGANISM, MODEL: T-800

NICK KAILOLA

MY CPU IS A NERO_NET PROCESSOR,
A LEARNING COMPUTER...THE MORE CONTACT
I HAVE WITH HUMANS, THE MORE I LEARN...

NICK KAILOLA

THANX FOR THE COMPETITION AND
I HAVE TO SAY THAT THIS PAIR GAVE
ME GREAT JOY WHEN I SAW THE
FINAL RESULT!   NICK K.

ARTIST: NICK KAILOLA
URL: WWW.LEYP.COM
SHOE: TERMINATOR HI
CITY: ROTTERDAM
INFO: ARNOLD JUST HAD TO BE ON THE SHOE! I GOT THE IDEA
         FOR THE PAIR A LITTLE WHILE AGO, BUT NEVER THOUGHT
         I WAS GOING TO MAKE THEM FOR REAL!

#1 NICK KAILOLA

Tell us about yourself? Where do you live? What do you do?
My name is Nick Kailola and I live in the Netherlands. Two years ago I got my degree in graphic design. I moved to Rotterdam right after I finished. It was hard getting started and settled at the same time. But all in all I'm having fun doing what I'm doing and will keep on doing it!

Tell us about your winning Terminator design?
I've always been an Arnold fan (leaving aside his political career), and last year I found this prank call site (see below) and played it over and over with a friend of mine... I don't know why, but it still cracks me up!
   And then you have his movies Running Man, Commando, Total Recall, Predator, Pumping Iron and, of course, Terminator. The connection was made! I didn't think I would really make them as shoes. Then along came the Kustom 99 Competition!

http://mckayness.com/~ray/Celebrity%20Prank%20Calls/

I must admit as soon as I saw it I started laughing, I wasn't expecting a 'comedy' entry to catch the judges eye! How did you stitch it together?
First I took away the Swoosh, painted them and put in new stitching. Then I painted the white parts, printed Arnold on fabric and the different parts for the back strap, tongue-label, inside and insoles. Then I cut the parts to size and put on stitching as the shoe had originally. Did the same with the computerised inside. I put the strap on the back (it's different than the original one), and glued fabric over the insoles, with text on top of a computer-image background. I did all the stitching by hand and can't say that it was a perfect job! But worth it though.

What's your background in customising shoes?
About a year ago, me and Nonski thought that we could do something. We had a friend who was having an Urban Festival in Amsterdam. We put our Sneakersart Expo together with some of our creative friends (Biros&Slum Peeters, Dumboh, Femku Smit, Lenny Schuurmans, Daan-banaan v/d Lelij, lexflex and Johan Klungel) We gave ourselves the name: Leyp (leip in Dutch means different, weird but in a good way. And we mde it just a little different than leip cause we leip with a y). For this expo I made the Anti and SuriMax and these designs were welcomed with open arms. The expo was good but we wanted more, so we've been busy with putting up our Leyp.com website! Next to this there have been 2 stores who have been giving me shoes to customise, either for sale or decoration.

What are your plans?
I hope that our site will be a success and that we can build on that. I have an idea about connecting people through shoes, the Max90, but that's a work in progress. Or maybe I could get a job at that company with the Swoosh and with any luck I'll make the orient-express railroad trip this summer.

How does it feel to be a world champion?
It just brings back feelings I haven't been feeling for a while. It's like watching He-Man and Buck Rogers on Saturdays or getting the AT-AT for your birthday... Joy!! Thanks SneakerFreaker for putting up this competition!

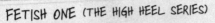

ARTIST: INSA
SHOE: NIKE AIR FORCE
CITY: SOUTH LONDON
URL: WWW.INSALAND.COM
INFO: IT WAS FAIRLY PAINSTAKING TO PAINT THESE SNEAKERS AS
I WANTED THE DESIGN TO COVER EVERY BUMP AND CURVE
OF THE SHOE AND NOT JUST USE THE FLAT PANELS...

INSA

THESE SHOES WERE DONE TO COMPLEMENT MY
LATEST WORK, 'THE HIGH HEEL SERIES', WHERE I TAKE
ON THE THEME OF GRAFFITI AS A FETISH, REPLACING
MY MUCH COVETED FOUR LETTERS (INSA) WITH
A MORE TRADITIONALLY FETISHISED OBJECT.

INSA

ALTHOUGH EACH ONE IS UNIQUE,
AS THE DESIGN ALWAYS TAKES ITS
OWN ROUTE, I WANTED THERE TO BE
BALANCE BETWEEN THE TWO SHOES

#2 INSA

Tell us about yourself?

I'm a graffiti artist, I go by the name of INSA. I am currently residing in
the realness of south east London. I have been painting for over 10 years
and live as an artist - getting up as well as getting commissions.

Tell us about your winning design? What's up with the high heels?

The design on my sneakers is from a theme of work I am doing at the
moment called 'the high heel series'. It comes from ideas I have about
graffiti being a fetish and the obsession I have with the four letters 'I N S A'
- constantly dressing them up and drawing their curves. So to represent
these ideas, I have replaced them with a more traditional fetishised
object, the high heel, and played around with it like I would my letters. The
sneaker is also a highly, though not traditional, fetishised object, so for
me to paint them with this design came naturally. Plus I thought the
continuous wraparound style of these fetish drawings would look bad on
a pair of my personal favorites: white Air Force One mid.

How painstaking is it to paint like that?

It was fairly painstaking to paint these sneakers as I wanted the design
to cover every bump and curve of the shoe and not just use the flat
panels. And although each one is unique as the design always takes its
own route I wanted there to be balance between the two shoes.

What's your background in customising shoes?

I don't really have a background in sneaker customising, although I have
painted several pairs now. I am just a big sneaker fan and think they are
a great object to use as a canvas for my artwork.

What else are you good at?

My main expression is painting with spray-cans. Check out my website or
www.fotolog.net/insa_fetish to see work from my high heel series.

What will you do next?

My plans from now are to enjoy my prize beer, continue with my artwork
and work on a few collaborations. I am planning to produce a limited
edition high heel with this design on, but now I wanna produce a Limited
Edition Air Force or maybe a high heel with an Air Force design on.
We'll just have to wait and see, but I'll be sure to keep you posted.

Anything else you want to say? How will you handle the glory?

This has really inspired me to work on a load more custom sneakers,
thanks for liking my work. Safe INSA!

*ALL 99 ENTRIES ARE LISTED OVER THE NEXT TEN PAGES
IN NO PARTICULAR ORDER·*

HARRY HITACHI

NAME: JAMES BEATTIE
ARTIST: DVATE
SHOE: ADIDAS SHELLTOE HI-TOP
CITY: MELBOURNE
INFO: COULD ALSO BE CUSTOMISED FOR OTHER COUNTRIES
WITH DIFFERENT TRAINS...

"WILD LIFE¦TYLE"

ARTIST: DREAM-ONE
SHOE: MENS LAWN BOWLING SNEAKERS
URL: WWW.FOTOLOG.NET/DREAMONETHEGREAT/
INFO: I SAW THAT THE SOLES WERE COMPLETELY FLAT
AND MUCH MORE INTERESTING TO PAINT!
I'D DEFINITELY SPORT A PAIR OF THESE!

AGAIN & AGAIN

NAME: MARTIN NG
ARTIST: AGAIN
SHOE: ADIDAS ROD LAVER
CITY: SINGAPORE

UNTITLED

ARTIST: JOR ONE
SHOE: JORDAN II
URL: WWW.JORI.COM
CITY: SAN FRANCISCO, CALIFORNIA

GREEN DEMONS!

NAME: CHRIS HUI
ARTIST: C2
SHOE: NIKE DUNK HIGH
URL: WWW.KICKSONLINE.COM/CUSTOMS/C2.HTML
INFO: I AM ONLY 14 YEARS OLD. I HAVE LIVED IN
MILWAUKEE, WISCONSIN MY WHOLE LIFE.

NASH

NAME: ALEX NASH
SHOE: NIKE AF1
CITY: LONDON
INFO: ALL HAND-STITCHED BY ME, THE MESH IS FROM
A WINDBREAKER!

DRP MINT

NAME: OLIVER MUNDAY
ARTIST: DRP
CITY: BALTIMORE
URL: WWW.DRPSNEAKERDESIGN.COM
INFO: THEY FEATURE A SCREEN PRINTED FABRIC DRP
LOGOTYPE ON THE BACK PANELS. THE REST OF
THE DESIGN IS HAND PAINTED.

AIR BITE

NAME: OVELIA TRANSTOTO
SHOE: NIKE AIR FORCE ONE MID
CITY: INDONESIA

KOI CARP vs WIND DRAGON

NAME: QUINCY RENON
ARTIST: KWINZ
URL: WWW.TECH-MATH.COM
INFO: THE INSPIRATION WAS DERIVED FROM JAPANESE
TATTOO-ART AND THE EXACT PLACEMENT OF
THE LINES IS NECESSARY OTHERWISE THE WHOLE
DESIGN IS SCREWED.

SNKRFRKR ASICS

ARTIST: LEXFLEX
SHOE: ASICS
CITY: AMSTERDAM AND LONDON
INFO: I MADE THESE FOR THE LAUNCH AT 90 SQM.
I LOVE SNKR FRKR! I LOVE REMKO!

FUNDAMENTALZ

NAME: SIR PATRICK FINKLESTEIN THE THIRD.
ARTIST: PEN ONE
SHOE: NIKE BLAZER
INFO: I LIKE GREEN OLIVES AND PICKLE JUICE.
THE SHOE IS ON DISPLAY IN HONG KONG
AND WAS CUSTOM MADE FOR HAMLET STORES.

EYELET OF THE TIGER

NAME: JUSTIN DALY
ARTIST: JAEDED
URL: WWW.USERS.BIGPOND.COM/DDALYJ/
SHOE: TIGER ASICS (SYNTHETIC AND SUEDE).
INFO: I AM AN ILLUSTRATOR LOOKING FOR WORK!

ARCTIC CAMMO-LONDON CHINATOWN EDITION

NAME: ALLISTER LEE
ARTIST: ALIST
INFO: COME PACKAGED IN CHINESE
TAKEAWAY BOX WITH LACES
AND A FORTUNE COOKIE

TRUE B-BOY

NAME: CHRISTIAN AZUL
INFO: HAND-MADE OVER THE PERIOD OF
4 YEARS, BY A TRUE AEROSOL WARFARE
B-BOY IN THE YARDS & ON THE DANCE FLOOR!
COMES WITH MIX CASSETTE!

RISING SUN

NAME: CHET-VOON HO
ARTIST: BIG C
SHOE: NIKE DUNK LOW
INFO: INSPIRED BY THE RAINFORESTS
OF ASIA

NIGHT SLITHERER

NAME: BRANDON LASKOWSKI
ARTIST: EVOLVED FOOTWEAR
SHOE: NIKE DUNK HIGH
INFO: FEATURES FLASHING LIGHTED SWOOSHES
AND FAUX SNAKESKIN TEXTURES

ABOVE THE CLOUDS

NAME: ATC
ARTIST: ABOVE THE CLOUDS
SHOE: NIKE AIR FORCE ONE
INFO: ENJOY THE SHOES AND THANKS FOR
THE POSSIBILITY OF RECOGNITION!

STEREO POPS

NAME: DECHAZIER & EDWARD GORDON
ARTIST: BLACK-MARMALADE & FAST EDDIE
SHOE: ADIDAS ZXZLEA'S
URL: WWW.STEREOTYPICS.COM
INFO: CLEAN, SIMPLE AND REFRESHING

AGPOON 2010

NAME: HOPI AGPOON-FERRER
ARTIST: AGPOON
SHOE: NIKE DUNK HIGH
URL: DEDICATED TO D.A.N, PIGGY, TIBET, HUG-G, AND ZAK

RICHONE

NAME: RICH
URL: WWW.CR8REC.COM
SHOE: CREATIVE REC KAPLAN
CITY: NEWPORT BEACH, CALIFORNIA

SOCIAL STUDY VANDAL

NAME: OLIVER MUNDAY
ARTIST: DRP
CITY: BALTIMORE
URL: WWW.DRPSNEAKERDESIGN.COM

PACE YOURSELF

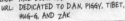

NAME: LAMAR R. SMITH
ARTIST: DIVINE (DIVINE DESIGNZ)
SHOE: NIKE AIR FORCE 1 HIGH
INFO: INDIANA PACERS COLOURS!

THE PATRIOT ACT

NAME: LAMAR R. SMITH
ARTIST: DIVINE (DIVINE DESIGNZ)
SHOE: NIKE AIR FORCE 1 LOW
INFO: PRESIDENTIAL ELECTION EDITION!

ILLYGRAPHY PART ONE

NAME: LUCA BARCELLONA
ARTIST: BEAN ONE
SHOE: NIKE AIR FORCE ONE
CITY: I'M FROM ITALY, MILAN. I HOPE YOU ENJOY IT.

MYSTERY MACHINES

NAME: MATT GRIPPO
ARTIST: AUTOMATIC
CITY: CINCINATI
SHOE: DUNK

STRIPE WAVE

NAME: JUSTIN DALY
ARTIST: EVOLVED FOOTWEAR
SHOE: ADIDAS TOURNAMENT (CANVAS)
URL: WWW.USERS.BIGPOND.COM/DDALYJ/

CLOWD

NAME: JOSEPH AU
URL: WWW.XANGA.COM/OUR_PUBLICATION
INFO: PEACE!

J4 RETRO

NAME: MATT TAYLOR
SHOE: JORDAN IV
URL: WWW.MATTTAYLOR.CO.UK
CITY: LONDON

SOCIAL STUDY BLAZER

NAME: OLIVER MUNDAY
ARTIST: DRP
CITY: BALTIMORE
URL: WWW.DRPSNEAKERDESIGN.COM

RASCAL EVILUTION

NAME: LAM WEN XIANG
ARTIST: RASCALBOY
CITY: SINGAPORE

UNTITLED

NAME: JOR ONE
URL: WWW.JORI.COM
SHOE: NIKE AIR FORCE ONE
CITY: SAN FRANCISCO, CALIFORNIA

LANDSPEED 816

NAME: DENNIS DOTY
SHOE: CONVERSE
INFO: I LIVE IN KANSAS CITY AND I ATTEND
THE KANSAS CITY ART INSTITUDE IN
THE UNITED STATES.

WORKHORSE PATTERN

NAME: LOGAN HICKS
URL: WWW.WORKHORSEVISUALS.COM
SHOE: NIKE AIR FORCE ONES
INFO: THESE CUSTOMS ARE PART OF AN UPCOMING
LIMITED RELEASE BY THE LOS ANGELES BASED
WORKHORSE STUDIOS.

JOE SCHAFER

NAME: JOE SCHAFER
SHOE: NIKE REVOLUTION MID
CITY: PITTSBURGH
INFO: THIS SHOE DESIGN WAS INSPIRED BY PAISLEY
FABRIC – I USED A PIECE OF LACE TO CREATE
THE DESIGN WITH SHOE PAINT.

KNIGHT

NAME: GAKU TSUYOSHI
URL: WWW.FLATLUX.COM
ARTIST: FLATLUX
INFO: DID LASER ON THE HEEL, AND
PUT PLASTIC AND RHINESTONE ON IT

UNTITLED

ARTIST: JOR ONE
SHOE: JORDAN
URL: WWW.JORI.COM
CITY: SAN FRANCISCO, CALIFORNIA

WINGS TO FLY

NAME: ROWENA MARYNISSEN
ARTIST: ROWENA M (YEAH NOT EXCITING)
SHOE: CONVERSE CHUCK TAYLOR ALL STARS- HI
CITY: SYDNEY
INFO: IF ONLY THE WINGS REALLY COULD WORK!

MELTOWN CLASSICS

NAME: DECHAZIER P. STOKES-JOHNSON
ARTIST: BLACK-MARMALADE
SHOE: ATHLETIC WOMENS / LOW CUT
URL: WWW.BLACK-MARMALADE.COM
INFO: BE ON THE LOOK OUT FOR FIT FOR A KING
MAGAZINE IN EARLY NOVEMBER

KOBE BRYANT AIR FORCE

NAME: EMMANUEL GOLDEN
ARTIST: EMMANUELABOR
SHOE: NIKE AIR FORCE ONE LOW

REVERSE DENIMS

NAME: DYLAN LIM
ARTIST: ZEPHYRII
SHOE: NIKE DUNK LOW PRO
INFO: INSPIRATION CAME FROM CAMPER TWINS, TOOK
ABOUT 20 HOURS TO COMPLETE, USE OF DENIMS
COZ I COULD NEVA AFFORD A PAIR OF DENIM SB!

JONAH STYLE

NAME: JONAH MILLER
ARTIST: J-MONEY
SHOE: NIKE AIR FORCE ONE, SIZE 10.5

MELBOURNE RULES

NAME: BONNIE GILLARD
CITY: MELBOURNE
SHOE: VANS SLIP ON
INFO: I HAVE A THING FOR MONSTERS. I DREAM OF
BRINGING THEM TO LIFE TO INVADE EARTH. ALL MY WORK
IS DONE BY HAND WITH A BRUSH. NO TWO ARE EVER ALIKE.

QUINTIN JEFFERSON

NAME: QUINTIN JEFFERSON
ARTIST: QREATIV
SHOE: NIKE AIR FORCE 1
URL: WWW.GRAND-HIGH.COM

UNTITLED

NAME: RITCHIE POERNOMO
ARTIST: EVOLVED FOOTWEAR
SHOE: CHUCK TAYLOR'S SZ 8

HEART REVIVAL

NAME: ROB CORDINER
ARTIST: LARDO
SHOE: DVS REVIVAL WHT/GRY
CITY: TASMANIA! THIS COMP WAS HELLA FUN

ODD SOX

NAME: TODD FINDLOW
CITY: MELBOURNE
SHOE: AIR FORCE LOW!
       (WITH ADDED STRAP)

GHOSTS & BONES

NAME: SIMON COURTNEY
ARTIST: DUST
URL: WWW.DUST.CO.NZ
SHOE: ADIDAS SUPERSTAR 3/4
INFO: I'M WORLD FAMOUS IN NEW ZEALAND!

SIMONE LEGNO

NAME: SIMONE LEGNO
SHOE: NIKE DUNK LO
CITY: LOS ANGELES

CONAN THE BARBARIAN

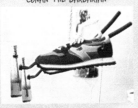

NAME: MIKE HUNT
ARTIST: WANKUSS
SHOE: KUSTOM DUNLOP KT26
INFO: BONGON IN 2005!

DIRTY 7'S

NAME: SIMON MOK
ARTIST: XYMON
SHOE: NEW BALANCE BB700
INFO: 'ATLANTA' COLOURWAY

DMITROV

NAME: DMITROV VAN DER WEIJDEN
CITY: AMSTERDAM
SHOE: NIKE AIR FORCE
URL: HELLO EVERYBODY, THESE ARE MY
      SHOES..... YOUR MAGAZINE IS GREAT!

SWAMP

NAME: TAKE7
ARTIST: EVOLVED FOOTWEAR
SHOE: NIKE DUNK HIGH
URL: WWW.TAKE7.COM

UNTHINKABLE

NAME: TSUBASA NOMURA
ARTIST: GRISMA
SHOE: NIKE DUNK HIGH
URL: WWW.PICTURETRAIL.COM/ALLTHINGSC

CAMMO

NAME: ANDRUE C. MYERS
ARTIST: DRU (SPECTRUM KICKZ)
SHOE: NIKE AIR FORCE ONE LOW

'HELLO I AM A...'

NAME: CHARLES WILLIAMS
ARTIST: PHATI
SHOE: NIKE DELTA FORCE
INFO: MY IDEA COMES FROM BEING A SNEAKER FREAK PLUS USING CLASSIC GRAFITTI LETTERS!

JULES

NAME: DREW
ARTIST: DREW FUNK
SHOE: NIKE
CITY: SELANGOR, MALAYSIA

PRO MODEL

NAME: JAKE
ARTIST: SUMO 178
CITY: MELBOURNE

VISUAL ORGASM

NAME: EDSON ANDRADE
ARTIST: E.D.S.O.N.
Exquisite_Design_Styles_Of_Nature
SHOE: NIKE AF1

VISUAL ORGASM #2

NAME: EDSON ANDRADE
ARTIST: E.D.S.O.N.
Exquisite_Design_Styles_Of_Nature
SHOE: NIKE AF1

KING MIDAS TOUCH

NAME: GEORGE WILLIAMS
ARTIST: DOUS F.S.C
SHOE: ZOO YORK

STONES ROSES WAFFLE

NAME: STEVEN HARRAN
SHOE: NIKE WAFFLE
CITY: MELBOURNE

GREEN EGGS AND SPAM

ARTIST: GONZO 247
SHOE: ADIDAS
CITY: HOUSTON

ELECTROPHANT

NAME: JAMES SEE
SHOE: AIR JORDAN I LOW
INFO: PLEASE EXCUSE DIRT ON THE SOLES. THESE CUSTOMS HAVE BEEN WORN.

JELLY TIP ICE CREAM

NAME: JANINE WILLIAMS
ARTIST: DIVA
SHOE: DELTA FORCE
INFO: MY IDEA COMES FROM AN ICE CREAM FLAVOUR WE HAVE HERE IN NZ!

PUMPKIN MIST

NAME: JOE
ARTIST: RETRO!NK.
SHOE: NIKE AF1

AFRO DUNKS

NAME: JOHNNIE MITCHELL II
ARTIST: 1/2 OF CREATIVE SOLE
SHOE: NIKE AF1 WHT/WHT
CITY: OAKLAND, CALIFORNIA
URL: WWW.CREATIVESOLE.COM

SFK99 - SPLATTER ATTACKER

NAME: STEVEN WARD (WARDY)
ARTIST: WAZODESIGNS
SHOE: SAUCONY - SPOT-BILT
URL: WAZODESIGNS.COM

UNTITLED

NAME: SHARIL, DANO BIN SABTU
ARTIST: STO404
CITY: SINGAPORE
SHOE: DUNK HI

D-SHELL'D SUPERSTARS

NAME: WAYNE WITH WORDS

MY WAY

NAME: BRIAN "BLAK" DIXON
ARTIST: TEAM BLAK-OUT CUSTOMS
URL: WWW.BLAK-OUT.COM
INFO: A MESSAGE TO PEOPLE TO DO THINGS
"THEIR WAY". I SAY IT ALL THE TIME!

GUERILLA BLACK

NAME: BRIAN "BLAK" DIXON
ARTIST: TEAM BLAK-OUT CUSTOMS
URL: WWW.BLAK-OUT.COM
INFO: SNEAKERS DONE FOR GUERILLA
BLACK RECORDING RAP ARTIST ON VIRGIN!

AIR- VERSION A

NAME: ANDY +DANI
ARTIST: UPROCK
SHOE: NIKE AIR FORCE I MID
INFO: TWO STYLES - BOTH EXPRESSING
ELEMENTS OF AIR!

REMEMBER THE ALAMO

NAME: CHRIS HUI
ARTIST: C2
SHOE: DUNK
CITY: MILWAUKEE, WISCONSIN

OL CHARLIE'S

NAME: CHARLES LIM
CITY: SINGAPORE
COLOUR: BLACK ON BLACK SUEDE/GOLD

BACK TO THE FUTURA

NAME: DARRIN UMBOH
SHOE: NIKE BLAZER
CITY: AMSTERDAM

BONDI BEAUTIES

NAME: DINO PLACIDO PARISI
SHOE: NIKE-LIBRETTO, INDOOR SOCCER SHOE
CITY: SYDNEY
INFO: IDEA CAME FROM THE LADIES
SUNBAKING AT BONDI BEACH.

JUMBLE "EMAC EDITION

NAME: ERIN MCCAN
SHOE: NIKE JUMBLE
ARTIST: EMAC
INFO: HAND CROCHET SIDE SWOOSHES,
TONGUE & BACK TAB SILVER SNAKESKIN TOE

DUNKACHEES

NAME: DAN KING
ARTIST: BAD KRU
INFO: HAVE YOU EVER SEEN A DUNK HI
WITH A HUARACHE STRAP LOOK SO
BEAUTIFUL?

BLUNT NAKED KICKS

NAME: HECTOR SERNA JR
ARTIST: BLUNT NAKED
SHOE: CONVERSE PRO LEATHER HI
CITY: KANSAS

4TH DAN

NAME: JJ
SHOE: KUNGFUSHOES
INFO: MY FRIEND IS QUITE A FUCKING
BRUCE LEE SO I CAME UP WITH A PAIR
OF SHOES, SO HE CAN WHOP SUMASS!

SHATTERED GREENS

NAME: CARLO BARRETO
ARTIST: KAELO

MONA, THE WUSHE MEMORIAL

NAME: LIN
SHOE: NIKE TERMINATOR MOWABB
LOCATION: TAIWAN

SUMO ONES

NAME: JAKE
ARTIST: SUMO 178
CITY: MELBOURNE

TERMINATORS

NAME: PETER MINA
SHOE: NIKE TERMINATOR

CLOUD NINE

NAME: FARTY JOHN
SHOE: AIR FORCE

OOMPA LOOMPAS

NAME: RIGO MARTINEZ
ARTIST: RIGATONI
SHOE: BLAZER MID
CITY: KANSAS CITY

TOP BUNK DUNK

NAME: RON LODEVICO
ARTIST: A.R.T.-ILLERY
INFO: PUMPKIN, FIRE WITH ART MUSIC
LOGO

DISKO DUNKS

ARTIST: WAYNE KING
SHOE: DUNK
CITY: TOOTGAROOK
INFO: LET'S GO DANCIN!

PRIMATES

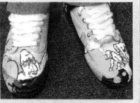

NAME: CHRIS PURNELL
SHOE: DUNLOP VOLLEY
CITY: MELBOURNE
INFO: I SPECIALIZE IN PRIMATOLOGY!

04TH DISTRICT❉ GREEN LANTERN

NAME: ANTONIO RODRIGUEZ
SHOE: TONI TONI
BRAND: ARTISTA KICKS

BITE ME!

NAME: RAPHAEL WEINBERG
SHOE: DUNK HI PREMIUM BLACK
URL: WWW.LIVINGMUTANTS.COM &
WWW.SOLEBOX.DE

PARAMOUNT DYNASTY

NAME: CHRIS HUI
ARTIST: C2
SHOE: AIR FORCE ONE
INFO: I AM ONLY 14 YEARS OLD.

HUNTED

NAME: SHARIL, DANO BIN SABTU
ARTIST: STO404
CITY: SINGAPORE
SHOE: TERMINATOR

RED RUMBLES

NAME: SHARIL, DANO BIN SABTU
ARTIST: STO404
CITY: SINGAPORE
SHOE: DUNK

SPRAYPAINT AND MARKERS

NAME: TUOMO LONGI
ARTIST: CLIENT 15
SHOE: ADIDAS CANVAS CAMPUS
URL: WWW.CLIENT15.COM

DRP DUNKS

NAME: OLIVER MUNDAY
ARTIST: DRP
CITY: BALTIMORE
URL: WWW.DRPSNEAKERDESIGN.COM